AF553570

TEACHING OF COMMERCE AND ACCOUNTANCY EDUCATION-II

TEACHING OF COMMERCE AND ACCOUNTANCY EDUCATION-II

Babu Muthuja
M.A., M.A., M.Ed.
Educational Advisor,
Arcot Sri Mahalakshmi Matric Hr. Sec. School,
Villapakkam, Vellore Dist.-632521 T.N.

R. Usharani
M.A., M.Ed.
Principal, Arcot Sri Mahalakshmi Matric Hr. Sec. School,
Villapakkam, Vellore Dist.-632521 T.N.

Dr. Shahid Akhtar
Lecturer, Deptt. of Commerce,
Mander College, Ranchi

CENTRUM PRESS
NEW DELHI-110002 (INDIA)

CENTRUM PRESS
H.O.: 4360/4, Ansari Road, Daryaganj,
New Delhi-110 002 (India)
Ph.: 23278000, 23261597

B.O.: No. 1015, Ist Main Road, BSK IIIrd Stage
IIIrd Phase, IIIrd Block,
Bangalore - 560 085 (India)
Tel.: 080-41723429
Visit us at: www.centrumpress.com

Teaching of Commerce and Accountancy Education-II

© Reserved

First Edition, 2009

PRINTED IN INDIA

Printed at Mehra Offset Press, Delhi

Contents

Preface

Commerce is a division of trade or production which deals with the exchange of goods and services from producer to final consumer. It comprises the trading of something of economic value such as goods, services, information or money between two or more entities. Commerce functions as the central mechanism which drives capitalism and certain other economic systems (but compare command economy, for example). Commercialization or commercialisation consists of the process of transforming something into a product, service or activity which one may then use in commerce.

Accountancy is the process by which financial information about a business is recorded, classified, summarized, interpreted, and communicated. The communication is generally in the form of financial statements that show in money terms that show the economic resources under the control of management. Such financial information is primarily used by lenders, managers, investors, tax authorities, and other decision makers to make resource allocation decisions between and within companies, organizations, and public agencies.

It involves the process of recording, verifying, and reporting of the value of assets, liabilities, income, and expenses in the books of account (ledger) to which debit and credit entries (recognizing transactions) are chronologically posted to record changes in value (see bookkeeping). Accounting has also been defined by the AICPA as "The art of recording, classifying, and summarizing in a significant manner and in terms of money, transactions and events which are, in part at least, of financial character, and interpreting the results thereof.

The strategic methods and techniques of teaching of commerce are elaborately explained in the present book. It will serve as a valuable reference tool for teachers, educationists, policy planners and students. An attempt has been made to cover up most of the topics included in B.Ed. syllabus of the Indian universities.

— Dr. Shahid Akhtar

UNIT-I

Commerce Education

Commerce Education

Commerce offers foundation for many professional careers like Finance, Planning, Accountancy, Tax Practitioners, Banking and Broking etc, besides academics, research, and many more. Persons having flair for accounting, finance, commodities, marketing and trading etc. generally choose Commerce as first career choice.

As a stream of study, Commerce can be studied right after 10 years of schooling. After the 10 years of schooling – commerce is available as an option in 10+2 or the Higher Secondary level. This paves the way for higher studies in commerce related subjects.

The undergraduate and postgraduate Education in Commerce is offered at University departments and colleges spread all across the country. Specializations are offered at post graduate and at research levels.

A number of subjects can be studied under disciplines of Commerce in conjugation like; accountancy, economics, mathematics, business, finance etc. Most commerce colleges in India offer the following subjects:

Business Economics: This would cover concepts like the laws of demand and supply, law of returns, elasticity, theory of pricing under different market forms etc.

Financial Accounting: This subject would deal with the preparation of profit and loss statements, balance sheets and final accounts of a company, knowledge of Indian and international accounting standards, calculation of depreciation and valuation of shares and goodwill of a company.

Cost Accounting: This would include process, job and contract costing, costing of overheads, standard and variance costing and budgetary control.

Income Tax: This would encompass the nature and basis of charge of income tax, tax planning, tax deduction, incomes not taxable etc.

Auditing: This would deal with vouching, valuation and verification of transactions, assets and liabilities. It will also include studying the auditing of different organizations like clubs, hospitals and charitable concerns.

Business Finance: This would include in its scope financial analysis as a diagnostic tool, the management of working capital and its components as well as capital structure leverages.

Business Law: This subject would discuss the different laws in India relating to, among others, the Companies Act and the Consumer Protection Act.

Marketing: This subject would deal with products, pricing methods, promotion, channels of distribution, logistics etc.

Need for Commerce Education

There has been a historic growth in the fields of commerce, industry and science in the recent past. This growth demands a specialised education in various fields concerned with science, commerce and industry. The dependence of commerce on science has been exemplified by pointing out the fact that "the management side of commerce is wholly dependent upon computers. In India too the computer is fully accepted by the business. Computer education has been introduced in the schools in India and with this it is expected that the school will become the machines of commerce education. However, at present commerce education in schools has not become so advanced that computers are used at school stage in bookkeeping or accountancy". In most of the advanced countries the commerce education is totally computerized.

Historical Development

During the last quarter of the last century, with rapid advances in technology more and more attention was paid towards the scientific management side of the business. A number of laws were passed by governments and so a need was felt for professionals in the field.

This created demand for professionalized commercial education. It is said, "Education of commerce was started by private commercial institutions. To start with only bookkeeping was taught. We find *Munims* used to train junior *Munims* under their apprenticeship. Later on private commercial institutes started teaching of bookkeeping and accountancy".

For such an education, Madras became a pioneer state where it started in 1886. The Government of Madras laid the foundation of education by setting-up commercial institute in Madras. Two other institutions were established during the next ten years (by L 8 96) one was set-up at *Calicut* and the other in the state of *Kerala.*

In the beginning of this century Calcutta Presidency College also introduced the teaching of commerce (1903). By about that time it a also introduced in Delhi. One more commercial institution was started in Bombay in 1912. At the graduate level the commerce education was introduced in 1913 in Sydenham College of Commerced Economics in Bombay.

In 1920's (1921-22) the first Fiscal Commission was set-up and this commission made certain important recommendations. In the light of these recommendations some major improvements were visible in various industrial fields specially in the field of iron and steel industry, tea industry, cotton industry and jute industry.

A very rapid growth of commercial educational institutions was rued during 1920-40. The Indian Institute of Bankers was established in 1926, the Institute of Chartered Accountants of India was In 1934. Later on in 1944,. Institute of Works and Cost Accountants of India was established. In 1955, the Federation of Insurance institutes were established.

Present Status in Secondary and Higher Education

To cope with the increasing demand for the trained people to transact to transact and governmental jobs, it became essential to introduce the commerce education at school level.

To start with the teaching of short-hand and typing was introduced in Government schools and aided schools and afterwards the teaching of commerce was introduced in such schools. Now the commerce education has been included in the school curriculum.

According to Dr. Khan, "Commerce education got some impetus in conjunction with the growth in the volume of the business. The constantly growing demand for typists, stenographers, book-keepers and clerical workers made commerce curriculum a very desirable addition on to secondary school programme. The tremendous spurt in commerce and industry with the planned economic development of the country made the possession of commercial competencies essential to commercial career. Now, there is a great demand for office workers who can type readily and accurately, take and transcribe notes quickly and correctly, keep financial records and operate business machines effectively. In addition it has been discovered that type writing and other commercial subjects can make valuable contributions to the general education of the students".

In the new scheme of education (I.C. 10+2+3 pattern of education) sufficient attention has been paid to commerce education in Indian schools. In addition to shorthand and typing some more subjects that have been included for teaching in commerce are as follows:

(I) Bookkeeping and Accountancy,

(II) Commercial mathematics,

(III) Secterial practice,

(IV) Commercial English / Hindi,

(V) Commercial Law,

(VI) Industrial law,

(VII) Taxation,

(VIII) Income Tax,

(IX) Salesmanship,

(X) Applied economics,

(XI) Public relations, and

(XII) Advertising.

The teaching of Commerce subjects starts from XI class and in class XII the syllabus is quite advanced. Many a commercial subjects are also taught in vocational institutes.

At present commerce education is considered as good education bemuse of the distinct advantages that a commerce student has over his counter-part in the arts faculty. It is believed that a commerce student not only achieves just training and perfection, but also a general professional intelligence.

Areas of Study of Commerce Education

Commerce education is concerned with the study of the structure and functions of commerce. Following three areas of study are of interest in the study of commerce education:

(i) Commerce education as a part of general education.

(ii) Knowledge about commerce as background understanding.

(iii) Commerce study as a specialized subject. These areas aro discussed in some details:

Knowledge About Commerce as a Part of General Education

This includes the knowledge about commerce that is needed by all people, non-commerce as also the commerce people. Such a knowledge is required by the individual for handling his commercial affairs more successfully. This type of knowledge also helps the individual to become an intelligent citizen.

It includes the topics such as money and banks, budgeting, record keeping, insurance, travel, communication, transport, commerce and community welfare, successful economic citizenship.

The above listed topics are much which introduce student to the activities of commercial enterprises. In addition to these some topics are listed below which include certain activities which are important for study from the over all social point of views and social welfare. Various topics which help in such study are as follows:

Commercial Law and Economics: Under the head *Commercial law* are included the topics such as contracts in every day life, a valid contract, how a contract operates, how to buy and sell goods, instalment and credit services, contracts of employment, life insurance contracts, cheques, drafts and negotiable instruments, buying or renting a home, business organisation contracts, remedyning wrongs.

In the study of *Economics* the topics generally included are as follows:

Consumption of goods and services, production, machine and management, exchange of goods, bank credit distribution of goods in rents wages and interest, labour unions, government taxes and wages etc.

The study of *Typewriting* and *shorthand* is also included in the study of commerce under this head of general education.

Knowledge about Background Understanding of Commerce

Under this head is included the study of general commerce, economics, economic geography, commercial law, bookkeeping, business management, accountancy, advertising and salesmanship, office practices etc.

Most of the topics included for study under this head serve to introduce the students to the activities of business enterprises and provide him material for discussions from the social points of views as also that of management.

Specialised Study for Commerce Students

Under this head are included the topics much as bookkeeping, typewriting, shorthand, office practice, cooperative commerce education, distributive education and office occupation. Most of the topics included for study under this head are much which helps the students to gain specialised education for vocational competencies on different business jobs which are likely to be available to the commerce graduates.

Teaching Basic Skills

The view expressed in various journals, and the views of some educationists about the nature of commerce education are given here to acquaint the students about the study of commerce education.

Leverett. S. Lyen defined commerce education as "any education which a business man has and which makes him a better businessman, is for him business education, no matter whether it" was obtained in the walls of a school or not".

According to Herbert A. Tonne, "For school teaching purposes the above definition is not satisfactory, in as much as it would label any useful thing learned by a business man as a form of commerce education. What Lyen was attempting to do in this definition was to indicate that the school can never do the entire job of training for business. In training for business, teachers must consider not only the specific training given, but also other learnings that may take place in and out of school, when viewed in this light, Lyen's definition is pre-eminently sound.

Paul S. Lomax (1928) writes, "Commercial education is mentally a programme of economic education that has to do with he acquirement, conservation and spending of wealth". Commenting on this definition Herbert A. Tonne observes, "that Lomax is obviously concerned with the total problem of specific education and so he is not thinking about narrower problem of specific education while making use of the word "Fundamentally" is his definition. He is interested to make is quite clear that commerce education includes more than clerical training. When this definition is read in its complete context it is quite clear and meaningful".

H.G. Shields (1930) defines commerce education as follows, "Real commerce education is economic education-economic education, not of academic sort, long on theory and short on facts, but economic education which will given the student a knowledge of the basic realities of business life and relationships. The basic science of business is economics and without a thorough grounding and awareness of economic problems much of the material included in secondary schools, Commerce course is purely additive and essentially superficial. We can not place technical and socio-business subjects on a dual basis science one is basic and the other is supplementary. We can not accept a two headed definition of the field, but must recognise that certain elements must be given most emphasis and these I take to be economic factors". According to Herbert A. Tonne "This interesting explanation is obviously given as a means of emphasizing the value of economic understanding as opposed to a limited skills training programme".

Fredrick G. Nichols defines commercial education as follows, "Commercial education is a type of training which, while' playing its part in the achievement of the general aims of education of any given level, has for its primary objective the preparation of people to enter upon a business career, or having entered upon such a career, to render more efficient service therein and to advance from their present levels of employment to higher levels".

Elaborating further Nichols writes, "There is no conflict between-preparation and efficient participation in productive activities and for wise use of resulting financial rewards. It is an obligation of business education to produce these results in the interests of the individual as a consumer of goods of business which produces what people will buy, and of society as a whole whose welfare is predicted upon a proper functioning of the forces of production distribution and consumption".

Before concluding we consider the view of Herbert A. Tonne on Commerce Education. According to him, "When the two statements of Nichols are placed next to each other, they may seem contradictory. In the complete text, however, Nichols makes very clear the relationship of what might be turned consumer education to vocational commerce education. It would be unfair to Nichols to relate these two statements without this caution, for it would result in a misrepresentation of his complete statement, obviously, Nichols does not deny Lyen's point of view, namely, that much useful learning has been acquired by the business man in non-school situations. Nichols, however, apparently feels that such learning is so diffuse and intangible that it is unwise to label it specifically as Commerce Education".

From the different views about commerce education it can be easily concluded that it is helpful in ones life as well as vocation. The skill in type-writing is most important and this is part of commerce education. Commerce education is useful for all professionals. It is necessary that every professional lawyer, doctor, engineer-can be benefited from commerce education.

Consumer Education

Consumer education is the preparation of an individual through skills, concepts and understanding that are required for everyday living to achieve maximum satisfaction and utilization of his resources. It is part of the formal school curriculum in many places and incorporates knowledge from many disciplines, including but not limited to.

- mathematics,
- economics,
- law,
- information theory,
- psychology, and
- game theory.

One magazine devoted to providing consumers with accurate reviews of products is *Consumer Reports*, not to be confused with *Consumers Digest*.

UNIT-II

Curriculum

Curriculum

If instructions in commerce is to be worthwhile it must be planned with the idea of achieving certain aims which represent values attained from its study. Selection of material should be made with a purpose that is to be served by commerce in the general scheme of education. In recent times we find significant changes in man's outlook on life. It is also essential here to clearly distinguish between 'course of study' and 'curriculum'. These two terms are used synonymously but they have different meanings. 'Curriculum' represents the subjects taught in department of school and 'course of study' represents the various topics which are prescribed for teaching. Thus the 'course of study' is a selection of topics for a particular subject where as 'curriculum' is the series of subjects in the curriculum of a stream.

The 'course of study' is a statement of objectives and outlines of the course content, e.g. there may be a vocational commerce curriculum meant for training the students for certain vocational careers.

Need for Curriculum

The word 'curriculum' is derived from the Latin word 'curresre' which means to run. So 'curriculum' is a course or path which one runs to reach a goal. Thus curriculum includes the subject matter and all learning experiences arranged by the school for a particular subject.

The needs of life go on changing, so is education, hence we can not go on with a static curriculum. The content has to be selected according to the changing needs of society in general and the subject in particular.

The curriculum has to be planned and organised in a scientific manner keeping in view the psychological requirements of the students.

If the curriculum is properly organised, it enables the students to know the subject matter which they have to study. On the other hand it also makes clear to teacher, the material that they have to teach to the students. It also provides the same facility to the examiner.

Principles Involved in Curriculum Construction

Following principles of curriculum construction were recommended by the Secondary Education Commission *(1952 53)*:

(i) The curriculum should be clearly understood. It specifies not only the traditional subjects taught in school but it includes the totality of experiences that peoples receive through the manifold activities that go on in the school, in the class room, library, laboratory, work shop, play grounds and in numerous informal contacts between teacher and the student. Thus the whole life of the school becomes curriculum that can touch the life of the students at all points and help in evolution of balanced personality.

(ii) Curriculum should have flexibility and variety so that it can be easily adopted for different needs and interests. It will help to keeping away a sense of frustration that generally creeps in the child if any attempt is made to teach him uncongenial subjects.

(iii) The curriculum should be vitally and organically related to community life, interpreting for the child, its salient and significant features and permitting him to come in contact with some of its important activities. *(activity curriculum)*.

(iv) The curriculum should be such as to help to train the students not only for work but also for leisure.

(v) It should be framed in such a way that there exist as much of interrelationship between different subjects and also between different topics in the same subject. It means that an attempt be made to keep the contents as "broad field" units so that it is easy to correlate than with life rather than narrow items of information.

Activity Centred Curriculum

Since most of the commerce subjects are vocation based so the activity curriculum is quite suitable for commerce. In the words of Rousseau, "Instead of making the child stick to his books keep him busy in workshop where his hands will work to the profit of his mind". Thus learning by doing 'by activity and experience is the first and the most natured form of learning. This has laid the foundation of activity curriculum. It is with this in mind that it was stated in Wardha Scheme of Education, "We have attempted to draft an activity curriculum which implies that our schools must be places of work experimentation and discovery and not of passive absorption imparted as second hand".

As activity curriculum generally is based on project method or problem solving method of teaching. This is quite significant in such areas as those of physical education, science, geography, history, mathematics etc. Various psychological needs of the child are satisfied to a large extent in an activity curriculum. Here we list some of the *merits* of activity curriculum.

(i) It helps to make the child interested in the process of learning.

(ii) It provides enough scope to the child to learn the things at his own speed.

(iii) It-provides the child various opportunities of working in a group.

(iv) It is need oriented

(v) It helps in development of a sound body.

(vi) It gives a totality of experiences to the pupil.

(vii) It helps to promote a democratic spirit in the child.

(viii) It help to create a self-confidence in the child.

(ix) It helps the child in making full utilisation of his leisure time.

(x) It helps to develop a school-community relationship.

Though there are many a merits of the activity curriculum yet it also has certain limitation. Sonic of the *limitations of activity curriculum* are as follows:

(i) It some times leads to fatigue and boredom.

(ii) In groups, it becomes difficult to achieve the aim. Sometimes misunderstanding may lead to jealousy among the participants. In such cases it becomes the duty of the teacher to coordinate the activity and remove the misunderstanding.

(iii) Some times an activity may not suit all the members of a group and this leads to lack of interest in some students.

(iv) In the activity curriculum there is always a possibility that the participant may not be able to master any thing those he knows something about various parts of the activity.

XI and XII Standard Commerce and Accountancy Syllabus

Before the Secondary Education Commission Report, the course content failed to keep pace with the changes in the social, political, economic, and industrial conditions. It could not keep pace with the latest developments in Education. Theory and practice courses were bookish and theoretical, they encouraged cramming. The instructions becomes lifeless and monotonous. This has been reflected in the following observations of Mudaliar Commission':

(i) The existing curriculum is narrowly conceived.

(ii) It is bookish and theoretical.

(iii) It is over-crowded and the content is not rich and significant.

(iv) It is the provision for practical work is not adequate.

(v) It is not in accordance with the needs and capacities of adolescents.

(vi) It is examination dominated.

(vii) It does not include technical and vocational subjects, which are so essential for industrial and economic development of the country.

The importance of inclusion of technical and vocational subjects was also emphasised in its report by Sapru Committee (1934). A thorough revision and diversification was undertaken on the basis of recommendations made by Mudaliar Commission.

Commerce Education being so closely related with our life its *curriculum* has to be the nucleus of all the activities. It should, therefore, include various subjects. At the middle level the following subjects be included

(i) Languages,

(ii) Social Studies,

(iii) General science,

(iv) Mathematics,

(v) Arts and Music, and

(vi) Craft and physical education.

At the secondary level there should be a few subjects to be taught as core subjects to be offered by all the students, the subjects to be included as core subjects be as follows

(i) Languages,

(ii) Social studies,

(iii) General Science, and

(iv) Craft.

For commerce education a separate stream be provided at higher secondary stage and the following subjects be included for being taught in this stream:

(i) Bookkeeping and Accountancy,

(ii) Elements of Commerce or Business Methods and Machinery,

(iii) Business Correspondence,

(iv) Economics,

(v) Commercial Arithmetic,

(vi) Short-hand,

(vii) Type writing,

(viii) Banking, and

(ix) Work-experience etc.

Most of these subjects have been included in their syllabus majority of Boards of Education of various states in India

In certain states the courses provide option to select there or four of these subjects e.g. as in Maharashtra which has been appreciated by Educationists. However, if this sort of freedom has to be given to the students then the schools should be fully equipped and staffed with the right type of teachers. Though all the subjects listed above are important for commerce education but four subjects namely type writing, short-hand, bookkeeping and general principles of commerce are basic to commerce and a knowledge of these subjects be imparted to all.

For "The persons joining specialised professions such as those of doctors, lawyers architccts etc. The commerce education be imported on the basis of utility". It is thus desirable that the course content in commerce programmes is broadly classified into two categories as under:

(i) Vocational Commerce Education, and

(ii) General Commerce Education.

Under the vocational commerce education the knowledge of following subjects be imparted:

(i) Stenography and Secterial practice,

(ii) Bookkeeping and accounts,

(iii) Clerical and general office work, and

(iv) Office practices.

The course content for general commerce education should include the following:

(i) Consumer information-Guidance,

(ii) Business administration and management,

(iii) Economics, and

(iv) Commercial geography etc.

The content and organisation of commerce course is expected to fulfil the following imperative needs if the students:

(i) It is capable of developing saleable skills amongst the pupils.

(ii) It develops such attitudes that makes the workers an intelligent and productive participant in economic life of the nation.

(iii) It develops in the student a clear understanding of his rights and duties.

(iv) It helps the student to understand, how to purchase and use goods and services intelligently ?

(v) It makes clear to the pupil the significance of the family for the individual and the society.

(vi) It helps the student to understand the methods of science and scientific methods of doing business.

(vii) It helps to develop the students capacity of appreciating the functioning of an office, business and industry.

(viii) It helps the students to develop respect for other persons.

(ix) It encourages the student to develop and maintain good health so that he can devote himself to his studies whole heartedly.

Curriculum in Commerce in High School

Keeping in mind various objectives of commerce education the following four sequences have been suggested:

(i) Stenographic sequence,

(ii) Clerical sequence,

(iii) Secterial sequence, and

(iv) Bookkeeping sequence.

The following scheme of teaching in different sequences in various classes have been suggested:

Stenographic Sequence

Class IX

1. Elements of Commerce
   or
   Business Methods and Machinery.

Class X

1. Type-writing and short-hand.

Class XI

1. Short-hand
2. Bookkeeping
3. Dictation and Transcription

Class XII

1. Office practice
2. Communication Skill
3. Work experience

Clerical Sequence

Class IX

1. ELements of Commerce
   or
   Business Methods and Machinery

Class X

1. Type-writing
2. Business Arithmetic

Class XI

1. Type writing
2. Book keeping
3. Communication skill

Class XII

1. Clerical Practice
2. Business Economics
3. Business Law
4. Work experience

Secterial Sequence

Class IX

1. Elements of commerce
   or
   Business Methods and Machinery.

Class X

1. Type-writing
2. Business Arithmetic/Economic Geography

Class XI

1. Bookkeeping
2. Shorthand
3. Type writing.

Class XII

1. Dictation and Transcription
2. Office practice
3. Communication skill
4. Business law
5. Work experience.

Bookkeeping Sequence

Class IX

1. Elements of Commerce
   or
   Business Methods and Machinery.

Class X

1. Type-writing
2. Business Arithmetic
3. Bookkeeping.

Class XI

1. Book keeping
2. Salesmanship.

Class XII

1. Communication skill
2. Book keeping
3. Work Experience.

Critical Appraisal of Curriculum of Commerce

India is a vast country and has a number of states and Union Territories. Education is in the concurrent list in Indian Constitution and so the states are free to have their independent education policies. However following general procedure is followed for framing of curriculum in commerce by different states.

"A curriculum committee is committee by the State Board or Secondary Education. The members of the committee are generally experts, who are nominated by the Board The members meet from time to time and prescribe the courses of study and curriculum in the commerce subjects. There is also a commerce committee of university teachers which recommend the courses of study. Their recommendations are examined at various stages in the Board and then the courses of study are prescribed.

There are some *defects* in the system of selection of courses and curriculum in commerce stream. Experienced school teachers are not represented. The business circle, for which learners are prepared, are also not represented. The result is that the courses of study suffer in quality and utility.

One of the recommendation made by kothari commission provides for the introduction of specialisation from class XI, but the boards of Secondary Education of most of the Indian states have introduced general education upto class X and specialisation from class XI. Commerce is also being incorporated as a subject of study and in several states it has already been done so in class XI and XII.

According to the growing needs of the economy and the employment opportunities available in the next decade, there is need of bringing about changes in the patterns and composition of the commerce programme.

At present, of the two sequences (i.e. Bookkeeping sequence and stenography sequence) only one sequence predominates (i.e. Book-keeping sequence) and the other sequence (i.e. stenography sequence) remains almost neglected. Even if it has been introduced in a very few schools the programme suffers considerably on vocational grounds.

Before finalisation of any syllabus in Commerce it is desirable to have a good deal of discussion among teachers, educators, planners and administrators so that every state may adopt it, maintaining uniformity in syllabus and standard of achievement in different sequences.

Status of Commerce Education in Secondary Schools in India

In India commerce education first started at the secondary level but its real growth and development took place at the college level, upto the middle of twentieth century. In India commerce was not considered as a separate discipline and it was reduced to an insignificant item of the twin departments Economics and Commerce, in which Economics had an upper hand. It hindered any real progress in the field of commerce for a pretty long time. Only after the report of Mudaliar Commission an expansion took place in commerce education. The multipurpose Higher Secondary School were opened and practical subjects were introduced in many fields including commerce.

To start with in Commerce education were introduced such subjects as letter writing, Business Methods, Shorthand and Typewriting. Later on many more subjects such as Bookkeeping Economics, Accountancy, Commercial Law, Taxation etc. were introduced.

Adopting the recommendation of Dr. V.K.RV. Rao Committee national Diploma in Commercial practice was started with a view to prepare qualified and skilled persons needed by the growing economy in the country.

With the rapid growth in the field of trade, commerce and industry, the need for proper education and right type of Commerce teachers was felt and to meet the needs of teachers of practical subjects a necessity was felt to have some special type of institutes. To provide for this type of institution N.C.E.R.T. and Regional Colleges of Education did a commendable job, Till about *1963* no facilities existed for providing training facilities in the field of commerce but now such training is available through regular training, in service courses, summer-cum-correspondence courses etc. but even now the practical aspect of commerce education programme is not quite satisfactory. An effort is needed to accelerate the teaching or shorthand and type-writing etc. in views of an enormously increasing demand in these fields.

There is a talk of *vocationalisation* and work-experience in Education. It is thus hoped that in recent future the commerce education will be much more oriented in favour of practical subjects. It would help to achieve the main objective of commerce education i.e. development of employable skills.

Academic and Vocational Curriculum—Vocational Areas Identified in the Tamil Nadu Higher Secondary Stage under the Heading "Business and Commerce"

Before the Secondary Education Commission report, the course con-tent failed to keep pace with the changes in social, political, economic and industrial conditions. It also failed to keep abrest of the latest development in Education. Theory and practice courses were theoretical and bookish and had little stuff to attract the students.

The Sapru Committee has pinpointed in 1934 for introduction *of diversified courses of studies* to solve the problem of unemployment in which other vocational subjects was emphasised.

The diversified courses of study should include the following seven groups. (I) Humanities, (II) Sciences, (III) Technical subjects, (IV) Commercial subjects, (V) Agricultural subjects, (VI) Fine arts, and (VII) Home Sciences.

It is on the basic of this organisation of the syllabus that commerce has been introduced at high or higher secondary schools.

After the Mudaliar Commission Report the content courses were reorganised and commerce occupied an eminent position among the vocational groups.

Objectives of the Content and Organisation of Commerce Courses

The content and organisation of commerce course should be such that it meets the following imperative needs of the students:

1. the Course content in the commerce programme should be arranged in such a way and so designed that it is capable of developing saleable skills among students and such attitudes that make the worker an intelligent and productive participant in economic life of the country. The student should be provided with supervised work experience and skills knowledge of their occupations.
2. All students must understand the rights and duties of the citizens of a democratic society, and be diligent and competent in' carrying out their obligations as a member of the community, state and the nation.
3. All students must know-how to purchase and used goods and service intelligently, understand both the values received by the consumer and economic consequence of their acts.
4. All students must understand the significance of the family for the individual and the society and the conditions that are conducive for successful family life.
5. All students must understand the methods of science and Scientific methods of doing business transactions.

6. All students need opportunities to develop their capacities to appreciate the functioning of an office, business and an industry.
7. All students should be trained in the use, of their leisure time well and to budget their time wisely and balance their activities, which yields satisfactions to the individual.
8. All-students must develop respect for other persons and grow an insight into ethical values and live co-operatively.
9. All students must grow their ability to think rationally and express their thoughts clearly.
10. All students must develop and maintain good health and physical fitness so that they can devote their attention to their studies.

Broadly, the course content in the commerce programme may be divided into the following two categories:

A. Vocational Commerce Education, and

B. General Commerce Education.

Vocational Commerce Education-should consist of the follow-ing concepts:

— Stenographic and Secretarial Works.

— Bookkeeping and accounting works. -Clerical and general office work.

— Office practice works-handling labour saving machines.

General Commerce Education-should consist of the following concepts:

— Consumer information-guidance.

— Understanding of business and its management.

— Understanding of economic systems within the country as well as outside. (Study of Economics).

— Study of the environment, regions, nations and the world (Study of Commercial Geography).

Critical Appraisal of the Suggested Curriculum in Commerce

A good deal of new thinking has been initiated on the point of the role of the commerce curriculum by the Government of India, plan-ning commission, educationist, magnets in the filed of commerce and last but not the least the Board of Secondary Examination as well as board of Secondary Education in every state in India. According to the growing needs of the economy and the employment opportunities available in the next decade, there is the need of bringing about great changes in the pattern and composition of the existing course con-tents of the commerce programme.

At present, though there are two sequences: Bookkeeping sequence and the stenographic sequence; only one sequence predominates i.e. the Bookkeeping sequence. The other sequence, i.e. stenographic sequence has been mostly ignored. Even if it has been introduced in a very few schools the programmes suffer considerably on vocational grounds.

Hence the above four sequences have been suggested, which may be offered at the high or higher secondary levels. If these sequences are offered at the school level, they will be able to meet the future needs and demands of the youth on the one hand and the society on the other.

In order to finalise the curriculum of the commerce programme, a good deal of discussing among the teachers,. educators, planners and administrators is vitally needed, so that every state may adopt it, maintaining uniformity in the syllabus and standards of achievement in different sequences.

Analysis of Multipurpose School Syllabus

Even after the adoption of diversified courses in commerce it was observed that the products of commerce schools and colleges are facing acute problems of unemployment. After reviewing the position in India it was suggested that a student of commerce must have a general knowledge of the programmes of commerce with specialisation in one or two subjects such system exists even in developed countries such as USA, England

and Germany. It simply means that the stu-dents be given a freedom to his subjects. He may be allowed to offer our subject of his choice but should be asked to take up the study of other subjects of commerce stream to acquire a general knowledge of all the subjects in thus improve his understanding of commerce.

Syllabus of Bookkeeping

The main deficiency in the syllabus of Bookkeeping is that it does not create a confidence in the business world about the ability and competency of students. Such a doubt crops up mainly due to negligence in developing proper concepts of Bookkeeping before teaching to students about: (i) Personal account, (ii) Real account, and (iii) Nominal account. It so happens because teacher wrongly presumes that students have the knowledge of accounts.

The other major defect in existing syllabus of bookkeeping in that its teaching starts with too many concepts by giving only a pre-view or general background of these concepts. It leads to utter confusion and the student fails to understand the basic concepts of book-keeping. Furthermore the present syllabus in bookkeeping is too narrow and too theoretical and so the students fail to do well in their practical life.

Presently a new thinking based on equation approach or Balance sheet approach has come up in the teaching of bookkeeping. In this approach certain basic concepts of bookkeeping are developed before introducing the teaching of journalising and ledger posting. It is thus more logical.

The introduction of three basic elements of bookkeeping i.e. *Assets, liabilities* and *capital* is quite useful to developed thinking, reasoning and analysing, power of the students. After developing 'what', 'how' and 'why' aspects on the new approach the student is introduced to the device of recording changes in assets, liabilities and capital through T-forms: Such an introduction is essential for creating a good background for introducing journalising. It is desirable to modify the syllabus in bookkeeping in the light of the above observations. In addition to what has been stated in foregoing discussion the syllabus in bookkeeping should include sufficient use of workbooks, practice sets and bookkeeping manual. The use of various types of forms and books of accounts should be mandatory. It would also be highly desirable to emphasise the use of business forms actually used in business houses.

Syllabus of Elements of Commerce

The existing syllabus is more theoretical and so fails to develop the skills of handling business activities. Any syllabus in elements of commerce is expected to pin point various equipments that a school must have for proper teaching of the subject. The possession of these teaching aids be mandatory for the schools.

The existing textbooks should be modified so as to include the new areas of business that have assumed importance. They should also included the upto date procedure of export, import licensing and Banking etc.

The practical training in commercial office, business office, bank etc. be made compulsory by making such a provision in the syllabus. The syllabus must have certain basic concepts e.g. mock trails, Group discussions, projects etc.

Syllabus of Economics

The existing syllabus develops the basic theoretical concepts of economics but fails to train the students in applied economics. The main objective of teaching economics is to develop in them economic understanding of the functions of production, consumption, exchange and distribution for making the individual and society 'better' and 'among other things' promote the general welfare and preserve democratic ideals. To achieve such an objective the knowledge of applied branch of economics is a must and to a paper in economics be included to cover the following.

(i) Various objectives of five year plans of India

(ii) The Industrial policy of Government of India and its impact on Indian Economy.

(iii) Agricultural contribution to the Indian Economy.

(iv) Export-import trade in India.

(v) Foreign trade policy of Indian Government.

To achieve anything concrete the syllabus needs a thorough screening and it should be framed in such a way as to develop, in the student, business economics understanding. It should also aim to develop students understanding and appreciation of role, the business plays in our daily life.

Syllabus in Economic Geography

We should emphasise, in it, the study of different region of the world putting more emphasis on different regions of India. The existing syllabus is too narrow and the data included in textbooks is outdated and obsolete some coordinated efforts in this direction are urgently required both on the part of Government and other educational publishers some way must be found that annual reports published by Government are made easily available to the students so that students may be able to know the economic resources of the country and ways and means of exploiting these resources.

The inclusion of projects in the syllabus will help the students in proper understanding of the knowledge. The syllabus should also aim at developing the students skills in drawing maps, charts and diagrams and for this purpose enough practice be given to the students by including such topics in the syllabus of economic geography.

It would be desirable of reform the syllabus in the light of above suggestion.

Syllabus in Short-hand

In the syllabus of short-hand more emphasis be laid on the vocational aspect of content area because it is a vocational subject. So far we have failed to make the syllabus more vocational oriented. Two systems exist in America (viz. (i) hand written symbol system and (ii) maching short-hand system). In India even the first system (i.e. hand written symbol system) has not fared well. This may be attributed to the defect of the content and the organisation of subject matter.

In short-hand teaching the book most commonly used in *Pitman short-hand Instructor* which does not suit our conditions. This book was written in England and includes many an English words which are not commonly used in India. The preparation and publication of book suitable for Indian students is the first and foremost need in this area. A thorough knowledge of short-hand and a good hand writing of the teacher who demonstrates the short-hand writings on blackboard is a must. The use of properly ruled blackboards should be made compulsory. Due emphasis be placed on reading manuscripts as well as printed outlines in short-hand. Proper place be given to all the three important activities (viz. Reading, Copying and transcribing).

Practice exercises in textbooks should be such as to accelerate the final learnings. There should be included in syllabus some student-teacher project on short-hand procedure.

Selection of Materials

The purpose of this policy is to serve as a guide to the Libraries/Learning Resource Centers/Educational Resources Support Services staff and Dallas County Community College District personnel for achieving consistent excellence in the choice of materials, in whatever format, and as a statement to the public of our purposes and standards in building collections.

- To assist librarians in providing current, diverse, balanced collections of materials to support the instructional, institutional and individual needs of students, faculty and staff.
- To provide access to materials in appropriate formats including print and electronic resources consistent with the college's fiscal resources.
- To encourage instructional faculty participation in collection development.
- To provide organized access to electronic resources.
- To serve distance education students and faculty by providing remote access to materials in the most appropriate and cost-effective manner.

Philosophy of Selection

Dallas County Community College District was established to help students equip themselves for effective living and responsible citizenship in a rapidly changing society. The Libraries/Learning Resource Centers/Educational Resources Support Services programs have been planned to provide support to the total college program in achieving its mission.

All materials acquired by the Libraries/Learning Resource Centers/Educational Resources Support Services should reflect resource needs of the Dallas County Community College District. This underlying principle will determine such basic matters as type, format, quantity and scope of resources to be acquired. In general, the resource needs of the College should reflect one or more of the following:

- curriculum support
- general reference needs
- research needs
- general or special professional growth
- cultural enrichment
- extracurricular interests

Responsibilities for Selection

Ultimate responsibility for selection of materials rests with the Librarians/Directors/Deans who operate within the framework of policies determined by the Board of Trustees. Selection is vested in the staff of the Libraries/Learning Resource Centers/Educational Resources Support Services who actively select the input and work with faculty and students in coordinating the selection of materials and helping to build a collection that truly reflects resource needs of the Colleges.

Principles of Resource Selection

The Libraries/Learning Resource Centers/Educational Resources Support Services are committed to the principles supported by the American Library Association's Library Bill of Rights in that it must provide materials:

- that will enrich and support the curriculum, taking into consideration the varied interests, abilities and maturity level of the users served;
- that will stimulate growth in factual knowledge, literacy appreciation, aesthetic values and ethical standards;
- on opposing sides of controversial issues, so that students may develop under guidance the practice of critical reading and thinking;
- representative of the many religious, ethnic and cultural groups and their contributions to the American heritage;
- on various learning and interest levels necessary to complement the open door policy of the community college.

Anyone within the user community may recommend purchase of library materials. The Libraries/Learning Resource Centers/Educational Resources Support Services reserve the right to make all final decisions on purchases.

Materials that meet the following evaluative criteria may be considered for inclusion in the collection:

- importance of subject matter to curriculum and contribution to the breadth or depth of the collection
- competent and qualified author, editor, compiler, publisher, producer, etc.
- accuracy of information
- readability
- cost of materials relative to the budget and other available material
- acquisitions and maintenance costs
- availability in alternate physical or online formats
- availability of material elsewhere in the college community
- availability of web sites originating from the creating or responsible organization/institution, not from a third party

- availability of commercial web sites that are unbiased and accurate, without aggressive or overly abundant advertising so educational use is not compromised
- historical value
- physical space requirements
- in compliance with the Americans with Disability Act of 1990. Pub.L. 101-336. 26 July 1990. Stat.104.37

Questioned Materials

Implementation of the concept of academic freedom in the Libraries/Learning Resource Centers/Educational Resources Support Services involves selecting some materials which may be considered controversial by some individuals or groups. Reasons often cited for materials considered offensive may include profanity, divergent viewpoints, controversial authors, sexual explicitness, use of nonstandard English and dialects, violence and criminal acts. The acquisition of such materials does not imply approval or endorsement of their contents. These materials are acquired to support the curriculum and to represent all sides of controversial issues.

The selection criteria must remain broad and flexible in order to provide a collection which supports the wide range of academic and technical programs and diverse backgrounds of its clientele. The Libraries endorse the American Library Association Library Bill of Rights, and the principles of that document are an integral part of this policy statement. The Libraries/Learning Resource Centers/Educational Resources Support Services do not add or withdraw materials that have been chosen or excluded on the basis of stated criteria at the request of any individual or group. Any individual or group questioning the appropriateness of materials in the collection should direct questions to the college Librarians/Library Directors/Deans.

Gifts/Donated Materials

The Dallas County Community College District will consider gifts/donated materials on the individual merit of each item. The same criteria that applies to selection of materials for the collection applies to gifts/donated materials. The Libraries/ Learning Resource Centers/Educational Resources Support Services have the right to reject any material on the basis of our stated selection policy. The Libraries/Learning Resource Centers/Educational Resources Support Services staff will not make appraisals of materials either for resale value or statements of donation on income tax reports. A letter of acknowledgement will be sent to the donor upon request.

Maintenance of the Collection

The Libraries/Learning Resource Centers/Educational Resources Support Services will retain control of all resources purchased through their budgets and/or placed in their inventories.

Multiple Copies

Need for duplicates at individual colleges will be determined by utilization, importance of materials to the curriculum, budget and/or price.

Replacement of Lost or Damaged Material

For lost or damaged material, the same general and specific criteria for selection will apply in determining if the material is to be replaced in the collections.

Deselection

Deselection of library materials is essential for the maintenance of a current, academically sound collection. The goal of collection assessment is to evaluate the appropriateness of the collection. Systematic withdrawals will be conducted using the following criteria:

- obsolescence
- physical condition
- insufficient use or basic value
- changing curricular needs
- physical space requirements
- maintenance costs

UNIT-III

Instructional Method-I

Lecture Method

The lecture is still the most frequently used method of instruction. However, presenting a lecture without pausing for interaction with trainees can be ineffective regardless of your skill as a speaker. The use of pauses during the lecture for direct oral questioning creates interaction between instructor and trainee. Unfortunately, when classes are large, the instructor cannot possibly interact with all trainees on each point. The learning effectiveness of the lecture method has been questioned because of the lack of interac- tion; but it continues as a means of reaching a large group at one time with a condensed, organized body of information. Providing trainees with lesson objectives before the lecture will enable them to listen more effectively.

It will help them to take concise, brief notes concerning the objectives rather than writing feverishly through- out the lecture. We discuss the lecture method first because the techniques involved serve as the basis for other methods of training.

Those techniques apply not only to lectures, but to many other kinds of presentations in which oral explanations play a secondary, but important, role. Every method depends on oral instruction to give information, to arouse attention and interest, and to develop receptive attitudes on the part of the trainees. Therefore, as an instructor, organize your oral presentations with the following techniques in mind:

1. Maintain good eye contact. As you speak, shift your gaze about the class, pausing momentarily to meet the gaze of each trainee. Make the trainees feel what you have to say is directed to each one personally. Your eyes as well as your voice communicate to them; and their eyes, facial expressions, and reactions communicate to you. Watch for indications of doubt, misunderstanding, a desire to participate, fatigue, or a lack of interest. If you are dealing with young trainees, you may sometimes need to remind them that they must give undivided atten- tion to the instruction.
2. Maintain a high degree of enthusiasm.
3. Speak in a natural, conversational voice.' Enunciate your words clearly. Make certain the trainees can hear every spoken word.
4. Emphasize important points by the use of gestures, repetition, and variation in voice inflection.
5. Check trainee comprehension carefully throughout the presentation by watching the faces of the trainees and by questioning. Observing facial expressions as an indication of doubt or misunderstanding is not a sure way of checking on trainee comprehension. Some trainees may appear to be comprehending the subject matter when, in reality, they are completely confused. Trainees who are in doubt often hesitate to make their difficulty known. They may hesitate because of natural timidity, fear of being classified as stupid, or failure to understand the subject matter well enough to explain where their difficulty lies. Frequently ask if the class has any questions, thus giving the trainees an opportunity to express any doubts or misunderstandings on their part. Based on your personal knowledge and past experiences, ask specific questions about those areas which might give trainees the most trouble. Some instructors make the mistake of waiting until the end of the presentation to ask questions. The best time to clear away mental fog is when the fog develops. Mental fog tends to create a mental block that prevents the

trainee from concentrating on the subject matter being presented. (Later in this chapter we discuss techniques related to asking questions, calling upon trainees to answer questions, and evaluating answers.)

6. Instruct on the class level. Use words, explanations, visual illustrations, questions, and the like, directed to the needs of the average trainee in the class.
7. Stimulate trainees to think. Think, as used here, refers to creative thinking rather than to a mere recall of facts previously learned. Use a number of instructional devices for stimulating trainee thinking. Among those devices are thought-provoking questions, class discussions, problem situations, challenging statements, and rhetorical questions (a question to which no answer is expected). Another device is the use of suggestions, such as "I want you to think along with me," and "Consider your reaction to this situation."

Demonstration Method

Use the demonstration or "doing" method to teach skills. Demonstrate step-by-step the procedures in a job task, using the exact physical procedures if possible. While demonstrating, explain the reason for and the significance of each step. To be effective, plan the demonstration in advance so that you will be sure to show the steps in the proper sequence and to include all steps.

If you must give the demonstration before a large group or if the trainees might have trouble seeing because of the size of the equipment involved, use enlarged devices or training aids. When practical, allow trainees to repeat the procedure in a "hands on" practice session to reinforce the learning process. By immediately correcting the trainees' mistakes and reinforcing proper procedures, you can help them learn the task more quickly.

The direct demonstration approach is a very effective method of instruction, especially when trainees have the opportunity to repeat the procedures

Techniques Used in the Demonstration Method

The basic method of instruction for teaching skill-type subject matter is the demonstration- performance method of instruction. This method is recommended for teaching a skill because it covers all the necessary steps in an effective learning order. The demonstration step gives trainees the opportunity to see and hear the details related to the skill being taught. Those details include the necessary background knowledge, the steps or procedure, the nomenclature, and the safety precautions. The repetition step helps the average and slow learners and gives the trainees an additional opportunity to see and hear the skill being taught. The performance step gives all trainees the opportunity to become proficient. In short, this method is recommended because it leaves nothing to chance. For convenience, we discuss the techniques for imparting skills in steps, rather than activities. When setting up an instructional plan, understand that, you don't have to follow these steps in the sequence given below; instead choose the steps in the sequence best suited to the needs of the trainees. Although you will always include a demonstration step and a performance step, you must use judgment in selecting techniques to make the various steps effective.

Lecture Cum Demonstration Method

Lecture Method

It is oldest teaching method given by philosophy of idealism. As used in education, the lecture method refers to the teaching procedure involved in clarification or explanation of the students of some major idea. This method lays emphasis on the penetration of contents. Teacher is more active and students are passive but he also uses question answers to keep them attentive in the class. It is used to motivate, clarify, expand and review the information. By changing Ms Voice, by impersonating characters, by shifting his posing, byusing simple devices, a teacher can deliver lessons effectively, while delivering his lecture; a teacher can indicate by her facial expressions, gestures and tones the exact slode of meaning that he wishes to convey. Thus we can say that when teacher takes the help of a lengthy-short explanation in order to clarify his ideas or some fact that explanation is termed as lecture or lecture method and after briefing about lecture method. Let's see what is a demonstration.

Demonstration Method

The dictionary meaning of the word "demonstration" is the outward showing of a feeling etc.; a description and explanation by experiment; so also logically to prove the truth; or a practical display of a piece of equipment to snow its display of a piece of equipment to show its capabilities. In short it is a proof provided by logic, argument etc.

Lecture Cum Demonstration Method

Definition: To define "it is a physical display of the form, outline or a substance of object or events for the purpose of increasing knowledge of such objects or events. Demonstration involves showing what or showing how". Demonstration is relatively uncomplica.ed process in that it does not require extensive verbal elaboration. Now it will be easy to define what is lecture cum demonstration method.

To begin with, this method includes the merits of lecture method and demonstration method. The teacher performs the experiment in tho class and goes on explaining what she does. It takes into account the active participation of the student and is thus not a lopsided process like the lecture method. The students see the actual apparatus and operations and help the teacher in demonstrating experiments and thereby they feel interested in learning. So also this mehod follows maxims from concrete to abstract Wherein the students observe the demonstration critically and try to draw inferences. Thus with help of lecture cum demonstration method their power of observation and reasoning are also exercised. So the important principle on which this method works is "Truth is that works."

Requirements of good Demonstration: The success of any demonstration following points should be kept in mind.

1. It should be planned and rehearsed by the teacher before hand.

2. The apparatus used for demonstration should be big enough to be seen by the whole class. If the class may be disciplined she may allow them to sit on the benches to enable them a better view.
3. Adequate lighting arrangements be made on demonstration table and a proper background table need to be provided.
4. All the pieces of apparatus be placed in order before starting the demonstration. The apparatus likely to be used should be placed in the left hand side of the table and it should be arranged in the same order in which it is likely to be used
5. Before actually starting the demonstration a clear statement about the purpose of demonstration be made to the students.
6. The teacher makes sure that the demonstration lecture method leads to active participation of the students in the process of teaching.
7. The demonstration should be quick and slick and should not appear to linger on unnecessarily.
8. The demonstration should be interesting so that it captures the attention of the students.
9. It would be better if the teacher demonstrates with materials or things the children handles in everyday life.
10. For active participation of students the teacher may call individual student in turn to help him in demonstration.
11. The teacher should write the summary of the principles arrived at because of demonstration on the blackboard. The black board can be also used for drawing the necessary diagrams.

These are some of the requirements of a good demonstrations. Steps needed to conduct a Lecture -cum demonstration lesson.

1. *Planning and Preparation:* A great care be taken by the teacher while planning and preparing his demonstration. He should keep the following points I mind while preparing his lesson.

   a. Subject matter.

   b. Questions to be asked.

   c. Apparatus required for the experiment

   To achieve the above stated objective the teacher should thoroughly go through the pages of the textbook, relevant to the lesson. After this he should prepare his lesson plan in which he should essentially include the principles to be explained, a lot of experiments to be demonstrated and type of questions to be asked form the students. These questions be arranged in a systematic order to be followed in the class. Before actually demonstrating the experiment to a class, the experiment be rehearsed under the condition prevailing in the classroom. Inspite of this, some thing may go wrong at the actual lesson, so reserve apparatus is often useful the apparatus has to be arranged in a systematic manner on the demonstration table. Thus for the success of demonstration method a teacher has to prepare himself as thoroughly as possible.

2. *Introduction of the Lesson:* As in every subject so also in the case of science the lesson should stat with proper motivation of the students. It is always considered more useful to introduce the lesson in a problematic way which would make the student's realise the importance of the topic. The usual way through which the teacher can introduce the lesson is by telling some personal experience or incident of a simple and interesting experiment. A good experiment carefully demonstrated is likely to leave an everlasting impression on the mind of the young pupils and would set the students talking about it in the school.

3. *Presentation:* The method presenting the subject matter is very important. A good teacher should present his

lesson in an interesting manner and not in an boring manner. To make the lesson interesting the teacher may not be very rigid too remain within the prescribed course rather he or she should make the lesson as much as broad based as possible. For widening the lesson the teacher may think of various useful application taught by him. He is also at the liberty to take examples and illustrations for allied branches of science like history, geography etc. Constant questions and answer should form a part of every demonstration lesson. Questions and cross question are essential for properly illuminating the principles discussed. Question should be arranged in such a way that their answers may form a complete teaching unit.

4. *Performance of Experiment:* A good observer has been described as a person who has learnt the use the senses of touch, sight, smell in an intelligent way. Through this method we want children to observe what happens in a experiment and to state it carefully. We also want them to make generalization without violating scientific spirit i.e. we should allow children from one experiment or observation. The following steps are generally accepted as valuable in conducting science experiment generally.
   a. Write the problem to be solved in simple words.
   b. To make a list of activities that has to be used to solve the problem.
   c. Gather material for conducting the experiment
   d. Work out a format of steps in the order of preocedu8re so that everyone knows what is to be done.
   e. Teacher should try the experiment before conduction. f. Record the findings.
   f. Assist students to make generalisation.

5. *Black Board Summary:* A summary of important results and principles should be written in the Blackboard. Use of blackboard should be also frequently used to

draw sketches and diagrams. The entire procedure should be displayed to the students after the demonstration.

6. *Supervision:* Students are asked to take the complete notes of the black board summary including the sketches and diagrams drawn. Such a record will be quite helpful to the student while learning his lessons.Such a summary will prove beneficial only if it has been copied correctly from the black boards and to make sure that it is done so the teacher must check it frequently during this stage.

Common Errors In Demonstration Lesson

A summary of the common errors committed while delivering a demonstration lesson is given below:

a) Apparatus may not be ready for use.

b) There may not be an apparent relation between the demonstration experiment and the topic under discussion.

c) Black board summary not up to the mark.

d) Teacher may be in a hurry to arrive at a generalisation without allowing students to arrive at a generalisation from facts.

e) Teacher may take to talking too much which will mar the enthusiasm of the students.

f) Teacher may not have allowed sufficient time for recording of data.

g) Teacher may fail to ask the right type of questions.

Merits of Lecture cum Demonstration Method

a) It is an economical method as compared to a purely student centered method.

b) It is a psychological method and students take active interest in the teaching learning process.

c) It leads the students from concrete to abstract situations.

d) It is suitable method if the apparatus to be handled is costly and sensitive. Such apparatus is likely to be handled and damaged by the students.

e) This method is safe if the experiment is dangerous.

f) In comparison to Heuristic, Project method it is time saving but purely Lecture method is too lengthy.

g) It can be successfully used for all types of students.

h) It improves the observational and reasoning sills of the students.

Limitations of Lecture cum Demonstration Method

a) It provides no scope for "Learning by Doing" for the Students as students are only observing the Teacher performing.

b) Since Teacher performs the experiment at his/ her own pace many students may not be able to comprehend the concept being clarified.

c) Since this method is not child centred it makes no provision for individual differences, all types of students including slow learners and genius have to proceed with the same speed.

d) It fails to develop laboratory skills in the students.

e) It fails to impart training in scientific attitude. In this method students many a times fail to observe many finer details of the apparatus used because they observe it from a distance.

Problem Method

Life is full of problems and we term one as successful, who is able to use the knowledge acquired and reasoning power to find solutions to these problems. Problem–solving may be a purely mental difficulty or it may be physical and involve manipulation of data. Problem-solving method aims at presenting the knowledge to be learnt in the form of a problem. It begins with a problematic situation and consists of continuous, meaningful, well-integrated activity. The problems are test to the students in a natural way and it is ensured that the students are genuinely interested to solve them.

- Mathematical Problem Defined as,

  A problem is a task for which:

  The person confronting it wants or needs to find a solution.

  The person has no readily available procedure for finding the solution.

  The person must make an attempt to find a solution.

- Goals Of Mathematical Problem-Solving: The specific goals of problem solving in Mathematics are to:

  1. Improve pupils' willingness to try problems and improve their perseverance when solving problems.
  2. Improve pupils' self-concepts with respect to the abilities to solve problems.
  3. Make pupils aware of the problem-solving strategies.
  4. Make pupils aware of the value of approaching problems in a systematic manner.
  5. Make pupils aware that many problems can be solved in more than one way.
  6. Improve pupils' abilities to select appropriate solution strategies.
  7. Improve pupils' abilities to implement solution strategies accurately.
  8. Improve pupils' abilities to get more correct answers to problems.

- Steps of Problem solving method:

  Recognising the problem or sensing the problem.

  Interpreting, defining and delimiting the problem.

  Gathering data in a systematic manner.

  Organising and evaluating the data.

  Formulating tentative solutions.

  Arriving at the true or correct solution.

Verifying the results.

- *Merits:* The merits or advantages of problem solving method are as follows:

  Method is scientific in nature.

  Develops good study habits and reasoning power.

  Helps to improve and apply knowledge and experiences.

  Stimulates thinking of the child.

  Students learn virtues such as patience, cooperation, and self-confidence.

  Learning becomes more interesting and purposeful.

  Develops qualities of initiative and self-dependence in the students, as they have to face similar problematic situations in real life too.

  Develops desirable study habits in the students.

- Limitations: the limitations are mainly due to ineffective use of the problem solving method. When a classroom is completely teacher dominated then in such a classroom the problem solving method will fail.

  Difficult to organise e contents of syllabus according to this method.

  Time consuming method.

  All topics and areas cannot be covered by this method.

  There is a lack of suitable books and references for the students.

  Method does not suit students of lower classes.

  Mental activity dominates this method. Hence there is neglect of physical and practical experiences.

Method Project

Project method is a natural hearted, problem solving and purposeful activity carried to completion in a social environment this is the most concrete of all types of activity methods. It is the revolt against the traditional, bookish and passive environment of school.

The project method of teaching is the practical outcome of the John Dewey's philosophy of pragmatism. Pragmatism has made a unique construction in the shape of project method enuciated by the Kilpatrick the follower of Dewey.

In project method, study through workshop and source methods are also studied, concrete activity rather than academic work take the dominant place in the project method. The project method also transcends the subject barrier which is not done by other methods. In project method the teacher instead of following the lecture method substitutes "the subject" with few outstanding problems and proceeds to solve the same by experiment method with the active co-operation of the students. The purpose of this method is to learn pupils into the trained investigators and prepare them for learning by living.

Importance of Project Method

1) *The Principle of Purpose:* A purposeful activity will stimulate and provide to the child to achieve the goal and to kindle interest in the activity and consequently accelerated the learning process.
2) *The Principle of Activity:* It is an activity oriented method. It enabler the pupil to plan independently and to carry out the project in the co-operation of the others.
3) *The Principle of Freedom:* The method provider free atmosphere to do activity since a project is a bit of real life that has been imported into school and freedom to choose activity according to the interests, need and capacities of the children give them a freedom of the free atmosphere.
4) *The Principle of Reality:* This method implies learning by doing. It meand the learning by doing is real. It introduces real life situation in the curriculum and the students.
5) *The Principle of Utility:* Knowledge for knowledge sake doesn't appeal to a young child thus this method enable the pupil to learn skills which may help them in the later part of their life.

6) *The Principle of Correlation:* Knowledge is artificially fragmented otherwise it is holistic in nature correlation of subject is possible in project method.

Definitions of Project Method

Ballard: "A project is a bit of real life that has been imported into the School".

J. A. Stevenson: "A project is a problematic act carried to the completion in its Natural setting".

Kilpatrick: "A project is a whole hearted purposeful activity proceeding in a social environment".

W.W. Charters: "In the topical organization principle are learned first while in the projects the problem are proposed which demands in the solution the development of principles by the learner as needed".

Different Types of Projects

The Producer Type: Here the emphasis is directed towards the actual construction of a material object or article.

The Consumer Type: Here the projective is to obtain either direct or vicarious experience such as reading and learning stories and also listening to a musical selection etc.

The Problem Type: Here the chief purpose is to solve a problem involving the intellectual process such as determining the density of a certain liquid etc.

The Dill Type: Where the objective is to attain a certain degree of skill in a reaction as learning a vocabulary.

Various Steps in Conducting Project

Creating the Situation: It is not right to force a project on the unwilling students. The students themselves should define state and choose their problems. Through mutual conversation the teacher helps in the making of a proposal by the students. The teacher would discover the taste, needs of the students and would provide situation wherein the students feel a spontaneous urge to carry out projects according to their felt needs.

Selection of Project: All the projects the children selects cannot be accepted and so only those projects which helps to meet the real needs of the students are selected. The teacher needs to participate and make the projects clearer to the students. For E.g. If teacher wants that there should be flower garden then he takes the student to a garden instead of ordering the students to plant a flower garden. The children thus are please to see the flowers and wonder why there are no flowers and the students select a project to have a flower garden. Thus in way teacher without ordering only by showing the situation can develop interest and select a project.

Planning: After the project is decided and accepted the teacher may develop an outline and ask the pupils to study it deeply at home. A class period may be devoted for this work. The teacher should draw attention of the students to the need of planning before undertaking the activity. The task of planning is difficult.

Good planning leads to better result reach child should be encouraged to give his suggestions. Different proposal should be discussed and alternative consider the proposal. The best plan is agreed upon after a good deal of discussion, suggestions counter suggestion and rejections. The teacher needs to divided the work among the students according to their interest and ability and see that they move towards accomplishing the task.

Education of the plan:In this the students start collecting the facts according to their own efficiency and the teacher nearly supervisor the task done by them. This is the stage at which the student perform many activities and learn many various useful experience. The children's are busy in collecting information, reading keeping accounts, calculating pries, visiting markets, museums etc For E.g.: Dramatizing the life of shivaji may be accepted as project in history. Where such a project is accepted the teacher may develop in broad outlines the life of shivaji and ask the pupils to study it thoroughly, children's should also be engaged in making maps of India showing the Mughal Empire. These maps may be utilized in the drama at the appropriate places.

Evaluating the project: The work is to be reviewed where it is completed. Here the pupil criticizer his own task and he decides are accomplished objectives that he sets out to achieve are occoueplished or not. They express their ideas before the teacher with freedom about their drawback.

Recording: In this steps a complete record of all activities connected with the project must be maintained. In this all the pupils write in details about their all the five steps of the project with mention of consulted books aids, details of task etc. the project book should be well maintained. The project book should give the procedure of providing a situation and of choosing the project, duties assigned difficulties felt and experience gained etc.

Merits of the Project Method

1. The project strategy is based upon the laws of learning:
   a. *Law of Readiness:* According to this law we learn most when our minds are already to receive. The project method prepares the mind of the students by providing them with suitable situation.
   b. *Law of Exercise:* Learning to be effective must be practised. The project method affords many opportunities to the students to learn by doing.
   c. *Law of Effect:* This law states that if learning is to be effective and fruitful it must be accompanied by satisfaction pleasure when they manipulate their own activities.
2. This method makes education effective because it is purposeful, meaning arouses curiosity etc. Learning becomes practical and intimately related with life. When meaningful purposeful activities are provided to the students get opportunities to acquaint themselves with the real problems of life. The students learn practical usefulness of different subject of the curriculum.
3. The pupil involves in real life problem practically. They are trained to face life in future since they work in natural conditions.

4. The project method gives unity of the curriculum. The subject do not remain isolated in this method, but instead they are co-related and thus students learn different learn different subjects in this method.
5. The pupil acquires knowledge which is useful for the present and future life in short time. The method providing sufficient opportunities to the students to work co-operatively for common purpose decision are arrived at democratic way.
6. This method imports training to the student to inculcate in there primary virtues like tolerance independence, open mind ness, resourcefulness etc.
7. It cause an all round development of the pupils and attributes like self dependence and self confidence.
8. Dignity of labour is engendered through the project method. The students have to perform their activities on their own and thus they develop a taste for all kinds of work. They learn that there is nobleness working and doing things with their own.
9. The students work with great enthusiasm for the competition of their self chosen project. They do not feel tried as there is good deal of Varity in their work and the atmosphere is full of the freedom. As the children busy with their self chosen work they do not get opportunities to think of the anti social ways.

Limitation of Project Method

1. A project with limited scope cannot develop on all around personality secondly no project can teach all the subject and so some times teaching becomes haphazard and discontinuous.
2. Neglecting intellectual work: There is a widespread misconception that the project method glorifies hard work at the cost of intellectual work. The critics argue is that the children are kept busy in model making only.
3. In this brilliant students lead other students who are passive and follow blindly.

4. This method practice and the development of skill in various subjects. The students do not get adequate drill in arithmetic, reading spelling drawing etc.
5. Preparation of books suitable for the project work is by no means an easy task. Moreover material required for the implementation of a project is very costly. The method is not suitable for the ordinary schools.
6. Some student who is not inclined to take responsibility may remain in the back ground and do very little work.
7. The school teaching can become disorganized and irregular because the method needs freedom and flexibility.
8. For the successful working of this method, very learned efficient teachers are needed. The method impose heavy burden and responsibility upon the teacher.

Method Inductive

What is the Inductive Method?

The inductive method, also referred to as the *scientific method*, is a process of using observations to develop general priciples about a specific subject. A group of similar specimens, events, or subjects are first oberved and studied; finding from the observations are then used to make broad statements about the subjects that were examined. These statements may then become laws of nature or theories.

An Example of the Inductive Method Is: Extensive observations of many species of land-dwelling turtles reveals that the observed turtles have shells, lay eggs, and eat a diet of plants as well as insects. From this, it could be induced that *all* land turtles have shells, lay eggs and eat plants and insects. The data gathered from observing **some** examples of land turtles is applied as a general rule about **all** land turtles.

How is the Inductive Method Used in the Classroom?

The inductive method is deeply entrenched in Science education. Traditionally science courses were taught deductively, with the teacher teaching the students the facts and theory, then moving to textbook exercises and finally application. Using the inductive method, the teacher presents the students with a specific challenge or problem, such as an experiment that needs to be interpreted, or a real-world problem that needs to be solved. The students must then use their base-knowledge to investigate, test, analyze and come to their own conclusion or solution. The inductive method, which is commonly interpreted in schools as the scientific method is widely used as a guide for observation and inquiry based learning. School Science Fairs universally adhere to inductive methods as a guideline for student investigation into Science. In Science classrooms, students are often guided through the process of induction by the following steps:

The Inductive (Scientific) Method

- *State the Question:* What information do you wish to obtain?
- *Make Observations:* Gather information that will help answer your questions by researching, making, and recording direct observations of the subject
- *Form a Hypothesis:* After gathering an adequate amount of information, apply what you have observed to form an educated guess or prediction of what the answer to your question is
- *Test:* Test your hypothesis by performing an experiment that includes a variable
- *Analyze:* Examine the results of your experiment to understand what they imply
- *Draw a Conclusion:* Based on the interpretation of your results, develop a general principle as an answer to your question.

Below is an Example of How the Above Steps of Inductive Reasoning Might be Applied in Science Classroom:

- *State the Question:* What type of artificial light will cause plants to grow the most: red, blue, green, or normal white light?

- *Make Observations:* Plants observed growing under normal white house lights often appear green, leafy, sturdy and healthy. However, plants grown in indoor white light usually don't appear as large or as healthy as plants that grow outdoors in natural sunlight. After reading about natural sunlight, I have found that the sun contains high amounts of red light.
- *Form a Hypothesis:* Based on my observations of plants already growing under two different types of light, I predict that plants grown under red light will grow the most, because red light is closest to natural sunlight.
- Test: As a test, a few plants are grown from seed under entirely red, blue, green, or white light. Plants are placed in the same amounts of soil, receive the same amount of water, and grow in identical environments. The only difference between the growth conditions of the plants is the light.
- *Analyze:* The plants grown under red light were the largest, leafiest, and sturdiest, followed by plants grown under white light, blue light, and green light.
- *Draw a Conclusion:* Based on the results from my tests and observations, I can conclude that: Red light causes plants to undergo the most growth.

Types of Inductive Teaching and Learning

Inductive teaching methods come in many forms and with many names. We have already mentioned inquiry-based and discovery learning. Besides those there are problem-based learning, project-based learning, case-based learning and just-in-time learning.

- *Inquiry-based Learning:* Students are presented with a challenge which will require knowledge that has not been completely covered. The challenge may come in a question that needs a solution, an observation that needs to explained, a data set that must be analyzed or a hypothesis that must be tested.
- *Discovery Learning:* Students are presented with a challenge and left to work out the solution on their

own. (Bruner 1961, French 2006) Students learn to use trial and error to analyze and resolve their findings. The instructor may provide limited feedback. In these situations, this process is referred to as "Guided Discovery."

- *Problem-based Learning:* As the name suggests, the students are presented with a real-world problem that needs to be solved. Problem-based learning generally incorporates collaborative learning by placing the students into teams. Collectively they formulate and evaluate their various solutions, select the best choice and present their argument for that solution. In problem-based learning students have not previously received the necessary background instruction and emphasis is not on a correct answer but on the investigative process.
- *Project-based Learning:* Students are presented with an assignment that requires that they design or produce a deliverable. The final product may be a formal written or oral presentation of their processes and outcomes. Project-based learning can be assigned to individuals or teams. Unlike problem-based learning, this style of inductive learning provides the student with the necessary background knowledge and is focused more on the solution.
- *Case-base Learning:* Students are presented with real-life scenarios, or cases, in which they hypothetically assume various roles. The cases tend to be very well structured filled with elaborate details to incorporate many of the variables real-life problems contain. Students learn to apply material that has already been covered in class and is somewhat familiar (Lohman 2002) Case-based learning can be assigned to individual students or to teams. Studies have shown that case-based instruction significantly improves student retention, reasoning and problem-solving skills (Fasko 20030, and higher-order skills on Bloom's taxonomy. (Gabel 1999)

- *Just-in-Time Teaching (JiTT):* Students are presented with conceptual questions at the beginning of class. These questions are usually done in an electronic or web-based mode so they can be accessed immediately. The teacher then uses the findings of that exam to adjust the lesson and address misconceptions the students may have about the subject content. This method is classified as inductive because the students are being asked questions about material they have not yet studied. This method is used primarily in higher education.

Is the Inductive Method an Effective Tool?

The inductive method is an extremely effective process for obtaining general, observation-based information about the world. In fact, the inductive method—whether guided in classrooms or occurring in non-academic settings—is one of the most common and natural forms of making logical assumptions about what we observe. Inductive reasoning allows us to gather ideas about an infinite number of events or phenomena in real life. Use of the inductive method as a teaching tool to guide students through critical thinking, awareness, evaluation of what they observe, and the drawing of logical conclusions and explanations is almost universally accepted in science education.

What are the Criticisms of the Inductive Method?

The main criticism of the inductive method is that is is not a valid means of obtaining *proof*. Because inductive reasoning encompasses broad statements based on smaller observations, the method can never completely prove that what is observed from a small set of data applies to the whole group. (For example, based on observation of mice, the inductive method can help us generalize that because the *observed* mice ate peanut butter that *every* mouse, *everywhere* must eat peanut butter.

However, the inductive method cannot provide absolute proof of this assumption.) Generalizations and principles arrived by means of the inductive method may certainly be tested. However, because conclusions drawn from inductive reasoning are based on observable data, if the data changes, the conclusion may change as a result.

What Does Research On Inductive Reasoning Say?

A significant amount of research indicates that the inductive method is highly effective and appropriate for some types of learning goals and a less accurate mode of thinking for others. Most research points to the idea that the inductive method is an effective way to:

- Understand how logical conclusions are drawn
- Apply small, concrete ideas to larger, abstract concepts
- Transfer conclusions and governing principles to newly encountered information
- Develop problem-solving skills

However, research suggests that inductive reasoning is not an effective means for the learning, development, or application of specific rules to small amounts of data or problems. Instead, deductive methods are more appropriate.

Method Deductive

Much like Sherlock Holmes, deductive methods involve beginning with a general concept or given rule and moving on to a more specific conclusion. Solving a math problem or conducting a science experiment is just like the mysteries presented by Sherlock Holmes. Clues are presented concerning the conclusion and using the information given as well as previous knowledge, you can solve the mystery!

Deductive reasoning is the process of reaching a conclusion that is guaranteed to follow, if the evidence provided is true and the reasoning used to reach the conclusion is correct. The conclusion also must be based only on the evidence previously provided; it cannot contain new information about the subject matter. Deductive reasoning was first described by the ancient Greek philosophers such as Aristotle. (from Wikipedia) "drawing conclusions by applying rules or principles; logically moving from a general rule or principle to a specific solution".

Comparison of Two Reasonings

Deductive reasoning works from the "general" to the "specific". This is also called a "top-down" approach. The deductive reasoning works as follows: think of a theory about topic and then narrow it down to specific hypothesis (hypothesis that we test or can test). Narrow down further if we would like to collect observations for hypothesis (note that we collect observations to accept or reject hypothesis and the reason we do that is to confirm or refute our original theory). In a conclusion, when we use deduction we reason from general principles to specific cases, as in applying a mathematical theorem to a particular problem or in citing a law or physics to predict the outcome of an experiment.

Inductive reasoning works the other way, it works from observation (or observations) works toward generalizations and theories. This is also called a "bottom-upýÿ? approach. Inductive reason starts from specific observations (or measurement if you are mathematician or more precisely statistician), look for patterns (or no patterns), regularities (or irregularities), formulate hypothesis that we could work with and finally ended up developing general theories or drawing conclusion. In a conclusion, when we use Induction we observe a number of specific instances and from them infer a general principle or law. Inductive reasoning is open-ended and exploratory especially at the beginning. On the other hand, deductive reasoning is narrow in nature and is concerned with testing or confirming hypothesis.

Properties of Deduction

In a valid deductive argument, all of the content of the conclusion is present, at least implicitly, in the premises. Deduction is nonampliative. If the premises are true, the conclusion must be true. Valid deduction is necessarily truth preserving. If new premises are added to a valid deductive argument (and none of its premises are changed or deleted) the argument remains valid. Deductive validity is an all-or-nothing matter; validity does not come in degrees. An argument is totally valid, or it is invalid.

Properties of Induction

Induction is ampliative. The conclusion of an inductive argument has content that goes beyond the content of its premises. A correct inductive argument may have true premises and a false conclusion. Induction is not necessarily truth preserving. New premises may completely undermine a strong inductive argument. Inductive arguments come in different degrees of strength. In some inductions the premises support the conclusions more strongly than in others.

Intuitive Reasoning: A third type of reasoning, intuitive reasoning, is what many young children use, as well as older children/adults in highly unfamiliar situations. Intuitive reasoning has to do with the way something appears to be, how something "seems" or "looks", and is based on unverified guesses. While it may seem to be very rudimentary, it is very useful in giving a starting point from which induction or deduction can proceed.

It is the chief type of reasoning used by early elementary students, and students must be shown the flaws in it by the use of cognitive conflict in order to learn to move past intuition towards induction and deduction.

Applications

In most subject areas, both deductive and inductive methods are taught as ways to reach a solution. In mathematic and science related subjects, the method of reasoning is most apparent. However, in all subjects of education, a method of reasoning is in place. The following are some resources to see how specific methods influence a variety of subject areas.

The deductive method in subjects of education:

- Mathematics.
- Language Arts
- Science
- Psychology
- The opposite of deductive methods is: Inductive methods.

Cultural Variations in Approaches to Learning

"Teachers may use inquiry methods that emphasize deductive approaches to learning, analytical examinations of details or parts, or the solving or the problems by examining the relationship of one part to another. This linear model, moving sequentially from the specific to the general and examining objects/concepts without a context may not be the preferred approach to learning for some children from groups of color. Students of color often use a more inductive problem solving and reasoning process. They may use observed instances in context to generate an idea or a concept. They move from whole to part from the general to the specific".

Case Study

A case study is one of several ways of doing research whether it is social science related or even socially related. It is an intensive study of a single group, incident, or community.Other ways include experiments, surveys, multiple histories, and analysis of archival information.

Rather than using samples and following a rigid protocol to examine limited number of variables, case study methods involve an in-depth, longitudinal examination of a single instance or event: a **case**. They provide a systematic way of looking at events, collecting data, analyzing information, and reporting the results. As a result the researcher may gain a sharpened understanding of why the instance happened as it did, and what might become important to look at more extensively in future research. Case studies lend themselves to both generating and testing hypotheses.

Another suggestion is that case study should be defined as a research strategy, an empirical inquiry that investigates a phenomenon within its real-life context. Case study research means single and multiple case studies, can include quantitative evidence, relies on multiple sources of evidence and benefits from the prior development of theoretical propositions. Case studies should not be confused with qualitative research and they can be based on any mix of quantitative and qualitative evidence. Single-subject research provides the statistical framework for making inferences from quantitative case-study data. This is also supported and well-formulated in (Lamnek, 2005): "The case study is a research approach, situated between concrete data taking techniques and methodologic paradigms."

Case Selection

When selecting a case for a case study, researchers often use information-oriented sampling, as opposed to random sampling. This is because the typical or average case is often not the richest in information. Extreme or atypical cases reveal more information because they activate more basic mechanisms and more actors in the situation studied. In addition, from both an understanding-oriented and an action-oriented perspective, it is often more important to clarify the deeper causes behind a given problem and its consequences than to describe the symptoms of the problem and how frequently they occur. Random samples emphasizing representativeness will seldom be able to produce this kind of insight; it is more appropriate to select some few cases chosen for their validity.

Three types of information-oriented cases may be distinguished:

1. Extreme or deviant cases
2. Critical cases
3. Paradigmatic cases.

Extreme Case

The extreme case can be well-suited for getting a point across in an especially dramatic way, which often occurs for well-known case studies such as in Freud's 'Wolf-Man.'

Critical Case

A critical case can be defined as having strategic importance in relation to the general problem. For example, an occupational medicine clinic wanted to investigate whether people working with organic solvents suffered brain damage. Instead of choosing a representative sample among all those enterprises in the clinic's area that used organic solvents, the clinic strategically located, 'If it is valid for this case, it is valid for all (or many) cases.' In its negative form, the generalization would be, 'If it is not valid for this case, then it is not valid for any (or only few) cases.'

Generalizing from Case Studies

The case study is effective for generalizing using the type of test that Karl Popper called falsification, which forms part of critical reflexivity. Falsification is one of the most rigorous tests to which a scientific proposition can be subjected: if just one observation does not fit with the proposition it is considered not valid generally and must therefore be either revised or rejected. Popper himself used the now famous example of, "All swans are white," and proposed that just one observation of a single black swan would falsify this proposition and in this way have general significance and stimulate further investigations and theory-building. The case study is well suited for identifying "black swans" because of its in-depth approach: what appears to be "white" often turns out on closer examination to be "black."

For instance, Galileo Galilei's rejection of Aristotle's law of gravity was based on a case study selected by information-oriented sampling and not random sampling. The rejection consisted primarily of a conceptual experiment and later on of a practical one. These experiments, with the benefit of hindsight, are self-evident. Nevertheless, Aristotle's incorrect view of gravity dominated scientific inquiry for nearly two thousand years before it was falsified. In his experimental thinking, Galileo reasoned as follows: if two objects with the same weight are released from the same height at the same time, they will hit the ground simultaneously, having fallen at the same speed. If the two objects are then stuck together into one, this object will have double the weight and will according to the Aristotelian view therefore fall faster than the two individual objects. This conclusion seemed contradictory to Galileo. The only way to avoid the contradiction was to eliminate weight as a determinant factor for acceleration in free fall. Galileo's experimentalism did not involve a large random sample of trials of objects falling from a wide range of randomly selected heights under varying wind conditions, and so on. Rather, it was a matter of a single experiment, that is, a case study.

Galileo's view continued to be subjected to doubt, however, and the Aristotelian view was not finally rejected until half a century later, with the invention of the air pump. The air pump made it possible to conduct the ultimate experiment, known by every pupil, whereby a coin or a piece of lead inside a vacuum tube falls with the same speed as a feather. After this experiment, Aristotle's view could be maintained no longer. What is especially worth noting, however, is that the matter was settled by an individual case due to the clever choice of the extremes of metal and feather. One might call it a critical case, for if Galileo's thesis held for these materials, it could be expected to be valid for all or a large range of materials. Random and large samples were at no time part of the picture. However it was Galileo's view that was the subject of doubt as it was not reasonable enough to be Aristotelian view. By selecting cases strategically in this manner one may arrive at case studies that allow generalization.

Informal Discussion

What is It?

Informal discussion is an opportunity to share information so that the person who was eliminated can understand and discuss the decision to eliminate him or her from consideration. It is intended to improve communication during the process and if an error is found, it can be corrected before a final decision is made. The person has the opportunity to raise concerns regarding his or her elimination and discuss this decision with the person responsible for this decision. Informal discussion is focussed on the person who was eliminated; therefore, the focus is on that person's own assessment, and not on a comparison to other persons in the appointment process.

Who Provides the Informal Discussion?

First and foremost, deputy heads are responsible for ensuring that the opportunity for informal discussion is provided within their organizations. In addition to this requirement, deputy heads must ensure that those persons to whom the authority to appoint has been sub-delegated, ensure that informal discussion is provided, upon request, when conducting internal appointment processes.

Informal discussion should be provided by the person responsible for making the decision to eliminate the person. This could be the manager or the person(s) who were responsible for the assessment. Depending on who was responsible for the decision or involved in the process, this could include other managers, a human resources advisor, or an assessment specialist. It is important that whoever is providing the informal discussion be able to sufficiently explain the decision to eliminate, to the person who requested the informal discussion. Keep in mind, informal discussion is intended to be informal. Consideration should be given to the fact that increasing the number of persons attending the informal discussion could affect the quality of the informal discussion. It could also make the process too formal and create an imbalance in the discussion.

The method of informal discussion can vary and be determined by the manager. The manager should take into consideration the request of the person and what is feasible. Informal discussion can be conducted in person, by telephone, by videoconference, electronically, or by any other method.

Managers or Person(s) Responsible for the Assessment

Preparing for the informal discussion:

- Obtain the appointment process file and review the documentation which has recorded the decision regarding the person who was eliminated from consideration;
- Review the PSC Policy on Informal Discussion;
- Review the PSC Guide to Implementing the Informal Discussion Policy;
- Check to see if the organization has a policy or procedures on Informal Discussion;
- Contact the person as soon as possible in order to ascertain his or her concerns;

- Determine the official language to be used in the informal discussion and if any accommodation is required;
- Discuss what method would be preferable and /or practical for the informal discussion; for example, in person, by telephone;
- If necessary, consult with other persons involved in the appointment process; for example, other assessment board members, the human resources advisor, etc.; and
- nquire as to whether anyone else will be attending the informal discussion.

During the Discussion

- Set aside enough time to conduct the informal discussion;
- Use a closed office or take measures to ensure privacy when conducting the informal discussion;
- Listen to the person and provide the opportunity for him or her to explain any concerns and present any supporting information;
- Always verify your understanding of the situation before responding;
- Remember, the discussion is an opportunity to exchange views, share information and explain your decision;
- Informal discussion is about the person who was eliminated, and not about others who are in the process; therefore, personal information about others cannot be disclosed unless that person consents to its disclosure;
- Stay focussed on what is relevant to the discussion: the requirements of the position, the merit criteria, how you assessed the qualifications and why the person was eliminated;
- Stick to the facts and ensure that you can support your statements;
- If an error has occurred and time is needed to reflect before making a decision, do so and reconvene or respond

to the person later; be prepared to make a decision as to what action to take;

- If unsure as to what, if any, action to take, seek advice from a human resources advisor and inform the person of the decision that is made and explain why;
- Remember fairness: fairness to the person in the informal discussion, fairness of any decision and the impact on others in the appointment process;
- Remember transparency: explain the decisions and provide information that will assist the person in understanding;
- If possible, and the person is amenable, you can use the opportunity to discuss general information that could be of use to him or her in future processes; for example, improving communication skills, interviewing techniques, suggestions for training etc; and
- Seek assistance if the issue is beyond what you feel comfortable dealing with or if the discussion goes beyond the decision to eliminate the person from the appointment process. For example, if it is an issue of longstanding conflict, it may be of benefit to set up a subsequent meeting with a third party, perhaps from an alternative dispute resolution (ADR) resource or from the Informal Conflict Management System (ICMS). This process would not be part of the informal discussion.

New or Different Information - what do you do?

There are no set rules on what you can or should do with information provided to you by the person in an informal discussion. Each situation will have to be addressed on a case-by-case basis. The circumstances will influence how and what should be done with the information. The important thing to remember is that the process must be fair and transparent, not only for that person, but for all persons in the process. If faced with a situation that you are unable to address immediately, take the time to seek advice from your human resources advisor on how to proceed. It is possible that the human resources advisor has dealt with, or knows of, similar situations. As well, there may be some basic principles flowing from jurisprudence that could influence your decision. Remember that because the informal discussion takes place during the process, if an error has occurred, it can be corrected before the appointment decision is finalized.

The following are some examples of situations that could occur during an informal discussion:

- a person provides additional information that was not submitted at the time of making a decision;
- a person clarifies information provided on his or her application;
- an error on the part of the assessment board is revealed;
- an apparent lack of clarity with respect to criteria is revealed;
- information provided to the board was not received due to a technical glitch or error; or
- contradictory information about a person who has not been eliminated is revealed.

The above list is not exhaustive; however, it does provide an indication of some of the situations that may arise. Even though informal discussion is intended to discuss the decision to eliminate the person, sometimes information brought forward could have a direct or indirect impact on other persons in the process, whether or not they were eliminated from the process.

When managers are faced with either new information or information which further clarifies that which was submitted, they must be mindful of the impact of any decision that is taken as a result. Managers should consider the following:

- Why was the information not submitted at the time of request?
- Are there circumstances which mitigate the failure to provide the information?
- Is there a chance that others fall under the same circumstances?

- Is the error one that requires reversing the decision? For example, even if the error were corrected, would it change the result?
- What level of confidence is there in the decision that was taken?
- Now that the information has been brought forward - would this lead to a different decision?

These are not easy situations and there are no easy answers, but this does illustrate the importance of planning and taking measures to ensure confidence in decisions made during the appointment process.

What Information can be Shared?

It is important for all persons involved in an informal discussion to be as open as possible to clearly explain the concerns with respect to the appointment process and, with respect to the manager, to clearly explain the decision taken; however, confidentiality issues must be taken into account so as to maintain the trust in informal discussion, as well as that of the appointment process.

Consideration must also be given to protecting proprietary information, such as standardized tests. Any disclosure of information will have to respect the Privacy and Access to Information Acts and the Public Service Employment Regulations established by the PSC concerning the disclosure of information obtained during the course of investigation. Informal discussion is intended to provide information on the decision to eliminate a person from the appointment process. Therefore, personal information about other persons must not be disclosed.

A person participating in informal discussion would normally have access to any personal information gathered in the appointment process relating to him- or herself.

Some basic tips include:

- In accordance with the PSC Policy on Informal Discussion, persons participating in informal discussion should be provided with sufficient information in order to understand and discuss the decision;

- Information to be shared would include any documents submitted by the person, the portions of rating guide that are relevant to the person's assessment, notes, and information on the person written by the assessment board. Any request for access or copies of standardized tests and how they are scored could be refused as it could compromise the integrity of the test or provide an unfair advantage. It is important to discuss any such request with your Access to Information expert and an expert from the Personnel Psychology Centre (PPC), or human resources advisor before conducting the informal discussion; and
- Under the Privacy Act, personal information about a third party is protected. The person who participates in the informal discussion should not be provided any assessment information regarding other persons since this could violate the Privacy Act. However, some personal information may be disclosed if its release is consistent with the purpose for which the information was gathered. For example, if a selection was made based on an organizational need to increase representativeness of the designated groups, and the person who is being considered for appointment has self-identified as a member of a designated group, the fact that this was the merit criterion applied, not information about the person who self-identified, can be shared in the informal discussion. When in doubt, seek assistance before sharing any information about a person other than the one with whom you are conducting the informal discussion.

Formal

In computer science and software engineering, formal methods are particular kind of mathematically-based techniques for the specification, development and verification of software and hardware systems. The use of formal methods for software and hardware design is motivated by the expectation that, as in other engineering disciplines, performing appropriate mathematical analyses can contribute to the reliability and robustness of a design. However, the high cost of using formal methods means that they are usually only used in the development of high-integrity systems, where safety or security is important.

Taxonomy

Formal methods can be used at a number of levels:

Level 0: Formal specification may be undertaken and then a program developed from this informally. This has been dubbed *formal methods lite*. This may be the most cost-effective option in many cases.

Level 1: Formal development and formal verification may be used to produce a program in a more formal manner. For example, proofs of properties or refinement from the specification to a program may be undertaken. This may be most appropriate in high-integrity systems involving safety or security.

Level 2: Theorem provers may be used to undertake fully formal machine-checked proofs. This can be very expensive and is only practically worthwhile if the cost of mistakes is extremely high (e.g., in critical parts of microprocessor design).

Further information on this is expanded below.

As with the sub-discipline of programming language semantics, styles of formal methods may be roughly classified as follows:

- Denotational semantics, in which the meaning of a system is expressed in the mathematical theory of domains. Proponents of such methods rely on the well-understood nature of domains to give meaning to the system; critics point out that not every system may be intuitively or naturally viewed as a function.
- Operational semantics, in which the meaning of a system is expressed as a sequence of actions of a (presumably) simpler computational model. Proponents

of such methods point to the simplicity of their models as a means to expressive clarity; critics counter that the problem of semantics has just been delayed (who defines the semantics of the simpler model?).

- Axiomatic semantics, in which the meaning of the system is expressed in terms of preconditions and postconditions which are true before and after the system performs a task, respectively. Proponents note the connection to classical logic; critics note that such semantics never really describe what a system *does* (merely what is true before and afterwards).

Lightweight Formal Methods

Some practitioners believe that the formal methods community has overemphasized full formalization of a specification or design. They contend that the expressiveness of the languages involved, as well as the complexity of the systems being modelled, make full formalization a difficult and expensive task. As an alternative, various *lightweight* formal methods, which emphasize partial specification and focused application, have been proposed. Examples of this lightweight approach to formal methods include the Alloy object modelling notation, Denney's synthesis of some aspects of the Z notation with use case driven development, and the CSK VDM Tools.

Uses

Formal methods can be applied at various points through the development process. (For convenience, we use terms common to the waterfall model, though any development process could be used.)

Specification

Formal methods may be used to give a description of the system to be developed, at whatever level(s) of detail desired. This formal description can be used to guide further development activities; additionally, it can be used to verify that the requirements for the system being developed have been completely and accurately specified.

The need for formal specification systems has been noted for years. In the ALGOL 60 Report, John Backus presented a formal notation for describing programming language syntax (later named Backus normal form or Backus-Naur form (BNF)); Backus also described the need for a notation for describing programming language semantics. The report promised that a new notation, as definitive as BNF, would appear in the near future; it never appeared.

Development

Once a formal specification has been developed, the specification may be used as a guide while the concrete system is developed (i.e. realized in software and/or hardware). Examples:

- If the formal specification is in an operational semantics, the observed behavior of the concrete system can be compared with the behavior of the specification (which itself should be executable or simulateable). Additionally, the operational commands of the specification may be amenable to direct translation into executable code.
- If the formal specification is in an axiomatic semantics, the preconditions and postconditions of the specification may become assertions in the executable code.

Verification

Once a formal specification has been developed, the specification may be used as the basis for proving properties of the specification (and hopefully by inference the developed system).

Human-directed Proof

Sometimes, the motivation for proving the correctness of a system is not the obvious need for re-assurance of the correctness of the system, but a desire to understand the system better. Consequently, some proofs of correctness are produced in the style of mathematical proof: handwritten (or typeset) using natural language, using a level of informality common to such proofs. A "good" proof is one which is readable and understandable by other human readers.

Critics of such approaches point out that the ambiguity inherent in natural language allows errors to be undetected in such proofs; often, subtle errors can be present in the low-level details typically overlooked by such proofs. Additionally, the work involved in producing such a good proof requires a high level of mathematical sophistication and expertise.

Automated Proof

In contrast, there is increasing interest in producing proofs of correctness of such systems by automated means. Automated techniques fall into two general categories:

- Automated theorem proving, in which a system attempts to produce a formal proof from scratch, given a description of the system, a set of logical axioms, and a set of inference rules.
- Model checking, in which a system verifies certain properties by means of an exhaustive search of all possible states that a system could enter during its execution.

Neither of these techniques work without human assistance. Automated theorem provers usually require guidance as to which properties are "interesting" enough to pursue; model checkers can quickly get bogged down in checking millions of uninteresting states if not given a sufficiently abstract model.

Proponents of such systems argue that the results have greater mathematical certainty than human-produced proofs, since all the tedious details have been algorithmically verified. The training required to use such systems is also less than that required to produce good mathematical proofs by hand, making the techniques accessible to a wider variety of practitioners.

Critics note that some of those systems are like oracles: they make a pronouncement of truth, yet give no explanation of that truth. There is also the problem of "verifying the verifier"; if the program which aids in the verification is itself unproven, there may be reason to doubt the soundness of the produced results. Some modern model checking tools produce a "proof log" detailing each step in their proof, making it possible to perform, given suitable tools, independent verification.

Criticisms

The field of formal methods has its critics. Handwritten proofs of correctness need significant time (and thus money) to produce, with limited utility other than assuring correctness. This makes formal methods more likely to be used in fields where it is possible to perform automated proofs using software, or in cases where the cost of a fault is high. Example: in railway engineering and aerospace engineering, undetected errors may cause death, so formal methods are more popular in this field than in other application areas.

At times, proponents of formal methods have claimed that their techniques would be the silver bullet to the software crisis. It is widely believed that there is no silver bullet for software development, and some have written off formal methods due to those overstated, overreaching claims.

Seminar

The second crucial component for Modeling Interdisciplinary Inquiry is a seminar run collaboratively by the postdoctoral fellows in the spring semester. That collaboration will be enriched by the multiple conversations among postdoctoral fellows and by their colloquy with mentors and other faculty involved in the postdoctoral program. The aim of the Theory and Methods seminar is to raise questions and address problems that face all of us involved in interdisciplinary research and teaching.

These questions will rise out of particular research problems and teaching experiences, but our aim is to generalize these issues so that the postdoctoral fellows and our own graduate students might join together in addressing such problems as the evolution of academic disciplines or the nature of historical methods. Core readings in theory and methods provide some of the common ground for each seminar; but discussion of current and on-going projects will allow the interrogation of such widely shared concerns as the nature of evidence, the problems of language in a post-deconstructive world, and the role of theory in guiding empirical research.

Our own experience in the Theory and Methods seminars of the Literature & History Program, the American Culture Studies Program, the Women and Gender Studies Program, and in the Mellon Dissertation Seminars, which have balanced theoretical discussion with case study, is valuable in guiding the initial formation of the Theory and Methods Seminar for the Modeling Interdisciplinary Inquiry. Inevitably this seminar will take on a life of its own informed by the research interests and teaching experience of the individual members of the seminar.

Running such a seminar is a challenging and important experience for the postdoctoral fellows and invaluable for our own graduate students who join in this effort. There has been much discussion of the role of theory in contemporary literary and cultural studies programs both on this campus and in other universities, and there have been individual efforts to join in that discussion -- in German, in Literature & History, and in Women and Gender Studies -- but there has been no sustained effort at Washington University to have our graduate students address the issues of theory and method as a group and across the humanities and the social sciences. The Theory and Methods Seminar will provide such an occasion both for the postdoctoral fellows and for our own graduate students and faculty.

Symposium

Symposium originally referred to a drinking party (the Greek verb sympotein means "to drink together") but has since come to refer to any academic conference, or a style of university class characterized by an openly discursive format, rather than a lecture and question–answer format. The sympotic elegies of Theognis of Megara and two Socratic dialogues, Plato's Symposium and Xenophon's Symposium all describe symposia in the original sense.

Symposium as a Social Activity in Antiquity

The Greek symposium was a key Hellenic social institution. It was a forum for men to debate, plot, boast, or simply to party with others. They were also frequently held to celebrate the introduction of youths into aristocratic society, much like debutante balls today. Symposia were also held by aristocrats to celebrate other special occasions, such as victories in athletic and poetic contests.

Symposiast in typical singing pose, accompanied by a flutist playing the aulos. The text reads "The boy is beautiful." Fifth century red-figure kylix by the Colmar painter.

Symposia were usually held in the men's quarters of the household. Singly or in pairs, the men would recline on couches arrayed against the three walls of the room away from the door. Free boys who participated did not recline but sat. Food was served, together with wine. The latter, usually mixed with water in varying proportions, was drawn from the krater, a large jar designed to be carried by two men, and served by nude servant boys from pitchers. Entertainment was provided, and depending on the occasion could include games, songs, flute-girls, slaves performing various acts, and hired entertainments. A symposium would be overseen by a symposiarch who would decide how strong or diluted the wine for the evening would be, depending on whether serious discussions or merely sensual indulgence were in the offing. Certain formalities were observed, most important among which were the libations by means of which the gods were propitiated.

In keeping with Greek notions of self-restraint and propriety, the symposiarch would prevent matters from getting out of hand. The playwright Euboulos, in a surviving fragment of a lost play has the god Dionysos describe proper and improper drinking:

For sensible men I prepare only three kraters: one for health (which they drink first), the second for love and pleasure, and the third for sleep. After the third one is drained, wise men go home. The fourth krater is not mine any more - it belongs to bad behaviour; the fifth is for shouting; the sixth is for rudeness and insults; the seventh is for fights; the eighth is for breaking the furniture; the ninth is for depression; the tenth is for madness and unconsciousness.

A game sometimes played at symposia was kottabos, in which drinkers swished the dregs of their wine in their kylikes (platter-like stemmed drinking vessels) and flung them at a target. Another feature of the symposia were skolia, drinking songs of a patriotic or bawdy nature, which were also performed in a competitive manner with one symposiast reciting the first part of a song and another expected to improvise the end of it.

What are called flute-girls today were actually prostitutes or courtesans who played the aulos, a Greek woodwind instrument most similar to an oboe, hired to play for and consort with the symposiasts while they drank and conversed. When string instruments were played, the barbiton was the traditional instrument.

Symposiasts could also compete in rhetorical contests, for which reason the term symposium has come to refer to any event where multiple speeches are made.

As with many other Greek customs, the framework of the symposium was adopted by the Romans under the name of comissatio. These revels also involved the drinking of assigned quantities of wine, and the oversight of a master of the ceremonies appointed for the occasion from among the guests.

Panel Discussion

Panel discussion for example, if an issue is too complex for one person to handle, a panel may be covered so a group of specialists can speak. Or perhaps the audience need to introduced or exposed to various people or viewpoints at the same session.

Panel discussions, however, differ from team presentations. Their purpose is different. In a team presentation, the group presents agreed-upon views; in a panel discussion, the purpose is to present different views. Also in a team presentations, usually speakers stand as they speak; in panel discussions, usually speakers sit the whole time. In panel discussion each speaker prepares separately, the other speakers here one another for the time at the session itself.

Technically, a panel discussion consists of questions and answers only, and a symposium consists of a series of prepared speeches, followed by questions and answers. The compare must monitor time and manage questions. If each participant is making a speech for a set period of time, he should signal the speakers at the one minute to go mark and at the stop mark. If a speakers goes more than one or two minute he can stop them to gave the equal rights to each speakers. The compare must be a biased person; he is neither in nor against the topic.

UNIT-IV

Instructional Method-II

Tutorial and Assignement Method

For teacher of every subject method is important. *Method* is nothing but a scientific way of presenting the subject, keeping in mind the psychological and physical requirements of the children.

For effective learning Commerce the method has to be as good as the content. It is through method only that it is possible to make a subject interesting and useful. Without a method, teaching would be hard. The arrangement of the subject and its presentation is very important for successful teaching

Method of teaching commerce differs from stage to stage and from age group to age group. The method to be adopted depend upon many factors which include the environment and the familiar situations or experiences that are to be correlated effectively. While teaching a set of pupils with varying interests, aptitudes and attitudes one has got to be aware of the psychological basis of teaching learning process.

The term 'method' can be thought of as the most effective and economic way of learning to take place among students. Communication of ideas and development of concepts in a precise manner based on a logical development of subject is the most important prerequisite in teaching a subject like commerce.

Generally students are afraid of studying commerce. There are various reasons for this, method being one of them. Pupils tend to learn commerce through a meaningful approach to commerce rather than by a mechanical process. Teaching is thus most difficult task and every body is not fit to *be* a teacher. Some persons may have a 'flair' for teaching and such persons have the ability to awaken interest and arrest the attentions of the students. Some others who are not so fortunate can improve their teaching through practice if they are fully acquainted with various methods of teaching. In order to make children learn effectively the teacher has to adopt the right method of teaching. For choosing right method for a given situation, the teacher must be familiar with different methods of teaching. In this chapter an effort will be made to discuss some common methods used for teaching of commerce.

Methods of Teaching of Commerce

"There are a large number if methods for the teaching of Elements of Commerce and it is as general and formal subject. Hanna and Stehr have laid down more than a score of methods for teaching general business. However, all the methods given by them are not important".

Some of the important methods are teaching of commerce are briefly discussed here.

1. Lecture Method

It is one of the oldest methods of teaching. It refers to the teaching procedure involved in the clarification or explanation to the students of some major ideas. It places more emphasis on the presentation of the content. In this method teacher is more active and the students are passive. In this method question answer procedure is used to keep the students attentive in the class. This method is used to clarify matter, to expand content and motivate the students. To effectively deliver his lecture teacher makes use of certain simple devices such as changing his voice, impersonating characters shifting his position etc. While delivering his lecture, a teacher can indicate by his facial expression, gestures and tones the exact shade of the meaning that he wishes to convey. Thus a lecture is a means of setting forth precisely, concisely and effectively the exact relationship leading to the subjective thought. Thus a lecture can save time, however, a poor lecture is actually time consuming and wasteful. Even a good lecture may fail in case sufficient background is lacking among students.

A good lecture contemplates complete exposition of a topic, principle, situation or the like. In order to achieve the goal, it must be effective and interesting, well expressed, concised, organised and systematised if the lecture is to become effective.

To make lecture method *effective and Inspirational* following points be given due consideration:

(i) Matter should be arranged in such a way as to leave a single clear impression on the minds of the students.

(ii) The teacher should have pauses in between the lesson so that the students may learn the new knowledge bit by bit.

(iii) The rate of exposition should be slow specially if the class is weak.

(iv) There should be abundant repetition.

(v) Children way of looking at things should be considered.

(vi) Language used should be familiar and suitable.

(vii) The lesson should be divided into sections which have a logical sequence.

(viii) Proper use of blackboard should be made.

(ix) Actual models, diagrams charts etc. should be used.

(x) Students should be encouraged to ask questions comparisons etc. should be used.

(xi) Verbal illustration such as examples, comparisons etc. should be used.

(xii) The aim of the lesson should be kept in view and the students should be made fully conversant with the aim.

Merits of Lecture Method

(i) It is economical and a large number of students can be taught at a time.

(ii) It saves time.

(iii) It is very effective in giving factual information.

(iv) It makes the work of teacher very simple.

(v) A good lecture not only stimulates students but lingers long in their imagination. It motivates students to become good orators.

(vi) It provides better scope for classification and for laying stress on significant ideas.

(vii) It brings a personal contact and touch to impress or influence the pupils.

(viii) It provides flexibility.

(ix) It gives students training in listening.

(x) It gives training to students in taking notes rapidly.

(xi) It provides opportunities of correlating events and subjects.

(xii) It enables the linkage of previous knowledge with new one.

Demerits of Lecture Method

(i) It provides little scope for pupil's activity.

(ii) It does not take into consideration the individual *differ*ences of pupils.

(iii) It is against the principle of 'learning by doing.'

(iv) It spoon feeds the students without developing their power of reasoning.

(v) Speed of the lecture may be too fast for learners to grasp the line of thought.

(vi) An average student may not be able to fix up his attention to a lecture.

(vii) A lecture may become monotonous to students after a while.

When to Use Lecture Method?

This method can be suitably used:

(i) For Communicating new facts or information to the students.

(ii) For completing the courses in time.

(iii) For reviewing and summarising a unit.

(iv) For expanding the unit by giving better explanation.

(v) For communicating such material to students which is not available in their textbook

Method of Presenting a Good Lecture

Following points should be given due consideration:

(i) Key terms be explained in details.

(ii) Reasonable task units be given.

(iii) Lecture should be delivered sequentially.

(iv) Teacher should prepare brief notes in good language before delivering the lecture.

(v) All out *efforts be* made to correlate the lecture.

(vi) Teacher should make frequent use of verbal imagery and oral illustrations.

(vii) Lecture should be delivered at proper speed.

(viii) Lecture should be delivered in well modulated tone and voice.

(ix) It should be followed by frequent inspection of students notes by the teacher.

Procedures to be Followed in Lecture Method

Thc following suggestion be kept in view while delivering a lecture:

(i) The teacher should stop after every 5-7 minutes so that students may be able to have control over the facts noted by them.

(ii) The teacher should start his lecture slowly and gradually increase his speed.

(iii) An outline of the lecture to be delivered be given to the students and they be encouraged to ask questions.

(iv) Voice-volume of the teacher should be tuned according to the need and importance of the point to be emphasised.

(v) The lecture should stimulate the emotions imaginations, feelings and creative tendencies of the learner.

2. Problem - Solving Method

Life is full of problems and successful person in life is one who is adequately equipped with knowledge and reasoning power to tackle problems rationally. The function of education is to prepare children for life. Problem solving therefore must be encouraged in schools.

Problem Solving may be defined as a planned attack upon a difficulty or perplexity in which a person uses his ability and capacity to find a suitable and satisfying solution.

In this method teacher motivates the pupils to make conscious, planned and purposeful efforts to arrive at an explanation or solution to some educationally significant difficulty.

Yoakam and Simpson define it as, "a problem that occurs in a situation in which a felt difficulty is clearly present and recognised by the thinker. It may be a purely mental difficulty or it may be physical and may involve the manipulation of data. The distinguishing thing about a problem, however, is that an individual who meets it as needing a solution, recognises it as a 'challange'. It is a method in which some difficulty to act in an educational setting is felt and an attempt is made in a conscious, planned and purposeful way to find its solution".

Gates has defined the problem thus, "A problem exists for an individual when he has a definite goal and he can not reach by the behaviours pattern which he already has available".

Problem Solving is not merely a method of teaching. It is in fact a method of organisation of subject matter.

Special Features of Problems

(i) Problems should have a direct bearing on the learning process.

(ii) Problem should be interesting, meaningful and worthwhile from the students point of view.

(iii) Problems should be correlated with the life of the children.

(iv) Problems should arise out of the real life needs of the children.

(v) Problems should be well defined.

(vi) Problems should have certain educational value.

Problem solving method involves active participation of students but in it physical activities are not necessary.

Problem solving method is the process of raising a problems in the mind of students which stimulates purposeful reflective thinking in arriving at a solution involving the following.

(a) Stimulation presenting difficulty, perplexity or doubt requiring the solution.

(b) A goal or end for which no ready answer can be given.

(c) A desire or motive that stimulates and attempts to find the answer.

Pre- requisites of Problem Solving

(i) It should emerge out of the felt needs of the students activities.

(ii) It should be clearly defined, interpreted and delimited.

(iii) For solving it sufficient data be collected in a systematic manner.

(iv) Data be then properly organised an evaluated

(v) Decision be made very coutiously and only after sufficient data has been collected and organised.

(vi) Results be verified to ascertain their correctness.

Steps in Problem Solving

Important steps in this method are:

(i) Selection of the problem.

(ii) Working on the problem.

(iii) Concluding step.

(1) Selection of the Problem

For making a proper selection of the problem following procedure is generally adopted:

The Formation and Appreciation of the Problem: The nature of the problem should be made very clear to the students. They must also feel a necessity of finding out a solution for the problem.

The Collection of Relevant Data and Information: The students should be stimulated to collect data in a systematic manner. Full Cooperation of students should be secured. They may be invited to make suggestions as to how they could collect the relevant data. The teacher may suggest many points to them. He may also ask them to read certain books. He may also ask them to organise a few educational trips to gather the relevant information.

(ii) Working on the Problem

It depends upon whether the work is to be done by adopting deductive or inductive method. It involves following steps:

Organisation of Data: The students should be asked to select the relevant material and to discard the superficial one and arrange the selected data in a scientific manner.

Making Hypothesis For Solution of the Problem: For this discussion should be arranged collectively or individually with each pupil. Panton suggests, 'The teacher's aim should be to secure that, as far as possible, the essential thinking is done by the pupils themselves and their educative process produces the particular solution, formulation or generalisation at state." Care should be taken that judgment is made only when sufficient data is collected.

(iii) Concluding Step

It includes checking and verifying results as also the application and summarisation of the conclusions.

Testing Conclusions

No conclusion should be accepted without being properly verified. The correctness of conclusions must be proved. The students must be taught to be critical, to examine the truths which they discover to see that they fit all the known data. We should keep our minds free of every bias in the process of problem-solving.

Teachers Role in Problem-Solving Method

Valentine Davis quotes Professor Pasher who suggests the following points in problem-solving:

(i) Give them (the students) a chance to define the problem clearly.

(ii) Aid them to keep the problem in mind.

(iii) Get them to make many suggestions by encouraging them

- (a) to analyse the situation in parts.
- (b) to recall previously known similar cases and general rules that apply.
- (c) to guess courageously and to formulate guesses clearly.

(iv) Give them time to evaluate each suggestion carefully by encouraging them

- (a) to maintain a state of doubt or suspended conclusion.
- (b) to criticise the suggestion by appeal to know facts, minister experiments. and scientific treatises.

(v) Get them to organise the material by proceeding

- (a) to build an outline on the board.
- (b) to use diagrams and graphs.
- (c) to formulate concise statement of the net outcome of the discussion.

For the success of this method we need teachers who have the ability to see the problems clearly, the power to analyse with a keen discernment and the facility to synthesise, draw conclusions with an uncanny accuracy.

Teaching Procedures in Problem-Solving Method

Following procedures may be adopted while teaching by this method.

(i) Introducing problem procedure.
(ii) Directing work procedure.
(iii) Application approach.

(1) Introducing Problem Procedure

(a) By setting the stage for the problem.
(b) By helping students in formulating an exact idea of the problem after the observation and comparison with their past experience.

(ii) Directing Work Procedure

(a) By motivating students and creating proper attitudes for work
(b) By helping the students in formulating the hypothesis.
(c) By helping the students in collection and proper arrangement of relevant data.
(d) By helping the students in evaluating the hypothesis.

(iii) Application Approach

(a) By suggesting to students various possible applications of the results of the problem.
(b) *By* summarising the findings of the students.
(c) *By* stimulating the students with a desire to use the knowledge gained.
(d) By arranging some suitable exercises for the practical application.

Merits of Problem-Solving Method

It is a psychological rather than a merely logical procedure. It has the following merits

(i) It helps in unit learning by correlating, using and integrating students knowledge and experience.
(ii) It increases the amount of experience or experiences of the students.
(iii) It takes into consideration the individual differences of the students.

(iv) It helps students to learn facts more meaningfully.

(v) It brings students to touch with life-like activities.

(vi) It enables students to think and reason.

(vii) It arouses the interest by stimulating students' urge from within.

Limitations of Problem-Solving Method

The scope of the method is limited in accordance with the needs of the students. The needs of the students are as follows

(i) Ability of the students.

(ii) Experimental background

(iii) Personal interest of the students.

(iv) Social attitudes of the students.

(v) Training of students.

3. *Project Method*

Project method is a natural, whole hearted problem solving and Purposeful activity carried to completion by students in a social environment under the guidance of their teacher.

Some of the definitions of this method given by Educationists are as follows:

A project is a bit of real life that has been imported in school. —Ballard

The problem is a project which results in doing. The motor element is not what makes the activity a project, but the problem solving of a practical nature accompanying the activity. —Burton

A project is a problematic act carried to completion is its natural setting. —J. A. Stevenson

Project is a unit of educative work in which the most prominent feature is some form of positive and concrete achievement. —Snedden

Characteristics of Project Method

(i) The project undertaken is complete in itself.

(ii) The project must be completed in its natural setting.

(iii) In a project there is a definite attainable goal.

(iv) Learning activities are life-like and purposeful.

(v) Students plan and direct their own learning activities.

(vi) It places emphasis as 'Learning by Doing'.

(vii) Project is a play-way activity.

(viii) Project is really life in its unity.

Main Principles of the Project Method

(I) The Principle of Purpose

Purpose motivates learning. Interest can not be aroused by aimless and meaningless activities. The child must have an ideal. "Why is he doing certain things".

(II) The Principle of Activity

Children love activity. They become active because of the instincts of curiosity, construction, pugnacity and herd. It is always better to provide children with certain activities both physical as well as mental. They should be allowed to 'do' and 'to live though doing'.

(III) The Principle of Experience

Experience is the best teacher. What is real must be experienced. The children learn new facts and information through experience.

(IV) The Principle of Social Experience

The child is a social being and he has to be prepared for social life. A training for corporate life should be given to him in his childhood. In the project method, child gets enough chance to work in groups.

(V) The Principle of Reality

Life is real and education to be meaningful must be real. The child should be fully prepared to live a real life and for this he should be trained through his education. The project method is a method of educating the child and, therefore, it must also be real.

(VI) The Principle of Freedom

The desire for an activity must be spontaneous and not forced by the teacher. The child should be free from imposition, restrictios or obstruction so that he may express himself fully and freely. He must be given freedom to choose an activity, to do an activity according to his interests, needs and capacities.

(VII) The Principle of Utility

Knowledge will be worthwhile when it is useful and practical, The project method develops various attitudes and values which are of great significance from the practical point of view.

(VIII) Principle of Democratic Procedures

In project method each member of the group has equal rights, duties and responsibilities. The procedures adopted for carrying out the project are democratic.

Classification of Projects

W.H. Kilpatrick classifies the projects in following four types.

(I) The Producer Type

In this type of projects the emphasis is laid on the actual construction of a material object or article.

(II) The Consumer Type

In this type of project the main objective is to obtain either direct or vicarious experience.

(III) The Problem Type

In this type of project the chief purpose is to solve a problem involving the intellectual processes.

(IV) The Drill Type

In such a project the objective is to attain a certain degree of skill.

Various steps in Project Method

(i) Providing a Situation

Teacher should discover the tastes, temperaments and needs of the students and should provide situations when in a student feels spontaneous urge to carry out projects according to their felt needs.

(ii) Choosing and Proposing

Proposing is very important. It is the centre round which the project moves. Under this the aims and objectives of the project are set. This step should be under the guidance and supervision of the teacher but freedom of choice and expression of ideas of students should be included.

The project selected must be such as to satisfy a definite need or purpose and the purpose as far as possible should be acceptable to students. Kilpatrick remarks, "The part of the pupil and the part of the teacher in most of the school work depend largely on who does the proposing. It is practically the whole thing".

Bossing states, 'The genius of the project lies in the wholehearted enlistment of the student in doing of it."

The project should always be chosen in a democratic way after discussing various situations. The teacher should merely guide and not thrust his opinion. The children must feel that the project is of their own choice.

(iii) Planning

The task of planning is a difficult one. Only a good planning leads to better results. Each child should be encouraged to give his suggestions. Different proposals should be considered and alternatives discussed. The best plan is agreed upon after a good deal of discussion, suggestion and counter suggestion, rejections etc. Planning may be discussed orally and final conclusion may be drafted in writing. It is essential that the teacher is ready with some proposal regarding the plan before hand so that he may be able to help the students in the best possible manner.

(iv) Executing the Plan

It is the longest step of this method and in this step actual activity is observed and learning takes place. For proper execution various activities of the project should be divided according to individual interests and abilities of the different children in the class.

While executing the project, students get a variety of experiences which help them in learning. The teacher should give sufficient guidance to students. He should not dictate them.

(v) Judging

Under this step the success or otherwise of the project is evaluated. In this step the students review the work, criticise for the wrong policy, present remedial measures for future projects. This enables the students to learn to criticise their own work. Self-criticism is a valuable form of training, the students should find out what they have learnt from the project.

(vi) Recording

A complete record of all activities connected with the project must be maintained. The project book should be well maintained. All the details in various steps should be noted down. The project book should give a comprehensive picture of the project as a whole. It should give the procedure of providing a situations, choosing the project, duties assigned, difficulties felt and experiences gained etc.

Role of Teacher in Project Method

The project to be successful must be based on a definite procedure. The first and main responsibility of a teacher is to provide those situations in which they feel a spontaneous urge to solve some of their practical problems. The teacher must be on the book out to discover their interest, tastes, aptitudes and needs.

Teacher should motivate the students in such a manner that there is whole hearted cooperation of students in the process.

Teacher helps the students in proper planning of the project and discuss with them all the *pros and cons* of the project. He highlights on the important aspects and hazards of the project.

The teacher supplies clues and also provides information to the students about the sources of materials for the project.

He also helps the students in evaluating the project and to draw inferences.

The relation of the teacher with his students is very closer in project method than in the ordinary class teaching. The teacher is like a friend, an elder brother who works together with the students and helps them to gain rich experiences. He acts in the capacity of a director of the student group and gives all types of necessary directions and does not behave as an autocratic teacher.

Essentials of a Good Project

Following points are essential for a good project.

(1) *Timely:* The project should be such as is related directly to the lesson and vocational interest. It should be in accordance with the mental and chronological age of the students Environmental and seasonal factors must also be given due consideration.

(ii) *Usefulness:* The project selected should be useful in life. The learning experience in a project must be capable of being applied in life.

(iii) *Interesting:* Project should be interesting from students point of view. They must make an appeal to the emotional hungers or drives of the students.

(iv) *Challenging:* Project should neither be too simple nor too long and difficult. They should be challenging. Challenging tasks are liked by youth.

(v) *Economical:* The project should be economical and should not unnecessarily tax the energy and pocket of the students.

(vi) *Rich in Experience:* The project should be able to correlate different subjects and practical activities of life.

(vii) *Cooperativeness:* In the project there should be enough scope for individual and cooperative thinking.

Merits of the Project Method

(i) It is based on the *laws of learning* i.e.

(a) the law of readiness,

(b) the law of exercise, and

(c) the law of effect.

(ii) It allows to students full freedom of expression and also of participation.

(iii) It bring and child to interact with real life situations.

(iv) It helps the students to learn the practical usefulness of different subjects of curriculum.

(v) It provides a correlation of all the subjects. While working on a project subjects do not remain isolated and learning comes as a bye product of purposeful activity.

(vi) It provides to the students a training in the democratic way of life.

(vii) Project method imparts training to the students to inculcate in them primary virtues like tolerance, independence, open mindedness, resourcefulness etc.

(viii) Dignity of labour is engendered through the project method They learn that there is nobleness in working and doing things with their own hands.

(ix) It discourages cramming and memory work. It stresses problem solving. It develops the thinking and reasoning power of the students.

(x) Project method provides a good relief to the backward children by providing them opportunities of participation in practical situations.

(xi) It develops *constructive discipline.* As the children

remain busy with their self-chosen work so they do not get opportunities to think of anti-social ways.

Demerits, Limitations, Difficulties of Project Method

(i) It leads to *neglect of intellectual work*

(ii) By project method learning is *not systematic and orderly.*

(iii) It *upsets the routine work* of the school.

(iv) This method *neglects drill* and development of skill in various subjects.

(v) The preparation of books suitable for project method is a difficult task. Moreover the material required for project work is quite costly.

(vi) Sometimes teachers bring about *artificial correlation* by over stretching the project beyond its natural limits and try to connect those topics which have remote connection with the project in hand.

(vii) Project method is *unsuitable for shirkers and shy students.* Such students are not inclined to take any responsibility and remain in the background and do very little work.

(viii) It puts *too much reliance on young children.*

(ix) For successful working of project method, learning, efficient and resourceful teacher are needed. It imposes heavy burden on the teachers.

(x) A child reading in an ordinary school finds it very difficult to adapt himself to a school that follows project method and vice-versa

(xi) There is no mastery over the area under this method.

(xii) It places more emphasis on manipulative activity and less on mental or critical thinking.

Unit Plan Method

This method is based on Herbart's concept of unit planning. According to him, it signifies, "Unity or wholeness of learning activities relating to some project or a problem". It emphasises learning by wholes. It meets the needs of the learners and is opposed to traditional, fragmentary lesson. *A unit plan* is a plan of instructions based on significant area of learning. It is an instructional procedure which implements the idea of learning the whole garment. The *unit* is a sustained well planned experience that lasts for days and weeks. The application of whole method in unit planning leads to whole and meaningful knowledge, skill and attitude on the part of the learner.

Characteristics of Good Unit

(i) The objectives of a unit must be stated very clearly and the unit should contribute to the achievement of stated objectives. *A* unit is expected to contribute in the development of problem solving skills, democratic behaviour, group action skills, significant concepts and understandings.

(ii) *A* good unit is one that includes sizeable topic related to the requirements and interests of students.

(iii) The unit should emerge out of the pervious experiences of the child

(iv) *A* good unit must help to broaden interests and training experiences of the child and to the continuity of child's learning.

(v) It should include various activities, materials and different modes of expression in order to meet the individual needs of the children.

(vi) It should provide opportunities of creative experiences.

(vii) It should allow the free use of textbooks and other learning materials.

(viii) It should be in accordance with the mental level of the students.

(ix) It should include various audio-visual aids.

(x) It should contribute sufficient learning.

Phases and Functions Developing Units

The three important phases of developing units are :

(i) Introductory phase,

(ii) Presentation phase, and

(iii) Concluding phase.

Functions

The two important functions are:

(i) It helps the teacher to break up the whole years work into a smaller number of units, and

(ii) It entails the procedures to be used in developing units.

Problems in Constructing Units

For planning a unit the teacher should be familiar with various types of units which can be developed and used.

(ii) The teacher should be familiar with the basis of selection of units.

(iii) Before adopting the units to class needs, the teacher must know the nature of learning activities which are used in different kinds of units.

(iv) After selection of unit there is problem of developing and understanding essential steps. The philosophies of education be used for unit planning.

Classification of Units

Mainly the units may be classified as

(i) Subject matter units,

(ii) Experience units, and

(iii) Resource units.

Steps in Unit Planning

The three important steps in unit planning are

(i) Introducing or Initiating the unit,

(ii) Developing the unit, and

(iii) Culminating the unit.

(i) Introducing the unit

Its purpose is to orient motivate the students and to initiate the work of the unit. During this step the main objectives are

(i) to emphasise the significant aspects of the unit.

(ii) to correlate new work with previous experiences of the child.

(iii) to make clear the relationship of unit to the work of the course.

(iv) to make an overview of the whole unit.

(ii) Developing the Unit

It aims at the attainment of the objectives set for the unit. It is devoted to learning experience so as to attain the objectives. Teacher should see that the learning experiences are unified and integrated and this period may be characterised as a period of functional learning.

(iii) Culminating the Unit

It aims at reteaching and remedial work self-evaluation etc. In this step the work of the unit is integrated.

Merits of Unit Method

(i) It helps in growth and development of activities and skills, in critical thinking, problem solving, discussing, reporting and experimenting.

(ii) It leaves a lasting impression of relationships, concepts etc.

(iii) It has significant content.

(iv) It involves students in learning process.

(v) It minimises individual differences among children because it provides on logically arranged system of instructions.

(vi) It modifies the behaviour of the students to such an extent that he can cope with new problems and situation more competently.

(vii) It fixes attention on important details of the specific subject. 5. Discussion Method

In this method the effective participation of students, is made possible, in the teaching-learning situation. In this method both the teacher and the students discuss the *pros and cons* of the problem and then arrive at some tangible conclusion. Thus "Discussion is a thoughtful consideration of relationships involved in the topic or the problem under study. These relations are to be analysed, compared, evaluated and conclusions are drawn. The discussion requires a statement or enumeration of the facts to be analysed. In discussion mere allegations unsupported by evidence are of little value."

Types of Discussion

Mainly there are two types of discussion

(i) Spontaneous discussion, and

(ii) Planned discussion.

(i) Spontaneous Discussion

It generally starts from students question about some current event that may be related to the topic under study. Such a discussion is quite helpful to students as it helps them to understand current events to analyse and relate facts to real life situations. In such a discussion the knowledge of facts is reviewed and an understanding is developed.

(ii) Planned Discussion

Such discussion may be initiated by the teacher by asking one student to present reports and others to discuss them in detail. This technique needs a careful planning by the teacher by including pertinent facts to the class and unitying them in the form of conclusions. An extensive list of questions is made by the teacher and these should be injected into the discussion at appropriate time. The teacher should at times emphasise a point and should see that all relevant points are covered during discussion.

Advantages of Discussion Method

(i) It follows a spiral of learning principles.

(ii) It is found to work well to the related content courses.

(iii) It helps in motivating the students through their participation in discussion.

(iv) It helps in developing students ability to express himself orally.

(v) It helps to develop the powers of thinking and reasoning in the students.

(vi) It helps the students in analysing critically and drawing conclusion judiciouly.

(vii) It helps in creating a healthy rapport between the teacher and the taught.

Disadvantages of Discussion Method

(i) In this method there is a chance that only a few students may dominate the whole discussion.

(ii) It is possible that discussion is initiated on those aspects of the problem with which few prominent students of the class are concerned.

(iii) In this method there are chances that the students may be drifted to unimportant and insignificant aspects of the problem.

(iv) This method is time consuming.

(v) This method is not adaptable to all teaching-learning situations.

(vi) In this method it is very difficult to assess all the students in terms of learning outcomes.

Organisation and Control of Discussion

Following procedure may be adopted for organisation and control of discussion

(i) The discussion may be started by the students by giving facts, describing a situation etc.

(ii) The teacher may introduce the topic by providing data. Discussion should be stimulated by way of questioning by the teacher.

(iii) The teacher in cooperation with the students should finalise important points and relevant facts.

(iv) For making the discussion interesting and lively it is desirable to cite the personal experiences of the students relating to the topic.

(v) Illustrative material to collected from various sources (e.g. museum other community resources etc.) and presented in the class.

(vi) Various proposed solution given by students be presented to the class.

(vii) The summary of the work done and problems discussed be prepared by student leaders.

(viii) Debate-discussion should be initiated by pairs of students on significant and controversial topics.

(ix) Panel discussions, round table discussions, open forums and symposia should be arranged as per nature of the study. Such type of discussions may have far reaching values for socialisation of classroom discussion.

The extent of success of the discussion depends primarily on the ability of the teacher in securing the whole hearted cooperation of the students and selecting, organising and conducting group discussions. In case teacher finds that student volunteers are not forthcoming, then he should ask students to relate their experiences in such a way the whole of the class is represented.

Limitations of Discussion Method

This method revolves round the contributions made by the teacher and the students and would be of insignificant value if the contribution by students is not quite significant. The success of this method is directly proportional to students reasoning, acquisition of understandings and socialisation of technique. This method has been quite successful in social sciences as also in physical and biological sciences. It has also been quite successful in the teaching of mathematics and languages etc.

Demonstration Method

In this method both senses of the students are appealed by the teacher which really accelerates the learning process. Though the method is quite suitable but it is always advisable to make use of this method for teaching a subject in which skills relating to manual dexterity are needed. In this method the following steps are involved.

Steps is Demonstration Method

(i) The teacher briefly describes the topic that he intends to demonstrate. He cautions the students to remain vigilant and to observe how he demonstrates.

(ii) Teacher arranges various articles, to be used during demonstration, as his table in some well ordered arrangement.

(iii) Teacher shows to the students the actual procedure of demonstration.

(iv) Students observe the demonstration and note down the conclusions.

(v) Students try to imitate the teacher and exhibit their demonstration firstly in groups and then individually. This procedure has to be followed till a mastery is achieved.

Basic Principles of Demonstration

(i) The teacher should be quite clear of the specific purpose of demonstration.

(ii) The teacher should have a rehearsal of the whole of demonstration procedure before actually demonstrating a lesson in a class.

(iii) The teacher should make sure that he has with him all of the equipment needed for the demonstration. He should also be sure that he has the essential knowledge of successful operation of all the equipments to be used during the demonstrations.

(iv) Teacher should himself check the various physical facilities and the classroom situation.

(v) For a complex demonstration, teacher should classify and clarify those problems in such a way that they can be easily grasped.

(vi) Teacher may ask some pre-planned questions so as to get a summary of the demonstration.

(vii) Lecturing and talking should be kept to the minimum in a demonstration.

(viii) Students be helped to make a brief and systematic note of demonstration.

(ix) The demonstration be presented in such a way that it appeals to all the five senses of the students,

Advantages of Demonstration

(i) It is the most useful method in teaching manual skills (e.g. filling of routine forms, typing skill etc.)

(ii) Demonstration helps in presenting a very realistic view of the process or working of the machine before the students.

(iii) It enhances the skills of the students.

(iv) It makes understanding of the complex ideas easier on the part of the students.

(v) It fosters a spirit of confidence among students and makes the learning alive.

(vi) In demonstration we need less supervision and more responsibilities are involved.

(vii) Demonstration method helps to develop a scientific attitude towards the world of work amongst the students.

(viii) It enhances the dignity of labour.

Question Answer Method

This method is quite important. Through question, an attempt is made to ascertain and evaluate the knowledge of students in regard to the subject. This method ensures participation. The teacher should ask question and the student should be encouraged to ask questions.

About this method a renowned author says, "If the teacher does not know the answer he should admit it and either he **ask** the students to find it in the textbook or offer to find out the answer himself. No teacher can answer all the question which can be asked in yes or no. The students should be asked such questions which compel them to think the matter over. If the students can not answer the question fully, his partial answer should be accepted and another student may be asked to improve upon it. The teacher himself be in regular habit of reading latest texts as students should also be asked to find answers in authoritative texts". In this method the teacher controls the situation. Generally informal lesson is developed by means of question-answer method.

Types of Questions

The real aim of teachers should be to help the students to revise the subject matter that they have been taught. Through these questions their knowledge about the topic may also be tested. While farming the questions, the teacher should keep in mind the age of the students. He should see that the questions are printed and meet the desired objective.

Some of the important types of questions are

(i) Compare and contrast type questions.
(ii) Relationship between cause and effect.
(iii) Classification type questions.
(iv) Statements of aims.
(v) Inference.
(vi) Out line.
(vii) Recall type questions.

This technique has been recommended by A.S. Daughtery for the following

(i) to check reading assignments,
(ii) to secure and maintain attention or contact,
(iii) to explore students background,
(iv) to develop informational background,
(v) to set the stage for discussion,
(vi) to involve non-responsive students in the class activities,
(vii) to reveal students difficulties, work-habits, interests and level of development,

(viii) to develop factual basis for principle or generalisation, (ix) to review the work,

(x) to motivate students to read assignments, and (xi) to prepare students for tests.

Advantages of Question-Answer Method

(i) It can be used in all teaching situations.

(ii) It helps in developing the power of expression of the students.

(iii) It is helpful to ascertain the personal difficulties of the students.

(iv) It provides a check on preparation of assignments.

(v) It can be used to reflect students background and attitude.

(vi) It is quite handy to the teacher when no other suitable teaching method is available.

Disadvantages

(i) It requires a lot of skill on the part of teacher to make a proper use of this method

(ii) It may some time mar the atmosphere of the class.

(iii) This method generally is quite embracing for timid students.

(iv) It is time consuming. 8. Analytical Method

In this method we proceed from known to unknown. The word 'Analytic' is derived from the word 'Analysis' which means to break up or to resolve a thing into its constituent elements. Thus in this method we break up the unknown problem into simpler parts and then see how these can be recombined to find the solution. Therefore, it is the process of unfolding of the problem or of conducting its operation to know its hidden aspects. In this process we start with what is to be found out and then think of further steps or possibilities that may connect the unknown with the known and find out the desired result. It is believed that all the highest intellectual performance of the mind is analysis.

Merits of Analytical Method

(i) It helps in developing reasoning power of the students.

(ii) It helps in clear understanding of the subject because the students have to go through the whole process themselves.

(iii) In this method students participation is encouraged.

(iv) It is a psychological method.

(v) No cramming is required in this method.

(vi) This method has little rather no scope for forgetting.

(vii) Teaching by this method, teacher carries the class with him.

(viii) It helps in' developing a spirit of discovery amongst the students.

(ix) It develops self-confidence in the pupil.

Demerits of Analytical Method

(i) It is a time consuming and lengthy method, so it is uneconomical.

(ii) It this method facts are not presented in a neat and systematic order.

(iii) This method is not suitable for all the topics in commerce.

(iv) This method does not find favour with all the students because below average students fail to follow this method.

Applicability

In commerce teaching this method is suitable for complicated problems.

It analyses the problem into sub-parts and various parts are reorganised and the already learnt facts are used to connect the known with unknown. This method is particularly suitable for teaching of Arithmetic, commercial mathematics. It puts more stress on reasoning and development of power of reasoning is one of the major aims of teaching of commerce.

Synthetic Method

In this method we proceed from known to unknown. Actually synthesis is the complement to analysis. The word "synthetic' is derived from the word `synthesis which means to combine together.

In this method we combine together a number of facts, perform certain mathematical operations and arrive at the solution. In this method we start with the known data and connect it with the unknown part. It is the process of putting together known bits of information to reach the point where unknown information becomes obvious and true. Thus in this method we proceed from hypothesis to conclusion.

Merits of Synthetic Method

(i) It saves time and labour.

(ii) It is a neat method in which we present the facts in a systematic way.

(iii) It suits majority of students.

(iv) It can be applied to majority of topics in teaching of commerce.

Demerits of Synthetic Method

(i) It makes the students passive Iistnes and encourages cramming

(ii) While teaching by this method teacher does not carry the class with him.

(iii) This is an unpsychological method.

(iv) In this method there is a scope for forgetting

(v) In this method, confidence is generally lacking in the students.

Application

This method suits the average teacher and the average student. It is a time saving and neat method so teachers usually prefer this method. However, if it follows the analytical method then it gives the best results.

Combination of Analytical and Synthetic Method

Analytical and synthetic methods are interdependent or complementary. One is incomplete without the other. Analytical method is a logical way to develop a solution as it accounts for each and every step. But if we follow only analytical method we fail to present the facts in a systematic way.

The analytical proof is lengthy but it is based on a sound footing and if forgotten it would be much easier for the pupil to recall and reconstruct the proof for himself.

In synthetic method we proceed from known to unknown and it is a neat and concise method. The synthetic proof is shorter but it has not sound footing Once forgotten it can not be reconstructed. Synthetic method shows that every step is true but does not reveal the process adopted and the reason for selecting a particular sequence for reasoning.

Therefore to make the teaching effective both the methods should be applied together. The students should be encouraged through Analytical method to cooperate with the teacher and then teacher may use Synthetic method to provide knowledge, Synthetic Method helps the students to learn the subject matter. If we use a combination of both the methods the teaching becomes interesting as well as complete. We quote here the words of Arthur Schultze to justify it, "Analysis is the method of discovery, synthesis is the method of concise and elegant, presentation."

Heuristic Method

This method involves finding out by the pupil, instead of merely telling every thing by the teacher. This method demands complete self-activity or self-education on the part of the learner. By this method student's learn to reason for themselves.

The word 'Heuristic' has been derived from the Greek word "Heuresco" which means 'I find'. This method implies that the attitude of student shall be that of the discovers and not of passive recipients of knowledge.

This method was originally introduced by Armstrong for learning of sciences. This method exphasises experimentation.

In this method the teacher becomes on looker and the child tries to move ahead independently without any help or guidance. This method makes the student self-reliant and independent. It imparts a sound training in the education of self.

The teacher's job is not to solve problems for the pupil, but to enable the student solve problems for himself. It aims at developing a scientific or Heuristic attitude in the pupil. It aims at training in the method of learning self-confidence, originality, independence of judgment and thinking power are to be developed in the individual to make him an ever successful pupil. The teacher and the student should not feel discouraged by the slow progress made by using this method.

Pre-requisites or Requisites of the Heuristic Method

Heuristic method cannot be used without certain prerequisites.

The teacher has to keep followings things in mind before using method. The pre-requisites of this method are

(a) The teacher should de, lot of preparation for it.

(b) The question should be so planned that it may be possible for the students to find the solution independently by proceeding in the proper direction. It is required because in this method the pupil is not told anything but he is led to see the solution through carefully planned and well-directed questions.

(c) This method is not suitable for the beginners because in the early stages, students need a good deal of guidance. This guidance should be planned in a scientific way.

(d) This method requires a lot of planning. Several precautions have to be observed so that things may be planned properly and the lesson may be effective.

(e) The teacher and the student should not be discouraged by the slow progress that is made in this method This method proceeds very slowly and the progress is not very marked.

(f) The teacher should realise his responsibility properly. He should know that is Heuristic method, the students are not to be left alone without any support. Their difficulty should be properly solved and they should be given a proper guide.

There are no definite steps to be followed in this method. The teacher gives a problem to the students, creates a learning situatior and asks the pupil to solve the problem with their own efforts. The teacher puts thought-provoking questions and stimulates pupil effort.

Merits of Heuristic Method

(i) This makes the student active participants in the process of learning and allows them to have independent thinking.

(ii) He learns by doing so there is a little scope of forgetting.

(iii) It is a psychologically sound method as the student learns by self-practice.

(iv) It inculcates in the students the interest for the subject and also develops willingness in them.

(v) It gives the student a sense of confidence and achievement.

(vi) It develops the powers of original thinking and reasoning in the pupil thus it develops scientific attitude.

(vii) The teacher is in contact with the whole of the class and there is very little of homework for the students.

(viii) It promotes self-discipline in the students as they feel responsible for their work.

(ix) The student acquire command of the subject. He has a clear understanding and notion of the subject.

Demerits of Heuristic Method

Some of the demerits of this method are as under:

(i) This method is un-suitable for certain types of students, because all the students cannot become independent thinkers. Discovery of thing needs hard work, patience, concentration, reasoning and thinking powers and creative abilities.

(ii) This method suits only hardworking and original thinking teachers. An average teacher cannot frame true heuristic questions and stimulate pupils' thinking

(iii) This method does not suit larger classes. If the number of students is large, individual attention by the teacher becomes impossible.

(iv) The method is slow. The students has to spend a lot of time to find out minor' results. The teacher may find it difficult to finish the syllabus in time.

(v) It is not desirable to discover everything. Mathematics is a vast subject. There are so many things have to be accepted as such. Moreover, the things discovered once, need not be rediscovered again and again.

(vi) The success of method depends upon well-equipped libraries, laboratories, and good textbooks written on heuristic lines but such facilities are lacking in our schools.

(vii) The results found out by the students *may* not be correct. In the absence of individual checking, all the mistakes may not be rectified.

(viii) If the teacher is not able to distinguish between false and true heuristic questions, he may do more harm than good.

Conclusion

The success of this method depends upon a number of factors which may be mentioned below:

(i) The teacher must cultivate heuristic spirit in himself. This will require hard work on the part of the teacher.

(ii) The questions should be well thought of and these should be of true Heuristic type and the questions should not be leading ones, e.g It would be wrong to ask a question like do you remember that the area of rectangle is equal to the product of length and breadth, rather the question be frame like, how to calculate the area of a rectangle ?

(iii) The work to be carried out by a student should be in accordance with his level and ability.

(iv) Teacher should provide only the minimum and necessary guidance.

(v) The teacher should plan his lesson in such a way that copying from the textbooks is not possible.

(vi) This method must be supplemented by other methods of teaching Facts may always be discovered.

(v) Psychological Method

In this method emphasis is put on the psychology of the student. Their aptitudes and facilities are kept in mind while teaching them the subject-matter. This method attaches a little importance to the teaching of subject-matter and lays more stress on the development of psychology and facilities of the child. Thus it is a more scientific and so useful method of teaching.

This method makes the teaching of subject-matter interesting because here the faculties of the students and their psychophysical requirements are kept in mind. While using this method following precaution be observed:

(i) The teacher should exercise certain limits and restrictions.

(ii) It should not be used in such a way that it leads to a total loss of the purpose of teaching and its only aim becomes the teaching method.

(iii) It should be used only as means and not as an end.

(vi) Dogmatic Method of the Teaching of Mathematics

Dogmatic method has a bearing on the attitude of the teacher as well as the mode of the presentation of the subject-matter. In this method, teaching of commerce is carried out by rigours. Students are made to practice things rigorously. Believers in this method are of the view that once the rigour is given up, the purpose of the entire method is defeated. In this method, the pupil are required to memorize formulae and cram up the rules and definitions.

Advantages of Merits of the Dogmatic Method

(i) This method saves time, energy and does not allow students to get involved in unnecessary thinking.

(ii) It gives exercise to memory and thus helps its growth. Moreover, rigour is quite useful for the development of the commercial aptitude of the students.

Disadvantages or Demerits of the Dogmatic Method

(i) This method is unscientific and unpsytchological.

(ii) This method kills the initiative in the students and makes them memorizing machine.

(iii) This method is unpsychological, since it puts more stress on the subject-matter and not on the students who are to be taught.

(iv) The main object of teaching is to develop certain qualities in the students. The method fails to achieve that object and so it is not of much use in practical life.

(v) If this method is applied and the students forget the rules they cannot solve a problem.

(vi) The method provides only information and does not allow students to do things independently.

(vii) The method makes the teaching uninteresting and dull and converts the whole atmosphere of the class into a mechanical atmosphere.

(viii) Through this method, only students with a good memory can make progress. Such of the students who did have a very strong memory shall not be able to use this method properly as they would not cram up the rules and memorize the problems.

Importance of this Method

In spite of the drawbacks, this method cannot be condemned wholly. It has its own utility, but at a proper stage. Given proper circumstances and situations this method can help the teacher to cover a good deal of syllabus in a short time.

Concentric Method

This is a system of organising a course rather than a method of teaching. It is, therefore, better to call it *concentric system or approach.* It implies widening of knowledge just as concentric circles go on extending and widening. It is a system of arrangement of subject matter. In this method the study of the topic is spread over a number of years. It is based on the principle that subject cannot be given an exhaustive treatment at the first stage. To begin with, a simple presentation of the subject is given and further knowledge is imparted in following years. Thus beginning from a nucleus the circles of knowledge go on widening year after year and hence the name concentric method.

Procedure

A topic is divided into a number of portions *which* are then allotted to different classes. The criterion for allotment of a particular portion of the course to a particular class are the difficulty of portion and power of comprehension of students in the age group. Thus it is mainly concerned with year to year teaching but its influence can also be exercised in day-to-day teaching. Knowledge being given today should follow from knowledge given yesterday and should lead to teaching on following day.

Merits of Concentric Method

(i) This method of organisation of subject matter is decidely superior to that in which one topic is taken up in particular class and an effort is made to deal with all aspects of the topic in that particular class.

(ii) It provides a framework from course which is of real value to students.

(iii) The system is most successful when the teaching is in hand of one teacher because then he can preserve continuity in the teaching and keeps his expanding circle concentric.

(iv) It provides opportunity for revision of work already covered in a previous class and carrying out new work.

(v) It enables the teacher to cover a portion according to receptivity of learner.

(vi) Since the same topic is learnt over many years so its impressions are more lasting.

(vii) It does not allow teaching to become dull because every year a new interest can be given to the topic. Every year there are new problems to solve and new difficulties to overcome.

Drawbacks

For the success of this approach we require really capable teacher. If a teacher becomes over ambitious and exhausts all the possible interesting illustrations in there introductory year then the subject loses its power of freshness and appeal and nothing is left to create interest in the topic in subsequent years.

In case the topic is too short or too long then also the method is not found to be useful. A too long portion makes the topic dull and a too short portion fails to leave any permanent and lasting impression on the mind of the pupil.

Conclusion

It is a good method for being adopted for arranging the_ subject matter. It should be kept in mind, by the organisers, while organising the subject matter no portion is too long or too short. It would also be much useful if the teacher teaches the same class year after year so that he can reserve some illustrative examples for each year and thus can maintain the interest of the students in the topic.

Topical Method

In this method a particular topic is started in a particular class and finished over there, however, this has failed to get approval from a majority of educational thinkers. In their opinion if this method is used, many irrelevant things may creep in and many relevant things may be left out. The students may be forced to study such things which are of no immediate importance to them. Moreover, if this method is adopted only a few topic will find a place in any particular class, because all types of problems on that topic shall have to be solved by the students in one class. In the opinion of such Educationists the Spiral Method of organisation of curriculum is preferable. In the Spiral Method a topic is divided into a number of small independent units to be dealt within different classes that suit the mental capacities of the pupils. In their opinion such a method is more natural and less tiring to the students. To support it they argue that in such a method student loses nothing in accuracy and gains a lot in power of application of the general rules to particular problems.

The criterion of difficulty lays more emphasis on the fact that topics should be arranged in order of difficulty. But to take the topic as a unit is not good arrangement. Topical arrangement is based on the unity of the topic i.e. exhaustion of the topic at the same time or at a stretch. However, it is unnatural and also impracticable to take a topic and exhaust all its possible portions and problems, simple as also complex, in the same class. For a good arrangement the follow ing be kept in view.

(i) Every topic should be divided into parts.

(ii) These parts should be graded according to difficulty.

(iii) Each part should be introduced at a proper stage.

These different portions be alloted to be taught in different classes according to their difficulty and maturity of minds of pupils. Such an approach is called *a Spiral approach.*

A portion is introduced when a sufficient back ground has been prepared for it. The remaining more tedious portions are left, for being taken up later on. Every thing is taken up at its proper stage and there is enough opportunity for revision. The precaution to be observed is that the portion should neither be too long nor too short.

Presently "Topical Method" is more a system of arrangement of subject-matter than a method of teaching. The topic is to be taught at a stretch, without a break or gap, continuous teaching of topic not only will save the students from divided attention and will also ensure their full and whole hearted concentration on the topic in hand. Thus a natural link will exist in the day-to-day work in the class room.

(xii) Some other Methods

Some other methods used in teaching of Commerce are

(a) Genetic Method.

(b) Play way Method.

(c) Montessori Method.

(d) Textbook Method.

The out lines of all methods are given here

Genetic Method: This method is nothing but an improved form of Heuristic Method. In this method attempt is made to retain the spirit of the Heuristic Method and do away with its limitations. Here the whole class is treated as a co-operating group rather than as a separate individual. This method is also a combination of several procedures that include questioning, providing information, explaining, guiding etc.

Play way Method: It is a method where teaching is carried out in play. While teaching commerce several games and plays are re-sorted to. This method may be useful for the teaching of commerce because it would facilitate the learning.

Students Motivated Technique

You can motivate students to learn in many different ways. First, take into account individual differences in ability, background, and attitudes. Then try to satisfy the physiological, safety, belongingness, and esteem needs of the students. Make the classroom environment conducive to learning. Take an interest in your students. Learn their names as fast as you can and let them feel that they belong in your classroom. Direct learning experiences toward feelings of success by encouraging achievement and a positive self concept. Give students positive, helpful feedback and help them set challenging but attainable goals. Use various techniques to motivate students and encourage self confidence and self direction at all times. Provide a learning-oriented environment. Do everything possible to create an environment that encourages your students to learn. Make it physically and psychologically safe.

Applying Motivation Techniques to Instruction

The techniques of motivation have application introduction, the presentation, and the summary.

Lesson Introduction

Use motivation at the beginning of a lesson in each part of a lesson presentation: the as a means of introducing the material, stimulating interest, arousing curiosity, and developing a specific direction. Besides showing the need for learning the information, the introduction should serve as a connecting link between the present lesson and previous lessons. Use the lesson introduction to discuss specific reasons why students need to learn the information you plan to present. To reinforce their desire to learn, show students how the information relates to their career advancement or some other need. Give the students specific examples. In many cases, you may motivate students by telling them they will need the information to understand future lessons. For most instructional methods, the lesson introduction should provide a road map for learning. You may find effective visual aids helpful at this point. A clear introduction can contribute greatly to a lesson by removing doubts in the minds of the learners about where the lesson is going and how they are going to get there. Tell students what you will cover or leave out and why. Explain how you have organized your ideas. Students understand better and retain more when they know what to expect. The purpose of the introduction is to motivate students to learn by listening to the information you will present in the body of the lesson.

7 Essential Student Motivation Techniques That You Must Use

As a teacher, one of your most important functions is to motivate your students to explore and learn. Teachers should try to instill in their students, the concept that learning is a lifelong adventure, but it can be a fun, satisfying and productive experience.

Teachers must keep the motivation for learning alive and growing in their students. From a very early age, children have that curiosity to explore everything around them. Teachers have a responsibility to their students to motivate them and develop that curiosity into a desire for knowledge.

There are so many ways for you to motivate your students but here are 7 methods or tactics that I have found very effective.

1. Establish a strong teacher-student relationship by showing your students that you care about them and are interested in what they do and accomplish. Respect them and hopefully they will respect you. Develop an atmosphere of trust in a positive learning environment.
2. Showing respect for your students means giving them more control over what they do and how it's done. Allow them to make some of their own decisions and choices, even if you have a better way and even if they make some mistakes. Just be sure that the choices are reasonable. Motivating students in this manner builds character and is extremely effective.
3. Prepare your students for the outside world by incorporating real world applications into your lesson plans, and your students class assignments and class projects. Students want to feel that they are spending their time on things that will be useful to them. As well, in our technology based society, take the opportunity to use computer applications such as Powerpoint for presentations, the Internet, video (You Tube), etc. to keep your students motivated, focused and interested.
4. A reward system is a terrific motivator for your students and can be of great benefit to you as well. Everyone wins. Introduce a reward system and allow your students to win simple and inexpensive prizes that you can buy at the dollar store. You can also offer other classroom awards such as giving "free time" or having

classroom parties. You'll need to adjust the rewards but all your students young and older will love it. You win by keeping your students motivated (at least by the prizes). Be sure to reward your students only if they finish their work, assignment, project,etc. and not just for taking part.

5. Classroom games and class meetings to discuss personal topics like hobbies are fabulous for motivating students and team building. It's amazing how it does wonders for students' self-esteem and camaraderie. Games and team building activities may also attract the unmotivated students you have in your class.
6. Another WIN-WIN for both teacher and students, is allowing them to help you out with many of the classroom jobs. Young and older students love to help the teacher and offering this as a reward, motivates them to try harder and do better with their work. It's a bonus for you too, since there's less for you to do.
7. Most kids love to show off to their peers, teacher and parents. So let them by displaying their work in the classroom. It makes them feel that the classroom belongs to them and it's great for motivating them to work harder and produce better results. Displaying your students work around the classroom will also create an inviting atmosphere in which to teach and learn.

Analytical Methods

The purpose of this chapter is to describe the **analytical** methods that are available for detecting, and/or measuring, and/or monitoring PCBs, its metabolites, and other biomarkers of exposure and effect to PCBs. The intent is not to provide an exhaustive list of **analytical** methods. Rather, the intention is to identify well-established methods that are used as the standard methods of analysis. Many of the **analytical** methods used for environmental samples are the methods approved by federal agencies and organizations such as EPA and the National Institute for Occupational Safety and Health (NIOSH). Other methods presented in this chapter are those that are approved by groups such as the Association of Official Analytical Chemists (AOAC) and the American Public Health Association (APHA). Additionally, analytical methods are included that modify previously used methods to obtain lower detection limits, and/or to improve accuracy and precision.

Methodology for PCB analysis includes several steps: sample collection and storage, extraction, cleanup, and determination (EPA 1995c, 1999k; Hess et al. 1995). Care must be taken to assure that the sample collection follows quality assurance protocols and that equipment and containers are free from contamination. Most sample collections are by grab sampling; however, PCBs may be concentrated from water or air onto sorbents. PCBs are typically separated from the sample matrix by solid-phase extraction (SPE), separatory funnel extraction, continuous liquid/liquid extraction (CLLE), Soxhlet extraction, or Soxhlet/Dean-Stark extraction. PCBs may be difficult to extract from oily matrices in which they are soluble. Some problems that may occur during extraction include evaporative losses during concentration, sorption onto labware, and contamination of samples.

Cleanup steps are necessary to remove compounds that may interfere with the determination. Chromatography (e.g., gel permeation, silica gel, Florisil, activated carbon, high-performance liquid) is often used to remove matrix interferences, and sometimes to fractionate PCBs into several groups. Cleanup by chromatography has been used extensively to separate the non-*ortho* and the mono-*ortho* CBs from the remaining congeners before quantitative analysis (Hess et al. 1995). The identification and quantitation of PCBs are most often accomplished by gas chromatographic (GC) techniques. Capillary or high resolution gas chromatography (HRGC) columns capable of separating a substantial proportion of the congeners are indispensable, and GC detectors possessing high selectivity and sensitivity for the PCBs are required. The more universal and less sensitive flame-ionization detector (FID) is used much less often than the electron capture detector (ECD), which has exceptional sensitivity to multiply chlorinated compounds. The mass spectrometer-selected-ion-monitoring

(MS-SIM) or ion-trap mass spectrometer (ITMS) detectors have sensitivities somewhat lower than ECD, and they have even greater selectivity for PCBs and can distinguish and individually measure homologs that may coelute on a particular HRGC column (EPA 1999k).

Some methods in use are multi-residue methods in which PCBs along with many other analytes such as pesticides, are determined. In general, PCB methods analyze for Aroclor mixtures, PCB homologs, or individual PCB congeners. Until recently, packed column GC/ECD was used most often for the determination of PCBs as Aroclor mixtures. The Webb-McCall technique was used for quantitation. The weight percent and homolog identification were determined for several Aroclors. Response factors were generated to calculate the amount in each sample peak; with packed columns, each peak contains several congeners. The amounts found in each sample peak were then summed (Webb-McCall 1973).

Alternately, the total area in the Aroclor region of the chromatogram was used for quantitation. However, Aroclor analyses are estimations that are prone to error as a result of the subjective assignment of Aroclor speciation and response factors. Also, the practice of comparing CB patterns in environmental samples with those of technical mixtures can be misleading since mixtures emanating from different sources are mixed at differing rates by diffusion, evaporation, and adsorption onto solids. Many congeners are metabolized, while others bioconcentrate in lipophilic material.

Therefore, the final pattern in the environment is often highly modified and may not resemble the original commercial formulation or mixture of formulations (Draper et al. 1991; Duinker and Hillebrand 1979; Hess et al. 1995). The maximum detection limits (MCLs) for Aroclors vary in the range of 0.054–0.90 µg/L in water and 57–70 µg/kg in soils (EPA 1995c). Another approach is to determine PCBs by level of chlorination (or homolog group). One PCB for each homolog (isomer group) is typically used for calibration. Total PCB concentration is obtained by summing isomer group concentrations (Alford-Stevens et al. 1986).

However, since the congener distribution is not determined with this method, an accurate calculation of PCB toxic equivalency (TEQ) can not be accessed. Recently, capillary or HRGC has made it possible to achieve lower detection limits and better separation of individual PCB congeners for quantitation (Frame 1997; Mullin et al. 1984; Newman et al. 1998), although complete separation of all PCB congeners on a single column has not yet been achieved (Duebeleis et al. 1989). The commonly used capillary columns (DB-5, C-18, DB-1701, SE-54, SIL-8, SP-2330, and CP-SIL-8) provide poor or no resolution for the following groups of congeners: 15/18, 28/31, 49/52, 66/95, 77/110, 84/90/101, 118/149, 138/163/164, 105/132/153, 170/190, and 182/187 (Liem 1999; Schantz et al. 1993b). Nevertheless, the trend is toward congener-specific analysis by HRGC. Recent advances include analytical methods that are able to quantify individual PCBs congeners to enable TEQ calculations (EPA 1999k; Frame 1999; Patterson et al. 1994). EPA Method 1668 (Revision A) is the current methodology used to measure individual PCB congeners in water, soil, sediment, and tissue by HRGC/high resolution mass spectrometry (HRMS) (EPA 1999k). Estimated detection limits (EDL) of selected PCB congeners range from 109 to 193 pg/L for water and 11–19 ng/kg for soil, tissue, and mixed-phase samples. . This method has been used to measure specific PCBs in EPA projects such as the assessment of PCBs in fish consumed by four Native American tribes in the Columbia River Basin in Washington state (EPA 1996f). As for all analytical methods, determining the quality and usability of Aroclor, PCB homolog, or specific congener data by formal data validation procedures is recommended; EPA has developed data validation guidelines for HRGC/ECD Aroclor data and HRGC/LRMS (low resolution mass spectrometry) PCB specific congener data (EPA 1994h, 1995g).

Brainstorming

Brainstorming is a group creativity technique designed to generate a large number of ideas for the solution of a problem. The method was first popularized in the late 1930s by Alex Faickney Osborn in a book called Applied Imagination. Osborn proposed that groups could double their creative output with brainstorming.

Although brainstorming has become a popular group technique, researchers have not found evidence of its effectiveness for enhancing either quantity or quality of ideas generated. Because of such problems as distraction, social loafing, evaluation apprehension, and production blocking, brainstorming groups are little more effective than other types of groups, and they are actually less effective than individuals working independently. In the Encyclopedia of Creativity, Tudor Rickards, in his entry on brainstorming, summarizes its controversies and indicates the dangers of conflating productivity in group work with quantity of ideas.

Although traditional brainstorming does not increase the productivity of groups (as measured by the number of ideas generated), it may still provide benefits, such as boosting morale, enhancing work enjoyment, and improving team work. Thus, numerous attempts have been made to improve brainstorming or use more effective variations of the basic technique.

Ground Rules

There are four basic rules in brainstorming. These are intended to reduce social inhibitions among groups members, stimulate idea generation, and increase overall creativity of the group.

1. *Focus on Quantity:* This rule is a means of enhancing divergent production, aiming to facilitate problem solving through the maxim, *quantity breeds quality.* The assumption is that the greater the number of ideas generated, the greater the chance of producing a radical and effective solution.
2. *Withhold Criticism:* In brainstorming, criticism of ideas generated should be put 'on hold'. Instead, participants should focus on extending or adding to ideas, reserving criticism for a later 'critical stage' of the process. By suspending judgment, participants will feel free to generate unusual ideas.

3. *Welcome Unusual Ideas:* To get a good and long list of ideas, unusual ideas are welcomed. They can be generated by looking from new perspectives and suspending assumptions. These new ways of thinking may provide better solutions.
4. *Combine and Improve Ideas:* Good ideas may be combined to form a single better good idea, as suggested by the slogan "1+1=3". It is believed to stimulate the building of ideas by a process of association.

Method

Set the Problem

Before a brainstorming session, it is critical to define the problem. The problem must be clear, not too big, and captured in a specific question such as "What service for mobile phones is not available now, but needed?". If the problem is too big, the facilitator should break it into smaller components, each with its own question.

Create a Background Memo

The background memo is the invitation and informational letter for the participants, containing the session name, problem, time, date, and place. The problem is described in the form of a question, and some example ideas are given.The memo is sent to the participants well in advance, so that they can think about the problem beforehand.

Select Participants

The facilitator composes the brainstorming panel, consisting of the participants and an idea collector. A group of 10 or fewer members is generally more productive. Many variations are possible but the following composition is suggested.

- Several core members of the project who have proved themselves.
- Several guests from outside the project, with affinity to the problem.
- One idea collector who records the suggested ideas.

Create a List of Lead Questions

During the brainstorm session the creativity may decrease. At this moment, the facilitator should stimulate creativity by suggesting a lead question to answer, such as *Can we combine these ideas?* or *How about looking from another perspective?*. It is best to prepare a list of such leads before the session begins.

Session Conduct

The facilitator leads the brainstorming session and ensures that ground rules are followed. The steps in a typical session are:

1. A warm-up session, to expose novice participants to the criticism-free environment. A simple problem is brainstormed, for example *What should be the CEO retirement present?* or *What can be improved in Microsoft Windows?*.
2. The facilitator presents the problem and gives a further explanation if needed.
3. The facilitator asks the brainstorming group for their ideas.
4. If no ideas are forthcoming, the facilitator suggests a lead to encourage creativity.
5. All participants present their ideas, and the idea collector records them.
6. To ensure clarity, participants may elaborate on their ideas.
7. When time is up, the facilitator organizes the ideas based on the topic goal and encourages discussion.
8. Ideas are categorized.
9. The whole list is reviewed to ensure that everyone understands the ideas.
10. Duplicate ideas and obviously infeasible solutions are removed.
11. The facilitator thanks all participants and gives each a token of appreciation.

The Process

- Participants who have ideas but were unable to present them are encouraged to write down the ideas and present them later.
- The idea collector should number the ideas, so that the chairperson can use the number to encourage an idea generation goal, for example: *We have 44 ideas now, let's get it to 50!*.
- The idea collector should repeat the idea in the words he or she has written verbatim, to confirm that it expresses the meaning intended by the originator.
- When more participants are having ideas, the one with the most associated idea should have priority. This to encourage elaboration on previous ideas.
- During a brainstorming session, managers and other superiors may be discouraged from attending, as it may inhibit and reduce the effect of the four basic rules, especially the generation of unusual ideas.

Evaluation

Brainstorming is not just about generating ideas for others to evaluate and select. Usually the group itself will, in its final stage, evaluate the ideas and select one as the solution to the problem proposed to the group.

- The solution should not require resources or skills the members of the group do not have or cannot acquire.
- If acquiring additional resources or skills is necessary, that needs to be the first part of the solution.
- There must be a way to measure progress and success.
- The steps to carry out the solution must be clear to all, and amenable to being assigned to the members so that each will have an important role.
- There must be a common decision making process to enable a coordinated effort to proceed, and to reassign tasks as the project unfolds.

- There should be evaluations at milestones to decide whether the group is on track toward a final solution.
- There should be incentives to participation so that participants maintain their efforts.

Variations

Nominal Group Technique

The nominal group technique is a type of brainstorming that encourages all participants to have an equal say in the process. It is also used to generate a ranked list of ideas.

Participants are asked to write their ideas anonymously. Then the moderator collects the ideas and each is voted on by the group. The vote can be as simple as a show of hands in favor of a given idea. This process is called distillation.

After distillation, the top ranked ideas may be sent back to the group or to subgroups for further brainstorming. For example, one group may work on the color required in a product. Another group may work on the size, and so forth. Each group will come back to the whole group for ranking the listed ideas. Sometimes ideas that were previously dropped may be brought forward again once the group has re-evaluated the ideas.

It is important that the facilitator be trained in this process before attempting to facilitate this technique. The group should be primed and encouraged to embrace the process. Like all team efforts, it may take a few practice sessions to train the team in the method before tackling the important ideas.

Group Passing Technique

Each person in a circular group writes down one idea, and then passes the piece of paper to the next person in a clockwise direction, who adds some thoughts. This continues until everybody gets his or her original piece of paper back. By this time, it is likely that the group will have extensively elaborated on each idea.

The group may also create an "Idea Book" and post a distribution list or routing slip to the front of the book. On the first page is a description of the problem. The first person to receive the book lists his or her ideas and then routes the book to the next person on the distribution list. The second person can log new ideas or add to the ideas of the previous person. This continues until the distribution list is exhausted. A follow-up "read out" meeting is then held to discuss the ideas logged in the book. This technique takes longer, but it allows individuals time to think deeply about the problem.

Team Idea Mapping Method

This method of brainstorming works by the method of association. It may improve collaboration and increase the quantity of ideas, and is designed so that all attendees participate and no ideas are rejected.

The process begins with a well-defined topic. Each participant brainstorms individually, then all the ideas are merged onto one large idea map. During this consolidation phase, participants may discover a common understanding of the issues as they share the meanings behind their ideas. During this sharing, new ideas may arise by the association, and they are added to the map as well. Once all the ideas are captured, the group can prioritize and/or take action.

Electronic Brainstorming

Electronic brainstorming is a computerized version of the manual brainwriting technique. It can be done via email and may be browser based, or use peer-to-peer software.

The facilitator sends the question out to group members, and they contribute independently by sending their ideas back to the facilitator. The facilitator then compiles a list of ideas and sends it back to the group for further feedback. Electronic brainstorming eliminates many of the problems of standard brainstorming, such as production blocking and evaluation apprehension. An additional advantage of this method is that all ideas can be archived electronically in their original form, and then retrieved later for further thought and discussion. Electronic brainstorming also enables much larger groups to brainstorm on a topic than would normally be productive in a traditional brainstorming session. Other brainstorming techniques are web-based, and allow contributors to post their comments anonymously through the use of avatars. This technique also allows users to log on over an extended time period, typically one or two weeks, to allow participants some "soak time" before posting their ideas and feedback. This technique has been used particularly in the field of new product development, but can be applied in any number of areas where collecting and evaluating ideas would be useful. Professor Olivier Toubia of Columbia University has conducted extensive research in the field of idea generation and has concluded that incentives are extremely valuable within the brainstorming context.

Directed Brainstorming

Directed brainstorming is a variation of electronic brainstorming. It can be done manually or with computers. Directed brainstorming works when the solution space (that is, the criteria for evaluating a good idea) is known prior to the session. If known, that criteria can be used to intentionally constrain the ideation process.

In directed brainstorming, each participant is given one sheet of paper (or electronic form) and told the brainstorming question. They are asked to produce one response and stop, then all of the papers (or forms) are randomly swapped among the participants. The participants are asked to look at the idea they received and to create a new idea that improves on that idea based on the initial criteria. The forms are then swapped again and respondents are asked to improve upon the ideas, and the process is repeated for three or more rounds.

In the laboratory, directed brainstorming has been found to almost triple the productivity of groups over electronic brainstorming.

Individual Brainstorming

"Individual Brainstorming" is the use of brainstorming on a solitary basis. It typically includes such techniques as free writing, free speaking, word association, and the "spider web," which is a visual note taking technique in which a people diagram their thoughts. Individual brainstorming is a useful method in creative writing and has been shown to be superior to traditional group brainstorming.

Other Variations

One of the problems can be to find the best questions to ask. This has been called *questorming*. Another of the problems for brainstorming can be to find the best evaluation methods for a problem.

Conclusion

Brainstorming is a popular method of group interaction in both educational and business settings. Although it does not provide a measurable advantage in creative output, brainstorming is an enjoyable exercise that is typically well received by participants. Newer variations of brainstorming seek to overcome barriers like production blocking and may well prove superior to the original technique. How well these newer methods work, and whether or not they should be classified as brainstorming, are questions that require further research.

Heuristic Method

Heuristic Method word meaning to discover). In Heuristic method, the student be put in the place of an independent discoverer. Thus no help or guidance is provided by the teacher in this method. In this method the teacher sets a problem for the students and then stands aside while they discover the. answer.

In words of Professor Armstrong, "Heuristic methods of teaching are methods which involve our placing students as far as possible in the altitude of the discoverer - methods which involve their finding out instead of being merely told about things". The **method** requires the student to solve a number of problems experimentally. To almost every one — especially children — experiments and science are synonymous. Once an idea occurs to a scientist he immediately thinks in terms of ways of trying out his ideas to see if he is correct. Trying to confirm or disprove some thing, or simply to test an idea, is the backbone of the experiment. Experiments start with questions in order to find answers, solve problems, clarify ideas or just to see what happens. Experimenting should be part of the elementary school science programme as an aid to helping children find solutions to science problems as well as for helping them to develop appreciation for one of the basic tools of science.

Procedure of the Method

The method requires the students to solve a number of problems experimentally.

Each student is required to discover everything for himself and is to be told nothing. The students are led to discover facts with the help of experiments, apparatus and books. In this method the child behaves like a research scholar.

In the stage managed heuristic method, a problem sheet with minimum instructions is given to the student and he is required to perform the experiments concerning the problem in hand. He must follow the instructions, and enter in his notebook an account of what he has done and results arrived at. He must also put down his conclusion as to the bearing which the result has on the problem in hand. In this way he is led to reason from observation.

Essentially therefore, the heuristic method is intended to provide a training in method. Knowledge is a secondary consideration altogether. The method is formative rather than informational.

The procedures and skills in science problem solving can only be developed in class rooms where searching is encouraged, creative thinking is respected, and where it is safe to investigate, try out ideas.

Teachers Altitudes

One of the most important aspects of the problem solving approach to children's development in scientific thinking is the teacher's attitude. H's approach should be teaching science with a question mark instead of with an exclamation point. The acceptance of and the quest for unique solutions for the problem that the class is investigating should be a guiding principle in the teacher's approach to his programme of science. Teachers must develop sensitiveness to children and to the meanings of their behaviour Teachers should be ready to accept any suggestion for the solution of problems regardless of how irrelevant it may seem to him, for this is really the true spirit of scientific problem solving. By testing various ideas it can be shown to the child that perhaps his suggestion was not in accord with the information available It can then be shown that this failure gets as much closer to the correct solution by eliminating one possibility from many offered by the problem.

In this method teacher should avoid the tempetation to tell the right answer to save time. The teacher should be convinced that road to scientific thinking takes time. Children should never be exposed to ridicule for their suggestions of possible answers otherwise they will show a strong tendency to stop suggestions.

For success of this method a teacher should act like a guide and should provide only that much guidance as is rightly needed by the student. He should be sympathetic and courteous and should be capable enough to plan and devise problems for investigation by pupils. He should be capable of good supervision and be able to train the pupils in a way that he himself becomes dispensable.

Merits of Heuristic Method

This method of teaching science has the following merits:

(i) It develops the habit of enquiry and investigation among students.

(ii) It develops habit of self learning and self direction.

(iii) It develops scientific attitudes among students by making them truthful and honest for they learn how to arrive at decisions by actual experimentations.

(iv) It is psychologically sound system of learning as it is based on the maximum, "learning by doing"

(v) It develops in the student a habit of diligency.

(vi) In this method most of the work is done in school and so the teacher has no worry to assign on check home task.

(vii) It provides scope for individual attention to be paid by the establishing cordial relations between the teacher and the taught.

Limitations of Heuristic Method

Main limitations of this method are as under:

(i) It is a long and time consuming method and so it becomes difficult to cover the prescribed syllabus in time.

(ii) It pre-supposes a very small class and a gifted teacher and the method is too technical and scientific to be handled by an average teacher. The method expects of the teacher a great efficiency and hard, experience and training.

(iii) There is a tendency on the part of the teacher to emphasize those branches and parts of the subject which lend brandies of the subject which do not involve measurement and quantitative work and arc therefore not so suitable.

(iv) It is not suitable for beginners. In the early stages, the students needs enough guidance which if not given, may greatly disappoint them and it is possible that the child may develop a distaste for studies.

(v) In this method too much stress is placed on practical work which may lead a student to form a wrong idea of the nature of science as a whole. They grow up in the belief that science is some thing to be done in the laboratory, forgetting that laboratories were made for science and not science for laboratories.

(vi) The gradation of problems is a difficult task which requires sufficient skill and training. The succession of exercises is rarely planned to fit into a general scheme for building up the subject completely.

(vii) Some times experiments are performed merely for sake of doing them

(viii) Learning by this method, pupils leave school with little or no scientific appreciation of their physical environment. The romance of modern scientific discovery and invention remains out of picture for them and the humanizing influence of the subject has been kept away from them.

(ix) Evaluation of learning through heuristic method can be quite tedious.

(x) Presently enough teachers are not available for implementing learning by heuristic method.

Simulation and Role Playing

A Training Technique

In several of the documents on this subject was recommended. We learn by reading, listening to someone talking, watching something being done, and doing something ourselves. Of course, different individuals have different ways of learning, and variable strengths according to how they obtain the information to be learned. This list is a rough generalization.

If you look at the various ways we have of learning, then reading appears to be at the bottom of the list. The information is difficult to absorb and understand, and retention tends to be short lived. Listening to a lecture appears to be far down on the list, almost as low as reading. Watching something being done, live, or video or on a film, is a little more effective – best if it is live. At the top of the list, when the trainee participates in the activity to be learned, absorption is faster, more complete and more concentrated, and retention is much greater.

In a classroom or workshop situation, however, it is not possible to exactly replicate a genuine field situation in which trainees can participate. That is one of the many reasons why training should not be all lumped together and the facilitator or mobilizer then expected to perform in the field. After doing some field work, mobilizers should be brought back to a training centre, allowed to share experiences, and obtain more training based upon what they have already done. Routine and regular follow-up training should be a standard element of all programmes for facilitating mobilization, capacity development, poverty reduction, management training and income generation.

Meanwhile, there is another, simulated form of participation that can be conducted in a class room, a workshop or training session. Role playing or simulation games have been found to be very effective. Such simulated participation should be used in the training of your facilitators and mobilizers, and used by those same facilitators and mobilizers in their work of capacity development, community mobilizing, income generation, and management training.

The Essence of a Role-Playing Game: A role playing game is a training session where the facilitator, perhaps with an assistant or two, sets up a scenario where the participants are assigned different roles, where those roles identify with those in the situation where participants will find themselves when they undertake their work in the field.

The play gives the training participants opportunities to act out various roles chosen to represent actual roles that would be in the field situation.

One important result is that training participants get an opportunity to see the field situation from perspectives other than those they might be taking in reality. That opportunity results in a greater sensitivity to the experiences of other persons in the field situation.

The follow-up session following the play gives the training participants an opportunity to analyse some of the social dynamics that occur. This objectivity is available both to those who take roles for a play session, and to those who might be observing the role-play session.

There are three stages to a standard role-play session: (1) the set up, (2) the play, (3) the discussion.

Setting Up the Play: In the set up stage, the facilitator sets the stage. This means describing the scenario and assigning roles to participants. If a participant plays a particular role in reality, in the field situation, it would be more effective to give a different role to that participant during the role-play session.

An optional part of the set up stage is to give some time for the key role players to get together to map out the general plot of their play. You as facilitator must decide this on the basis of what you want to emphasize, and this should be decided when you design the workshop in which the role-play will be carried out.

Another option is to put together a single page description of the scenario to be worked out by the players. Another option is to write one-paragraph descriptions of the key role players. A description can include the main objectives and concerns of the person in that role, perhaps can include some key dialogues or a statement to be read by the person playing the role. The possible variations are numerous; use them.

Alternatively, it may be useful for the persons playing all the roles to be spontaneous and think up their separate acts in the heat of the moment. In this case there will be no time for the actors to plan their plot, and no written descriptions or guidelines.

The Play Stage: The second, or play stage of the session is when the trainee participants act out their roles and the play is carried out.

If the play becomes too long, then the facilitator can give the actors a time warning of one or two minutes, and then end the play after that.

Alternatively, the play may be too short, and the facilitator must encourage the actors to embellish their acting, and to add speeches, a soliloquy and actions that make their play less skimpy.

The Follow Up: The third stage is the follow-up. This is important and can not be omitted.

It is important for all the trainee participants to discuss what happened. They may question individual role-players to ask why they took a particular position, made a certain statement, or undertook an action. The explanation and the resulting discussion is important for the participants to obtain a greater understanding of the social dynamics related to a particular field situation.

In some role play sessions, a certain amount of heat (anger, dismay, disagreement) may be generated, especially if some role-players take the play too seriously, and take hard line positions. The follow-up discussions offer the facilitator an opening to cool off the group a little, and explain that the heat was generated by the structure of the situation, not by the stubbornness (or evil) of the individuals playing the roles.

That heat is not a bad thing to be avoided; it is an opportunity to reveal the nature of some field situations, and to encourage participants to be sensitive to the different assumptions, values, goals and positions that may be taken by different persons actually in the field.

The Value of Humour: In both the set up and the discussion stages, the facilitator should encourage a light touch. Remember that a "play" by definition is not reality, and should not be taken seriously. Humour is encouraged.

Humour can defuse an anxious situation, and it allows participants to take a more arms-length approach to analysing the potential field situations they might experience later.

Participants should be encouraged to "ham it up," (play with their roles; over act), and to enjoy playing.

When to Use Role Playing?: As mentioned above, role playing games should be used in the training of mobilizers and facilitators, and used by mobilizers and facilitators in their work in the field. Role playing should not be limited to initial training or awareness raising sessions.

They are very useful during annual and semi-annual reviews of various programmes. They are useful in follow-up and ongoing training of community workers after they have been in the field for some time. They are useful for heads of programmes, managers, programme managers, planners and head office staff and officers, especially if they can be included in sessions along side of field workers in the programmes they administer. In a single training session or workshop, you may wish to set up more than one role playing game. If so, make it different, using a different scenario, and with different structure (eg whether or not you hand out written instructions; whether or not you give time for the players to prepare their plot; whether or not you use all or some of the participants).

Simulation Games: Simulation games are more elaborate than simple role playing. Perhaps one of the earliest simulation game, developed for a class in political science, is "The Power of Suns."

One of the most elaborate simulation games was one funded by CIDA, held on Camp Shylo, a military wilderness area in southern Manitoba, where a hundred or so secondary students from across Canada were set up in five "nations," with various characteristics, with facilitators and chaperones, equipped with radio handsets, in a game that lasted several weeks.

Relative to the output, the raised awareness of participants, perhaps the elaborate setting up of simulation games does not warrant them being used in training of and by facilitators and mobilizers in community mobilization, poverty reduction, capacity development and income generation.

Conclusion: During training workshops and routine reviews, role playing games are an effective method of increasing awareness, enhancing participant analysis of field situations, and familiarizing participants with the roles, aims, perspectives and positions of people whom they will meet in the field.

While not directly participatory in the sense that they are real situations, they are participatory in their implementation, and provide considerable and valuable benefits in a training programme.

Team Teaching

In many higher education institutions, including CityU, the usual pattern of teaching is still largely based on an individual lecturer bearing responsibility for students in a course module or unit, possibly supported by part-time staff tutors. At some levels of learning though, for example in postgraduate seminars, this model is replaced by a team teaching approach which involves a number of lecturers (usually between two and five) and possibly non-teaching professional support staff as well. To carry out effective team teaching requires a re-orientation on the part of individual staff members and departmental administrators.

What is Team Teaching?

In team teaching a group of teachers, working together, plan, conduct, and evaluate the learning activities for the same group of students. In practice, team teaching has many different formats but in general it is a means of organising staff into groups to enhance teaching. Teams generally comprise staff members who may represent different areas of subject expertise but who share the same group of students and a common planning period to prepare for the teaching. To facilitate this process a common teaching space is desirable. However, to be effective team teaching requires much more than just a common meeting time and space.

(i) Why Should I Use Team Teaching?: In view of the additional complexity which team teaching initiatives introduce into departmental organisation and in view of the time needed for staff to adapt to the new structures, it is relevant to ask what benefits accrue from team teaching. How, for instance, does team teaching benefit lecturers, part-time tutors, students, and departments as a whole?

- For Lecturers, who so often work alone, team teaching provides a supportive environment that overcomes the isolation of working in self-contained or departmentalized class-rooms. Being exposed to the subject expertise of colleagues, to open critique, to different styles of planning and organisation, as well as methods of class presentation, teachers can develop their approaches to teaching and acquire a greater depth of understanding of the subject matter of the unit or module.

- Part-time staff can be drawn more closely into the department as members of teams than is usually the case, with a resulting increase in integration of course objectives and approaches to teaching.
- Team teaching can lead to better student performance in terms of greater independence and assuming responsibility for learning. Exposure to views and skills of more than one teacher can develop a more mature understanding of knowledge often being problematic rather than right or wrong. Learning can become more active and involved. Students could eventually make an input into team planning.
- Team teaching aids the professional and interpersonal dynamics of departments leading to closer integration of staff.

In the following extract, the authors describe the instructional advantages of working in teams.

"Team Teaching: An Alternative to Lecture Fatigue"

Team teaching is an approach which involves true team work between two qualified instructors who, together, make presentations to an audience. The instructional advantages of team teaching include:

(1) Lecture-style instruction is eliminated in favour of a dynamic interplay of two minds and personalities.

Lectures require students to act as passive receptors of communicated information, but team teaching involves the student in the physical and mental stimulation created by viewing two individuals at work. . . .

(2) Teaching staff act as a role models for discussion and disagreement.

Teaching staff members demonstrate modes of behaving in a disagreement as well as exposing students to the course content.

(3) Team teaching makes effective use of existing human resources.

Acquisition of additional expensive resources or equipment is not required to implement this method: only reorganisation is required to put the team into operation.

(4) Team teaching has the potential for revitalizing instructional capabilities through a process of dialogue.

Team teaching begins with the recognition that the instructor/student link is critical and offers an approach that has been shown to stimulate and provoke, while expanding and enriching student understanding.

(5) Interest in traditional courses can be stimulated as students share the enthusiasm and intellectual discourse that the lecturers communicate.

Team teaching is not boring. Students are drawn into the situation from the first moment.

(6) The effective use of facilities is possible.

The impersonal nature of large lecture halls can be brought to life by an interactive and dynamic situation.

(7) Team teaching provides opportunities for interaction with the audience.

Implementation

Implementing a team teaching approach requires administrative encouragement, acceptance of an initial experimental quality, and willingness to take risks. Proof that team teaching works comes not only from the instructors' self-judgment, but from students' evaluations. Above all, team teaching cannot be accomplished by administrative fiat — but administrators need to encourage it.

Adapted from: Quinn, S. and Kanter, S. (1984) "Team Teaching: An Alternative to Lecture Fatigue", Innovation Abstracts, Volume 6, No. 34, Eric Document: ED 251 159.

(ii) *Is There Only One Way To Team Teach?:* In its fullest sense, team teaching is where a group of lecturers

works together to plan, conduct, and evaluate the learning activities of the same group of students. However, it would be a mistake to think that team teaching is always practised in the same way. Its format needs to be adapted to the requirements of the teaching situation. Some possible options are where:

- two or more teachers teach the same group at the same time;
- team members meet to share ideas and resources but generally function independently;
- teams of teachers share a common resource centre;
- a team shares a common group of students, shares planning for instruction but team members teach different sub-groups within the whole group;
- certain instructional activities may be planned for the whole team by one individual, for example planning and developing research seminars;
- planning is shared, but teachers each teach their own specialism or their own skills area to the whole group;
- teams plan and develop teaching resource materials for a large group of students but may or may not teach them in a classroom situation.

Planning to Implement Team Teaching

Planning, conducting and evaluating team teaching are all important activities. Some of the most important aspects of planning which need to consider in advance of implementing teams are the concerns of staff; the selection of team members; and setting realistic goals for any teaching team in the first instance.

(i) Understanding Staff Concerns: Like any other change or innovation in a department, team teaching will raise concerns among staff members. The full range of concerns will only become clear over time after initial worries are dealt with and team members become comfortable with the innovation. A basic premise of

team teaching is that its adoption is not something that happens at one point in time — it extends over time. As users go through the adoption process there will be changes in their concerns.

From a team perspective, the ultimate aim will be to have individual team members reach a stage where they accept joint responsibility for the basic instruction of a group of students. There will be concerns, however, the relevant literature suggests that one way of dealing with these concerns is to recognise that they seem to follow a time cycle.

Early concerns usually appear to be procedural e.g., determining roles, setting agendas, keeping records, setting procedures for communicating with outside people, and scheduling teamwork, etc. Next to appear are student-related concerns such as meeting students' needs, planning to deal with individual students, etc.

These are followed by concern among team members for their own professional growth and finally there is concern for the collective well being of the team. This last level is reached when teams are seen as (i) a means of professional self development, (ii) a forum at which ideas about instruction and coordinating curriculum can be shared, and (iii) when students are involved in decision making.

Here are some common concerns about team teaching along with suggestions of what to do to improve the likelihood of overcoming them. The first three of these concerns are usually expressed before the team actually begins functioning while the last is usually expressed after it has functioned for a time.

I Do not know Enough about Team Teaching

Explain the concept of team organisation and the rationale for implementing it. This should include an explanation of how it is envisaged that team teaching will fit with the rest of the departmental programme. Staff need to have a clear idea of the kinds of teaching teams envisaged, what their responsibilities will be and how much of their time will be occupied in teaching in this way.

How will I Manage My Teaching in the Light of the Proposed Change?

Supplying information usually leads teachers to express personal concerns. Take these concerns seriously. If you do not they become potential barriers to effective implementation. Personal concerns usually expressed about team teaching include:

- not all team members will contribute equally;
- teachers do not understand how to make the team work;
- there will be personality conflicts to deal with in addition to the teaching itself;
- a preference for working alone;
- all the work will fall on the team leader/senior subject expert;
- it will be too difficult to cover all the course content;
- team meetings will be a waste of time.

All in all, concerns usually revolve about inter-personal problems — issues of self doubt, team management and group processes in addition to whether the teaching carried out by this method will be worthwhile.

How is the Team Going to be Managed?

Management questions are concerned with who will be on the team, who will lead it, what will be expected and in what timeframe, how meetings will be conducted, how teaching activities and events will actually be planned, and so on. These should be dealt with as early as possible and not in a casual manner, so that everyone is clear about what their roles and responsibilities will be. As well, once the team begins to function, more routine issues will surface: staff may be bothered by the amount of time involved, the difficulty of keeping track of students, coordinating materials and the work of other team members.

Concern may arise and have to be dealt with while the team is actually functioning or at the time of periodic course reviews. Rather than a single concern, it may be more useful to see it as a category of concerns that focus on the consequences of team actions.

It would be most unusual for the team to find that everything has proceeded as they planned. More usually, they find that there are outcomes as a result of team teaching which they had not anticipated. These outcomes may be to do with student learning or with how the team is functioning. If there are differences between what was planned and what the students are achieving then the team will need to refocus on what is important. To do this the team will have to monitor continually how students are reacting to the team teaching experience. Conscious decisions will have to be taken to emphasise points that may have been missed or correct mistaken impressions. However, concerns may arise apart from those related to student learning. There may be a need for the team to deal with issues of collaboration among its own members. In the same way that the goals associated with student learning need to be monitored and reviewed where necessary, so too do aspects of team behaviour. In both these examples it is apparent that regular meetings of the team need to take place where constructive, professional reflection is encouraged which is itself a team teaching strength.

(ii) *Selecting Team Members:* The composition of any teaching team is a matter which must be considered carefully if that particular team is going to function effectively. While it is possible that teams can be arbitrarily formed it is far more fruitful if they come together in response to needs and interests. Thought needs to be given to selecting team members and defining team roles and these decisions need to be evaluated periodically. The following questions are indicative of the sorts of issues which should be considered:

- *on what basis should team members be selected?:* Team members should not be clones of each other. Why? Because differences in subject expertise, interests, perspectives, back-grounds, and qualification levels, can contribute to the collective strength of a team and the growth of individual team members. Furthermore, the 'mix' of personalities and characteristics add to the experience the students get from interacting with the team.

- *What is the role of the team leader?:* Basically the team leader will be concerned with (i) internal functioning — setting agendas, keeping records, coordinating schedules ensuring the team 'stays on task' i.e. that it achieves what it sets out to achieve; and (ii) external functioning — communicating with department heads to ensure that the team is resourced, supported, and meeting departmental goals/expectations, etc.
- *What is the role of team members?:* Team members need to contribute to the team in ways other than simply turning up for classes and meetings. It is essential that all team members contribute to formulating and achieving team goals. To do this, each member must take responsibility for participating in team discussions and planning session and following through on decisions made by the team within the timeframes decided by the team. It is only in this way that a spirit of co-operation and collaboration can be maintained.

(iii) *Setting Realistic Team Goals:* Teams need to have a sense of direction. One finding from the relevant literature of particular interest relates to the time required to develop an effective level of team teaching. When teams are formed from teachers with no previous team experience, it seems to take about three years for them to develop the team teaching process to an efficient and effective level. Hence in setting a time line for teams to achieve realistic goals it is important to ask what will be the aims of team teaching during the first year or semester and what are the longer term goals? The answers to such questions are important in determining priorities for the development of teams. It is unrealistic to expect that all goals and expectations will be met immediately. Rather it is better to consider what it is reasonable to undertake as teachers and to expect from students and at what stage?

The Team in Action

(i) Planning for Teaching

Assume that it has been decided that team teaching will go ahead in your department and that you have agreed and been selected to be a member of a team. Assume also that the issues surrounding teams discussed earlier have been attended to and the team is now ready to begin work. Decisions facing yourself and your teaching partners now will focus undoubtedly on planning teaching/learning activities.

You may ask, for instance, in what way will the team use small and large group contexts or independent study? Will it use a large group in an auditorium setting to introduce a topic or convey basic information and background material which all the students need to know? Will the team decide to use a single teacher to make the presentation or will several teachers be used?

Will small group discussions relate to large group presentations, or demonstrate skills, or develop a seminar discussion group etc? What of independent study? It is not always taken into consideration but it provides a student or group of students with the opportunity to research or explore a topic of special interest in greater depth outside the formal teaching situation. How will the team use independent study?

This short list of questions underlines the decisions to be made in this area.

- What are the programme, unit, and lesson objectives?
- What lesson content is to be presented and in what order?
- Which content is to be presented by large group presentation?

- Which methods and resources are to be used to present the content?
- Who will make large group presentations?
- What will be discussed during small group meetings?
- How will small groups be organized?
- Who will be assigned to each small group?
- What types of independent study will be appropriate?
- What blocks of time will be assigned to large-group, small group and independent study activities?
- How will students be assessed?

All of these questions are to do with ongoing interaction with students. A little later the team will have to consider questions such as:

- How can the activities be improved?
- What specific problems have arisen with particular groups of students and how can they be solved?

Irrespective of who asks these questions, they are very realistic and they need to be answered, but the critical issue is who by and how.

(ii) Assigning Roles and Responsibilities

Effective teams are systematic in their division of labour, not forgetting that roles may be rotated on a regular basis. In allocating roles, strengths and weaknesses of individual team members need to be taken into account. A brief questionnaire gathering an idea of these strengths and weaknesses might be a good idea before a draft list of responsibilities for the team is discussed.

(iii) Catering for Students

While team teachers and their students are usually happy with the community spirit that teams can provide, teamwork also has a considerable effect on classroom management. For example, by planning together, team teachers can clarify teaching policies and behavioural expectations that are applied to students. Difficult management situations can be analyzed and resolved together resulting in richer discussions and sounder solutions. Teams of teachers can think of ways of improving student motivation, a sense of responsibility, and overall student performance.

(iv) Conducting Meetings

Team teaching is group work and as such teams need to develop as functioning groups. In dealing with other team members teamwork is seldom without conflict — professional or personal points of view may clash. Blending differences constructively is a challenge to all team members. To do this it is important to acknowledge team members' strengths, interests, personal and professional goals both in assigning responsibilities and in the conduct of meetings.

Running Meetings

For a team to function effectively the team meetings need to run well. They need to clarify expectations for how the team will operate, i.e. clarify management issues and set ground rules for meetings such as:

- how will items get on the agenda?
- what should be recorded in the minutes?
- who will do the recording?
- how will decisions be reached?
- how should communication with other teams and members of the department be managed?
- how will a team calendar/schedule be compiled?

Making Decisions

The main problem encountered in meetings which prevents decisions from being made effectively and efficiently is the difficulty of keeping all team members on task. The team leader needs to ensure that:

- problems are defined clearly;
- there is time for brainstorming alternatives for action;
- each alternative is subject to critique

- a plan of action is selected, implemented and subsequently evaluated

(v) Evaluating Progress

In a small team, a formal evaluation of progress often seems inappropriate. However, all teams need to set aside some time to evaluate their progress in terms of both teaching the module and with their own development as an effective team. An outside facilitator could be called in to manage this where appropriate. Some questions which might be asked in the context of such an evaluation are:

- are the goals set for the team's work realistic?
- have the goals been achieved? to what extent?
- do all team members participate equally in team decisions?
- have decisions been carried out?
- are responsibilities shared among team members?
- do students benefit from the team's work?
- what areas need more attention?

(vi) Maintaining Continuity From Year to Year

In order to ensure the continuity of the module/course when it is presented a second and subsequent times the team needs to maintain clear documentation of the course including:

- the course outline or syllabus;
- weekly timetables;
- teachers' notes for each unit;
- students' notes;
- teaching materials/written bulletins;
- copies of tests and examinations;
- final course evaluations;
- student evaluations.

Carefully maintaining these course documents will ease the task of the course leaders, facilitate the induction of new teachers into the team, and simplify the task of revising the course/module in a rational manner.

Conclusion

Teams take a variety of forms in different contexts, however, successful team teaching must go beyond sharing a group of students and scheduling a common meeting time if it is to make positive contributions to the quality of learning and staff development.

Effective team teaching takes time to develop to its fullest potential. Staff who are unfamiliar with it need time to work through the basic issues and routine matters before they can turn their attention fully to issues which affect students and to the impact which their teaching has on the department as a whole. This is time well spent because team teaching can be a valuable source of personal and professional development for those who engage in it. It can also be a source of considerable frustration if its goals are unrealistic, meetings are not productive and decision making is not well handled by team leaders.

These pitfalls and others can be avoided or at least not encountered more than once if adequate staff development support is available and the relative complexity of demands which team teaching places on people is recognized both by the individuals themselves and their departmental leaders.

Microteaching

Microteaching is a training technique whereby the teacher reviews a videotape of the lesson after each session, in order to conduct a "post-mortem". Teachers find out what has worked, which aspects have fallen short, and what needs to be done to enhance their teaching technique. Invented in the mid-1960's at Stanford University by Dr. Dwight Allen, micro-teaching has been used with success for several decades now, as a way to help teachers acquire new skills.

In the original process, a teacher was asked to prepare a short lesson (usually 20 minutes) for a small group of learners who may not have been her own students. This was videotaped, using VHS. After the lesson, the teacher, teaching colleagues, a master teacher and the students together viewed the videotape and commented on what they saw happening, referencing the teacher's learning objectives. Seeing the video and getting comments from colleagues and students provided teachers with an often intense "under the microscope" view of their teaching.

Why Microteach?

Microteaching is organized practice teaching. The goal is to give instructors confidence, support, and feedback by letting them try out among friends and colleagues a short slice of what they plan to do with their students. Ideally, microteaching sessions take place before the first day of class, and are videotaped for review individually with an experienced teaching consultant. Microteaching is a quick, efficient, proven, and fun way to help teachers get off to a strong start.

How to Microteach?

As many as six teachers from the same or similar courses can participate in a single microteaching session. Course heads, a few experienced instructors, and a Bok Center staff member are usually invited to serve as facilitators. While one person takes his or her turn as teacher, everyone else plays the roles of students. It is the job of these pretend pupils to ask and answer questions realistically. It is the job of the pretend teacher to involve his or her "class" actively in this way.

Such a scenario typically runs for five to ten minutes. When finished, the person conducting the class has a moment or two to react to his or her own teaching. Then everyone else joins in to discuss what they saw that they especially liked. Finally, the group may mention just a few things that the practice teacher might try doing differently in the future.

Like all Bok Center tapes, videos of these sessions are for the benefit of those taped and will not be seen by anyone else without the explicit permission of the practice teacher. Session tapes can even be erased immediately if the practice teacher wishes. Nearly everyone, however, finds it extremely helpful to make an appointment to view and discuss their tape together with a Bok Center consultant.

What to Prepare?

Most course heads provide microteachers with scenarios to prepare in advance. If not, think of a few minutes of material that you especially would like to make sure your students understand by the end of your next class. As always, you should not only plan out how to treat the subject matter, but also give some thought to how you are going to present yourself, manage the class, and involve the students. There are, of course, many different ways of teaching a given lesson well. That is why participants find that, along with what they learn from their own experience practice teaching, they can also pick up many helpful ideas from observing fellow microteachers.

Individualized Instruction Methods

Individualized instruction is a method of instruction in which content, instructional materials, instructional media, and pace of learning are based upon the abilities and interests of each individual learner.

Individualized instruction *is **not*** the same as a one-to-one student/teacher ratio or one-to-one tutoring, as it may seem, because economically, it is difficult, if not impossible to have a teacher for each student. Even tho most expensive public school system in the United States (Washington, DC, 2003, approximately $11,000 per student per year) would require at least 5 students per teacher to pay teacher salaries, without anything left for buildings or non-teaching staff.

In a traditional classroom environment, lectures consume approximately 80% of an average teacher's in-class time, to say nothing of the time needed to prepare lessons. Yet lecturing is an inherently inefficient method of conveying information. The average student retains only approximately 10% of what is presented in a lecture, but without substantial reinforcement that figure falls to an abysmal 2%, or less, within 24 hours. Therefore, throughout the history of education the notion of lecturing has been challenged as a time-effective method of teaching, and alternative pedagogical models have been proposed. For example *Educational Research Associates* has concluded that placing greater reliance upon well-designed instructional materials – whether audio, video, multimedia Computer-assisted instruction (CAI), or simply a good textbook – can hardly be less efficient than the lecture method, but yields a huge net benefit by freeing teachers to focus upon the needs and problems of individual students.

In this way, individualized instruction is like direct instruction, which also places greater reliance upon carefully prepared instructional materials and explicitly prepared instructional sequences. But where direct instruction is very rigidly structured for use with children in primary school, individualized instruction is recommended only for students of at least junior high school age, and presumes that they have greater self-discipline to be able to study more independently. Thus, individualized instruction has points of contact with the constructivism movement in education, started by Swiss biologist Jean Piaget, which states that the student should build his or her learning and knowledge. Individualized Instruction, however, presumes that most students of secondary school age still lack the basic knowledge and skills to direct most of their own curriculum, which must be at least partially directed by schools and teachers.

In a traditional classroom setting, time (in the form of classes, quarters, semesters, school years, etc.) is a constant, and achievement (in the form of grades and student comprehension) is a variable.

In a properly Individualized setting, where students study and progress more independently, achievement becomes more uniform and time to achieve that level of achievement is more variable.

Where implemented according to Educational Research Associates' recommendations, Individualized Instruction has been found to improve student accomplishment substantially even while reducing cost dramatically. (Oregon Department of Education, 1976)

The coming of computer- and Internet-based education holds the promise of an enormous increase in the use of individualized instruction methodology.

Method

As theories of learning and instruction develop and mature, more and more consideration is given to the way in which learning occurs. In an attempt to account for the way that students learn, instructors may apply a combination of theories and principles in preparing instruction. This can influence whether instruction is designed for one homogenous group, or is flexible, in anticipation of individual differences among learners. In the majority of cases, instruction is designed for the average learner, and is customized ad-hoc by the teacher or instructor as needed once instruction begins. This type of instruction, although it does give some consideration to individual differences among learners during instruction, does not fall into the typically accepted definition of individualized instruction. For instruction to be considered individualized, the instruction is usually designed to account for specific learner characteristics. This could include alternative instructional methods for students with different backgrounds and learning styles.

To help clarify this point, the instructional method used can be considered in terms of extremes. In the first extreme, one instructional method is used for everyone. Terms like *inclusion* and *mainstreaming* have been used to describe this first case. In the second extreme, a specific instructional method is used for each individual. Between these extremes lie situations where students are arranged into groups according to the their characteristics. These groups can vary in size, and the instructional method is tailored to each group.

Methods Suitable for Teaching Accountancy

Accounting is the primary language used to process, integrate, and disseminate information throughout the veins of today's businesses. Modern accounting teachers must strive to achieve a balance between the extensive content and the need for new emphasis on using accounting information in decision-making, developing critical thinking skills, enhancing communication skills, and working in groups. It is hoped that this site will assist in providing new or continuing teachers with the resources to investigate new concepts, strategies, and methodologies for use in a dynamic and creative learning environment.

New methodology has enhanced emphasis on critical thinking, analysis, and communication skills. With access to traditional methods in business education classes becoming increasingly rare, new teachers are often left to their own resources to plan curriculum and instruction. This site also seeks to provide resources for teachers to investigate accounting curriculum and methodologies, compare and contrast methods of instruction, and examine the latest textbooks and software in the field.

New teachers just entering education from college programs or industry and veteran teachers returning to update skills will benefit from opportunities to investigate new methodologies, teaching strategies, and other resources.

Professional Resources

Professional organizations offer a variety of resources, including conferences, publications, web links, and the latest research, many of which are recommended resources in this paper. If you are a current or potential business education teacher, it is strongly recommended that you become a member of one or more of the professional associations for business educators and accounting professionals.

Skills, Competencies, & Standards for Accounting

In the early 1980's, the American Accounting Association (AAA), a professional organization for accounting educators, appointed a commission to study accounting education. Their concern was that the curriculum was not keeping up with the dynamic changes of the profession. Other professional organizations joined and funded several studies to help research accounting education and implement recommended curriculum changes. In 1994, the Institute of Management Accountants (IMA) presented "What Corporate America Wants in Entry-Level Accountants." In the late 1990's, AICPA released its "Core Competency Framework for Entry into the Accounting Profession." The intent was to establish a framework to assist educators in developing a broad-based accounting curriculum. "New Competencies for Accounting Students" summarizes primary components from this framework. (Foster, Bolt-Lee, 2002)

Ethics in Accounting

With the major ethical problems that have been developed in recent years, it is extremely important that this topic be included in accounting classes to ensure that accounting students understand the importance of ethics in their field.

Relationship to the Knowledge Base, National, and State Goals

In 2001, the National Business Education Association published the 2nd Edition of the National Standards for Business Education. Students today are challenged to exercise critical-thinking skills, develop problem-solving skills, master workplace competencies, and become independent learners. These standards are designed to help develop these skills for student.

The Achievement Standards set for accounting students, Levels 3– 4 (grades 9 – 14) are:

- Complete and explain the purpose of the various steps in the accounting cycle.
- Apply generally accepted accounting principles to determine the value of assets, liabilities, and owner's equity.
- Prepare, interpret, and analyze financial statements using manual and computerized systems for service, merchandising, and manufacturing businesses.
- Apply appropriate accounting principles to payroll, income taxation, managerial systems, and various forms of ownership, and

- Use planning and control principles to evaluate the performance of an organization and apply differential analysis and present-value concepts to make decisions.

Teaching Strategies and Resources

In today's classroom, instructors are no longer just the disseminators of information. The old paradigm positioned the instructors as the vessels of all knowledge for students to access. The student was limited to this level of information. Modern instructors are more like captains, guiding the student's journey through a learning process to mastery of various outcomes. The teacher becomes a facilitator for the student's journey and should not be concerned that the student may surpass his/her knowledge level.

As students learn in a variety of ways, instructors need multiple strategies to facilitate students in the learning process. Resources available can connect teachers with research on methods for teaching practical accounting and bookkeeping skills as well as facilitating students in understanding those skills.

UNIT-V

Educational Technology

Programmed Learning

Programmed Learning is a learning technique first proposed by the behaviorist B. F. Skinner in 1958. According to Skinner, the purpose of programmed learning is to "manage human learning under controlled conditions". It is similar in some ways to the Saxon method used in some math courses; both methods teach information in small bites rather than trying to tackle an entire subject at once, though programmed learning places less emphasis on repetition than Saxon.

The technique involves self-administered and self-paced learning, in which the student is presented with information in small steps called "frames". Each frame contains a small segment of the information to be learned, and a statement in which the student must fill a blank section, and after each frame the student uncovers the correct answer before advancing to the next frame.

Personalized System of Instruction also known as the "Keller Plan" 1960s, Fred Keller, built on earlier models of personalized instruction (e.g., Winnetka plan in Illinois) geared toward K-12 Keller Plan designed more for higher ed. at University of Brasilia many large university courses follow the model today

The Personalized System of Instruction is a mastery learning model which seeks to promote mastery of a pre-specified set of objectives from each learner in a course. Students work through a series of self-paced modules.

PSI Steps:

- instructor designs course policy statement
- instructor breaks content into topical chunks or units
- instructor develops study guides for each unit (historically print-based unlike A-T)
- study guides include: objectives, study procedures, questions
- self-paced, individual work through guides

PSI study guides were historically print-based, although they may take different forms today from computer-based to internet-based instruction. Students work through modules at their own pace.

PSI Steps:

- as students complete a unit, they are tested
- immediate feedback is provided by proctor with an opportunity to review and re-test
- student move on to new units after they master previous, prerequisite units, self-pacing through course
- lectures limited, provide for interaction and motivation more than content-dispensing.

In PSI units, "live" proctors grade student tests and provide immediate feedback on their performance. This one-to-one support is the key component that makes the model "personalized." Lectures are limited in PSI courses.

PSI Outcomes:

- some evidence that tutored students learn "more" than lectured students
- students favour individual pacing and appreciate individual attention from proctors
- individualized attention for gifted/special ed. most common, traditionally viewed as too expensive for average classes

Students in PSI courses have been shown to learn more than lectured students. Students typically favour some degree of control over the pace of their instruction, although younger or less mature students will likely need to be monitored to stay on task. Through personalized attention from proctors, students can learn good study habits and strategies.

Role of Technology

- systems designed to track student progress, help teacher manage class
- technology used to provide extensive resources to students "on demand" (no longer reliant on print)
- technology can support proctors in providing tests and feedback, but "audio" feedback could "de-personalize" course

Although the PSI model was designed in the late 1960's, educational technologies allow similar systems to be designed and efficiently delivered today.

A database system to track student progress through units can be established. PSI recommends students who access and master each module be given a grade of "C." Grades of "B" and "A" can be reserved for students who complete extra work, problems, or an examination.

Print is no longer the medium of choice for PSI, but rather, computer-based or internet-based modules. Students can access richer resources in multimedia formats and potentially more information through computers.

Technology can also support TA's or course proctors by allowing quizzes to be graded automatically. Computer-based feedback, however, is not as responsive to a diversity of student questions as live feedback from a proctor. Still, computers could engage students in discussing, debating, or questioning course content with other students, with an instructor, or with a TA, all from a distance.

Criticisms:

- like audio-tutorial, most PSI units geared toward mastery of specific objectives
- application of higher-order thinking skill not explicitly a part of the models

- guided design model was created to include this "missing" component
- in guided design, students still expected to master material, but also to APPLY it

While this model does not prohibit the acquisition of higher-order thinking skills, most units designed within its framework have emphasized lower-order knowledge acquisition. This is a common criticism of both the audio-tutorial model and the personalized system of instruction. Another mastery learning model, the guided design model, formally recommends and emphasizes the application of knowledge to a project or problem after basic knowledge components have been mastered. The application of basic knowledge to real tasks is highly recommended regardless of the model chosen. Students will be more likely to retain knowledge and will develop necessary thinking skills to solve a diversity of realistic problems.

Branching

Branching, tagging, and merging are concepts common to almost all version control systems. If you're not familiar with these ideas, we provide a good introduction in this chapter. If you are familiar, then hopefully you'll find it interesting to see how Subversion implements these ideas.

Branching is a fundamental part of version control. If you're going to allow Subversion to manage your data, then this is a feature you'll eventually come to depend on. This chapter assumes that you're already familiar with Subversion's basic concepts (Chapter 2, Basic Concepts).

What's a Branch?

Suppose it's your job to maintain a document for a division in your company, a handbook of some sort. One day a different division asks you for the same handbook, but with a few parts "tweaked" for them, since they do things slightly differently.

What do you do in this situation? You do the obvious thing: you make a second copy of your document, and begin maintaining the two copies separately. As each department asks you to make small changes, you incorporate them into one copy or the other.

You often want to make the same change to both copies. For example, if you discover a typo in the first copy, it's very likely that the same typo exists in the second copy. The two documents are almost the same, after all; they only differ in small, specific ways.

This is the basic concept of a branch—namely, a line of development that exists independently of another line, yet still shares a common history if you look far enough back in time. A branch always begins life as a copy of something, and moves on from there, generating its own history.

Branches of Development

Subversion has commands to help you maintain parallel branches of your files and directories. It allows you to create branches by copying your data, and remembers that the copies are related to one another. It also helps you duplicate changes from one branch to another. Finally, it can make portions of your working copy reflect different branches, so that you can "mix and match" different lines of development in your daily work.

Developing Branching Strategy and Codeline Policy

This section defines the critical concepts of a codeline policy, a codeline owner and a branching strategy. Three main attributes of a branch are identified and discussed to assist in the formulation of codeline policy: branchpoints, merging policy and branch life span.

A codeline policy describes the rules governing check-ins, merges and other uses of a codeline. Each branch has an associated codeline policy dictating how it should be used. [WING98] advocates codeline policy, and recommend that one should branch on incompatible policy. Therefore, a new branch should be created when changing development needs require a change in the current codeline's policy. A branch provides a mechanism by which one can support a newly required set of policies without changing the policies that are already in effect.

Codeline policies should not be arbitrarily invented. They are derived from the organization?s software development requirements. They are shaped by the answers to a number of detailed questions about how a company releases its software, how they plan to develop their software, and what range of software packagings they need to produce. Within an organization, certain sets of these answers will define common approaches to development, and many codeline policies will resemble each other. Bear in mind that not all codeline policies apply in all company?s environments.

[APPL98] and [WING98] both recommend that each codeline have a codeline owner. It is the codeline owner's job to rule on any questions regarding the codeline policy and to ensure that any maintenance issues defined or inferred in the codeline policy are successfully carried out. Sometimes the codeline owner will do the integration, but he is at least responsible for delegating it.

A branching strategy consists of the guidelines within an environment for the creation and application of codeline policies. Creating a branching strategy consists of:

* identifying the categories of development that can be easily characterized,
* defining the differences and similarities between them,
* defining how they relate to each other, and
* expressing all of this information as codeline policies and branches.

In addition, there needs to be an owner of the branching strategy who will have final judgment on changing policy guidelines. A codeline policy identifies how a branch should be used, but this assumes that the branch exists. The branching strategy sets parameters for the issues relating to branches creation, interaction, and retirement. These aspects of the branch's lifetime are represented by the branchpoint, the merging policy, and the branch life span.

Generally, the branchpoint is fully defined before the branch is created for use. The full specification of a branchpoint usually occurs through a label, but can also be described by date and time or specific version numbers. Although other branchpoint creation strategies exist, they are not within the scope of this discussion.

Identification of the need for a branchpoint occurs when the need for a different type of project causes a change in branch policy. Any new project or type of project on any branch carries with it the possibility to require a new branch, and therefore to define a branchpoint.

Merging is the process by which one codeline is integrated into another. Merging occurs when there is utility in applying any set of changes on one branch to another branch. Generally, merging is relevant when the source and target branches have common ancestors. Ancestral relationships beyond those having a common immediate branchpoint have varying levels of support in SCM tools.

The merge policy of a branch describes how frequently the branch is merged to other branches. This policy can be divided into the import policy and the export policy. The import policy for a branch defines when the codeline owner should have work on other branches merged to it. The export policy is usually defined with respect to recognizable characteristics of the development assigned to the branch, such as stability or completeness. It also may be responsive to other events, such as imports and other incoming merges, time intervals, or the branch's life span.

Life span refers to the amount of activity between branch creation and decommissioning. Life span is a qualitative attribute, not a quantitative measure. A branch?s life span is discussed as it compares to that of other branches.

In summary, a codeline policy defines the rules governing the use of a codeline or branch. A branching strategy consists of the guidelines for creating and applying codeline policies within an organization. Its primary purpose is to define a collection of template codeline policies that can be applied to form a coherent development environment. As a codeline has an owner to resolve ambiguities in a codeline?s policy, a branching strategy should also have an owner to resolve conflicts between codeline policies and to mentor the creation of new ones.

Personalized System of Instruction (PSI)

Fred S. Keller first described the Personalized System of Instruction (PSI) in 1968. It is often called simply "the Keller Method." PSI was developed a few years earlier by Keller, Gil Sherman, and other professors at the University of Brazilia for college instruction there while Keller was a visiting professor.

PSI is characterized by a well-defined set of objectives, and insistence on mastery of discrete units of content before moving on to new units of instruction. It is thus student-paced. Students take tests as soon as they think they have learned the material, and the tests are immediately graded with immediate feedback. If there is less than mastery, the students review the material in which they are having trouble, and retake the test as often as necessary.

Instruction relies on writeen content material, and lecture serves a different role than in typical college teaching, primarily for interaction and motivation.

Definition

The Personalized System of Instruction fits into several paradigms, but is most closely aligned with direct instruction. It fits with direct instruction by requiring student to work on course modules independently. It fits slightly with social constructivism by also requiring students to meet weekly in peer teams with a proctor to answer questions and take a quiz on the content studied. Students do not engage in considerable team work as most social constructivist models advocate, rather, they only correct one another's responses to proctor-led questions.

Design and Development Tips

Since PSI units are self-paced and typically designed for students in large lecture classes, technologies that can be accessed by many students in any location are preferable. For instance, web pages or CD-Rom modules in computer labs allow for multimedia modules to be easily accessed. To compile multimedia elements, it may also be necessary to work with audio editing software, video editing software, and image editing software.

Future of PSI

PSI in Distance Education. One area where PSI is gaining popularity is in distance education. Grant and Spencer (2003) illustrate why PSI is an ideal format for distance education. In most distance education classes, like PSI, the written word is the primary method of communicating course-related content. Further, many distance education courses use timed tests or mastery-based tests taken over the internet as their primary assessment measure. These courses are already intentionally or unintentionally similar to PSI. Instructors could easily integrate PSI more systematically into these courses by setting the unit tests to cover a small amount of material, be mastery-based, and self-paced (see Liu, 2003 for a comprehensive example). Proctoring could be accomplished in a variety of ways including synchronous or asynchronous chats, discussion board postings, individualized test feedback, or preprogrammed test feedback if live feedback is not feasible or desirable. Lectures for motivational purposes can be given through streaming video, podcasts, discussion board posts, or other methods.

The PSI experience could be further enhanced by incorporating programmed instruction into a PSI course. The students could go through the course using a programmed online text where they fill in the word which the computer would recognize as correct or incorrect. They would work their way through a given unit and be given remedial work for any section not mastered. They then could take a unit test over the same material which they would have to master before the next section of the programmed text became available. Another alternative would be to use a standard text, but have a programmed instruction tutorial available. That is, a student would read the standard text and then take a unit test over a given unit. For any items missed on the test, the student would complete a programmed instruction tutorial over these concepts. The programmed instruction tutorial in this case would serve to replace the live proctors. Many of the computer-programmes listed above, along with several not discussed in this paper, would be capable of being used for a distance education PSI course. Most university students already learn to use a course platform such as WebCT[R] and Blackboard[R] and may use these platforms for regular on-campus classes, hybrid classes, and totally online classes. It would not take much effort to modify any given instructor's course to be a true PSI course. Other programmes such as CAPSI have also been successfully used for distance education classes (Pear & Kinsner, 1988).

Conclusions

Will PSI become popular once again, or are its days of glory long past? The question of whether PSI will rise again to the level of prominence it once had in the education system will likely rest on how the current generation of PSI researchers resolves the questions that stymied the original PSI innovators. There are many paradoxes yet to be solved, especially with the self-pacing and mastery components. Computers appear to have resolved one the major hurdles to effective PSI course management by automatically grading multiple-choice tests and providing feedback, as well as facilitating the grading of short-answer tests. The computer has also helped PSI move into new venues such as the rapidly expanding field of distance education and online courses where the instructor's traditional role of "lecturer" has been changed into one of "mentor" and "learning facilitator," consistent with Keller's vision and with the administration's blessing. Thus, although there are many problems yet to be resolved, it appears that there may just be the demand and market in the new millennium for this type of innovative approach. We will see in another decade or so if this resurgence of interest blossoms into a full-scale revival or was simply a fleeting fancy.

Computer-Assisted Instruction

Not so long ago, the microcomputer was a rare and exotic sight in American classrooms. Then, during the 1970s, many schools began acquiring microcomputers and putting them to use for instruction, drill and practice, recordkeeping, and other applications. The use of microcomputers expanded rapidly during the 1980s. Between 1981 and the end of the decade:

- American schools acquired over two million microcomputers.
- The number of schools owning computers increased from approximately 25 percent to virtually 100 percent.
- More than half the states began requiring—or at least recommending—preservice technology programmes for all prospective teachers (Kinnaman 1990).

"The 'information age' has clearly arrived," notes Kinnaman, "and in the '90s the educational use of computer technology will surely continue to grow." While this is no doubt an accurate prediction, many educators, legislators, parents, and researchers have expressed concern about the educational effectiveness of using microcomputers in schools. Because the acquisition of computer hardware and educational software programmes involves a considerable monetary investment, these groups want assurance that computers in the schools are more than expensive and entertaining toys; they desire evidence that educational microcomputer use truly enhances learning in demonstrable ways.

Fortunately, a great deal of research has been conducted during the 1970s, 1980s, and early 1990s on the effects of computer use on student achievement, attitudes, and other variables, such as learning rate. This research covers a wide range of topics, from computerized learning activities which supplement conventional instruction, to computer programming, to computerized recordkeeping, to the development of databases, to writing using word processors, and other applications.

The main focus of this report is the most commonly used and most frequently researched kind of educational computer use—computer-assisted instruction (CAI). Findings about other educational computer applications are presented as they relate to this main focus.

Definitions

It will be helpful, before discussing the research findings, to offer some definitions of CAI and other kinds of learning activities involving computers. As Kulik, Kulik, and Bangert-Drowns point out in their 1985 research summary, "the terminology in the area is open to dispute" (p. 59). This is putting it mildly. Those seeking to make sense of the array of terms used by educators and researchers—computer-assisted instruction, computer-based education, computer-based instruction, computer-enriched instruction, computermanaged instruction—can easily become confused. The following definitions are a synthesis of those offered by Bangert-Drowns, et al. (1985), Batey (1987), Grimes (1977), Samson et al. (1986), and Stennett (1985), and represent commonly accepted (though certainly not the only) definitions of these terms:

- Computer-based education (CBE) and computer-based instruction (CBI) are the broadest terms and can refer to virtually any kind of computer use in educational settings, including drill and practice, tutorials, simulations, instructional management, supplementary exercises, programming, database development, writing using word processors, and other applications. These terms may refer either to stand-alone computer learning activities or to computer activities which reinforce material introduced and taught by teachers.
- Computer-assisted instruction (CAI) is a narrower term and most often refers to drill-and-practice, tutorial, or simulation activities offered either by themselves or as supplements to traditional, teacherdirected instruction.
- Computer-managed instruction (CMI) can refer either to the use of computers by school staff to organize student data and make instructional decisions or to activities in which the computer evaluates students' test performance, guides them to appropriate instructional resources, and keeps records of their progress.
- Computer-enriched instruction (CEI) is defined as learning activities in which computers (1) generate data

at the students' request to illustrate relationships in models of social or physical reality, (2) execute programmes developed by the students, or (3) provide general enrichment in relatively unstructured exercises designed to stimulate and motivate students.

The CAI Research Base

The findings offered in this summary emerge from an analysis of the 59 research reports cited in the Key References section of the annotated bibliography. Each of these reports documents some relationship(s) between computer-based learning and student outcomes. Twentyeight are research studies, 22 are reviews, and 9 are meta-analyses of research studies. Twelve of the documents focus on elementary students, 19 are concerned with secondary students, 7 cover the elementary-secondary range, 5 involve subjects spanning the elementary-postsecondary range, and the age/grade levels of subjects are not specified in 16 of the reports.

Most of the studies involved American students, but Israeli and Canadian subjects are also represented. Other specific populations serving as subjects in the documents include economically disadvantaged students (4), special education students (5), remedial students (2), and Hispanic students (2). The rest of the documents either concerned general student populations or did not specify characteristics of their subjects.

The 59 reports were concerned with the effects one or more of the following types of educational computer use on student outcomes: CAI (35), CBE in general (15), the use of word processors for written composition (5), computer-managed instruction (3), programming (2), and simulations (4).

The effects of computer use on a large number of outcome areas were examined, including academic achievement in general (30), in mathematics (13), in language arts (8), in reading (3), in science (2), in problem-solving skills (2), and in health and social studies (1 each). Studies also focused on students' attitudes toward the content of courses in which computers were used (21), toward computers themselves (19), toward school in general (6), toward the quality of instruction in courses with computer activities (4), and toward themselves as learners (4). Other outcome areas include learning rate (10), learning retention (9), locus of control and motivation, computer literacy, and cooperation/helping (4 each).

Beyond these outcome-focused reports, the General References section of the bibliography cites 18 additional reports on related topics, such as teacher training to conduct CAI effectively, cost-effectiveness of CAI, discussions of current and potential applications of computers in education, and examinations of students' favorable attitudes toward computer activities.

Research Findings

Microcomputer Use and Student Achievement

The single best-supported finding in the research literature is that the use of CAI as a supplement to traditional, teacher-directed instruction produces achievement effects superior to those obtained with traditional instruction alone. Generally speaking, this finding holds true for students of different ages and abilities and for learning in different curricular areas. As summarized in Stennett's 1985 review of reviews, "well-designed and implemented D&P [drill-andpractice] or tutorial CAI, used as a supplement to traditional instruction, produces an educationally significant improvement in students' final examination achievement" (Research support: Bahr and Rieth 1989; Bangert-Drowns 1985; Bangert-Drowns, et al. 1985; Batey 1986; Bracey 1987; Burns and Bozeman 1981; Braun 1990; Capper and Copple 1985; Edwards, et al. 1975; Ehman and Glen 1987; Gore, et al. 1989; Grimes 1977; Hawley, Fletcher, and Piele 1986; Horton, Lovitt, and Slocum 1988; Kann 1987; Kulik, Kulik, and Bangert-Drowns 1985; Martin 1973; Mevarech and Rich 1985; Mokros and Tinker 1987; Office of Technology Assessment 1988; Okey 1985; Ragosta, Holland, and Jamison 1982; Rapaport and Savard 1980; Rupe 1986; Samson, et al. 1986; Stennett 1985; Way 1984; White 1983; Woodward, Carnine, and Gersten 1988.)

Some writers also reported on research which compared the effects of CAI alone with those produced by conventional instruction alone. Here, results are too mixed to permit any firm conclusion. Some inquires have found CAI superior, some have found conventional instruction superior, and still others have found no difference between them. (Capper and Copple 1985; Edwards, et al. 1975; Rapaport and Savard 1980.)

Other researchers and reviewers compared the achievement effects produced by all forms of computerbased instruction (sometimes alone and sometimes as a supplement to traditional instruction) as compared with the effects of traditional instruction alone. While the research support is not as strong as that indicating the superiority of CAI, the evidence nevertheless indicates that CBE approaches as a whole produce higher achievement than traditional instruction by itself. (Bangert-Drowns 1985; Bangert-Drowns, et al. 1985; Braun 1990; Hasselbring 1984; Kulik 1983, 1985; Kulik, Bangert, and Williams 1983; Kulik and Kulik 1987; Roblyer, et al. 1988; Swan, Guerrero, and Mitrani 1989.)

This group of findings supports the conclusion drawn by Dalton and Hannafin in their 1988 study to the effect that "while both traditional and computer-based delivery systems have valuable roles in supporting instruction, they are of greatest value when complementing one another" (p. 32).

Researchers concerned with student writing outcomes have determined that writing performance is superior when the teaching approach emphasizes "writing as a process," rather than focusing only on the end product—the finished composition. The writing-as-a-process approach encourages students to engage in prewriting activities, followed by drafting, revising, editing, and final publication, with each step receiving considerable attention and often feedback from teachers or peer editors. Word processing programmes, with their capability to add, delete, and rearrange text, are seen as being far more congruent with the writing process than more laborious pencil-and-paper approaches. And indeed, most research in this area indicates that the use of word processors in writing programmes leads to better writing outcomes than the use of paper-and-pencil or conventional typewriters. Specific positive outcomes associated with the use of word processors in writing include:

- Longer written samples
- Greater variety of word usage
- More variety of sentence structure
- More accurate mechanics and spelling
- More substantial revision
- Greater responsiveness to teacher and peer feedback
- Better understanding of the writing process
- Better attitudes toward writing
- Freedom from the problem of illegible handwriting.

(Batey 1986; Bialo and Sivin 1990; Collins and Sommers 1984; Dickinson 1986; Kinnaman 1990; MacGregor 1986; Office of Technology Assessment 1988; Parson 1985; Rodriguez and Rodriguez 1986; Sommer and Collins 1984.)

Researchers are careful to point out that these desirable outcomes are obtained when computers are used as part of a holistic, writing-as-a-process approach. Only using computers for drill and practice on isolated subskills, such as grammar and mechanics, is not associated with improved writing achievement. As expressed by Sommers and Collins in their 1984 article on computers and writing, "microcomputers are counterproductive when used in a theoretical vacuum".

Learning Rate

As well as enabling students to achieve at higher levels, researchers have also found that CAI enhances learning rate. Student learning rate is faster with CAI than with conventional instruction. In some research studies, the students learned the same amount of material in less time than the traditionally instructed students; in others, they learned more material in the same time. While most researchers don't specify how much faster CAI students learn, the work of Capper and Copple (1985) led them to the conclusion that CAI users sometimes learn as much as 40 percent faster than those receiving traditional, teacher-directed instruction. (Batey 1986; Capper and Copple 1985; Edwards, et al. 1975; Grimes 1977; Hasselbring

1984; Kulik 1983, 1985; Kulik, Bangert, and Williams 1983; Kulik and Kulik 1987; Rapaport and Savard 1980; Rupe 1986; Stennett 1985; White 1983.)

Retention of Learning

If students receiving CAI learn better and faster than students receiving conventional instruction alone, do they also retain their learning better? The answer, according to researchers who have conducted comparative studies of learning retention, is yes. In this research, student scores on delayed tests indicate that the retention of content learned using CAI is superior to retention following traditional instruction alone.

(Capper and Copple 1985; Grimes 1977; Kulik 1985; Kulik, Bangert, and Williams 1983; Kulik, Kulik, and Bangert-Drowns 1985; Rupe 1986; Stennett 1985; Woodward, Carnine, and Gersten 1988.)

Attitudes

Much of the research that examines the effects of CAI and other microcomputer applications on student learning outcomes also investigates effects upon student attitudes. This line of inquiry has brought most researchers to the conclusion that the use of CAI leads to more positive student attitudes than the use of conventional instruction. This general finding has emerged from studies of the effects of CAI on student attitudes toward:

- Computers and the use of computers in education (Batey 1986; Ehman and Glen 1987; Hasselbring 1984; Hess and Tenezakis 1971; Kulik 1983, 1985; Kulik, Bangert, and Williams 1983; Roblyer 1988; Way 1984)
- Course content/subject matter (Batey 1986; Braun 1990; Dalton and Hannafin 1988; Ehman and Glen 1987; Hounshell and Hill 1989; Rapaport and Savard 1980; Roblyer, et al. 1988; Rodriguez and Rodriguez 1986; Stennett 1985)
- Quality of instruction (Kulik, Bangert, and Williams 1983; Kulik and Kulik 1987; Rupe 1986; White 1983)

- School in general (Batey 1986; Bialo and Sivin 1990; Ehman and Glen 1987; Roblyer, et al. 1988)
- Self-as-learner (Bialo and Sivin 1990; Mevarech and Rich 1985; Robertson, et al. 1987; Rupe 1986).

Other Beneficial Effects

The effects of CAI on other student outcomes have not been as extensively researched as CAI's effects on achievement, learning rate, retention, and attitudes. Some researchers have, however, investigated CAI's influence on other variables and found it to confer benefits on:

- Locus of control. Capper and Copple (1985), Kinnaman (1990), and Louie (1985) found that CAI students have more of an internal locus of control/sense of self-efficacy than conventionally instructed students.
- Attendance. CAI students had better attendance in Capper and Copple's 1985 study, Rupe's 1986 review, and the 1990 ISTE study.
- Motivation/time-on-task. Bialo and Sivin (1990) and Capper and Copple (1985) found that CAI students had higher rates of time-on-task than traditionally instructed controls.
- Cooperation/collaboration. Cooperative, prosocial behaviour was greater with CAI in the work of Dickinson (1986); Mevarech, Stern, and Levita (1987); and Rupe (1986).

CAI and Different Student Populations

Is CAI more effective with some student populations than others? Many researchers have conducted comparative analyses to answer this question and have produced findings in several areas. Younger versus older students. Most comparative studies have shown that CAI is more beneficial for younger students than for older ones. While research shows CAI to be beneficial to students in general, the degree of impact decreases from the elementary to secondary to postsecondary levels. (Bangert-Drowns 1985; Bangert-Drowns, et al. 1985; Becker 1990; Bracey 1987; Ehman and Glen 1987; Hasselbring 1984; Kulik, Kulik, and Bangert-Drowns 1985; Okey 1985; Stennet 1985; Swan, Guerrero, and Mitrani 1989.)

Lower-achieving versus higher-achieving students. These comparisons show that CAI is more effective with lower-achieving students than with higher-achieving ones. Again, both lower-and higher-achieving students benefit from CAI. However, the comparatively greater benefits experienced by lower-achieving students, like those experienced by younger students, are largely due to the need these groups have for elements common to the majority of CAI programmes—extensive drill and practice, privacy, and immediate feedback and reinforcement. (Bangert-Drowns 1985; Bangert-Drowns, et al. 1985; Edwards, et al. 1975; Kinnaman 1990; Kulik, Kulik, and Bangert-Drowns 1985; Martin 1973; Okey 1985; Roblyer 1988.)

Economically disadvantaged versus higher-SES students. Researchers note that CAI confers greater benefits on economically disadvantaged students than those from more privileged backgrounds. Lower SES students, too, benefit greatly from opportunities to interact privately with CAI drill-and-practice and tutorial programmes. (Bangert-Drowns, et al. 1985; Becker 1990; Mevarech and Rich 1985; Ragosta, Holland, and Jamison 1982; Stennett 1985.)

Lower-versus higher-cognitive outcomes. Closely related to the above is the finding that CAI is more effective for teaching lower-cognitive material than higher-cognitive material. This research makes essentially the same point—that CAI is particularly effective for reinforcing the basic, fact-oriented learning most often engaged in by younger, lowerachieving, and/or lower SES students. (Ehman and Glen 1987; Hasselbring 1984; Schmidt, et al. 1985-86.)

Handicapped learners. Research conducted with learning disabled, mentally retarded, hearing impaired, emotionally disturbed, and language disordered students indicates that their achievement levels are greater with CAI than with conventional instruction alone. In some of this research, handicapped CAI students even outperformed conventionally taught, nonhandicapped students. (Bahr and Rieth 1989; Bialo and Sivin 1990; Hall, McLoughlin, and Bialozor 1989; Horton, Lovitt, and Slocum 1988; Schmidt, et al. 1985-86; Woodward, Carnine, and Gersten 1988.)

Males versus females. This comparison was not addressed by enough researchers to draw firm conclusions. The 1988 meta-analysis of 82 studies of CBE conducted by Roblyer, et al. concluded that effect differences slightly favour boys over girls, with differences falling short of statistical significance.

CAI and Different Curricular Areas

A few researchers undertook to compare the effectiveness of CAI in different curricular areas. Their findings, though not conclusive, indicate that CAI activities are most effective in the areas of science and foreign languages, followed, in descending order of effectiveness, by activities in mathematics, reading, language arts, and English as a Second Language, with CAI activities in ESL found to be largely ineffective. (Capper and Copple 1985; Kulik, Kulik, and BangertDrowns 1985, Roblyer, et al. 1988; Rodriguez and Rodriguez 1986.)

Why Students Like CAI?

An earlier section of this report offers research evidence showing that CAI enhances student attitudes toward several aspects of schooling. Some researchers took these investigations a step further by asking students what it is about CAI that they like. The following is a list of reasons given by students for liking CAI activities and/or favoring them over traditional learning. These student preferences also contribute to our understanding of why CAI enhances achievement.

Students say they like working with computers because computers:

- Are infinitely patient
- Never get tired
- Never get frustrated or angry
- Allow students to work privately
- Never forget to correct or praise

- Are fun and entertaining
- Individualize learning
- Are self-paced
- Do not embarrass students who make mistakes
- Make it possible to experiment with different options
- Give immediate feedback
- Are more objective than teachers
- Free teachers for more meaningful contact with students
- Are impartial to race or ethnicity
- Are great motivators
- Give a sense of control over learning
- Are excellent for drill and practice
- Call for using sight, hearing, and touch
- Teach in small increments
- Help students improve their spelling
- Build proficiency in computer use, which will be valuable later in life
- Eliminate the drudgery of doing certain learning activities by hand (e.g., drawing graphs)
- Work rapidly—closer to the rate of human thought.

(Bialo and Sivin 1990; Braun 1990; Lawton and Gerschner 1982; Mokros and Tinker 1987; Robertson, et al. 1987; Rupe 1986; Schmidt, et al. 1985-86; Wepner 1990.) Many of these items point to students' appreciation of the immediate, objective, and positive feedback provided by computer learning activities by comparison with teacher-directed activities. As Robertson, et al. (1987) point out: "This reduction in negative reinforcement allows the student to learn through trial and error at his or her own pace. Therefore, positive attitudes can be protected and enhanced".

Cost-effectiveness

While cost considerations are not a major focus of this report, it is worth noting that some of the research on effectiveness also addressed the cost-effectiveness of CAI and other computer applications. Ragosta, Holland, and Jamison (1982) concluded that equal amounts of time of CAI reinforcement and the more-expensive one-to-one tutoring produced equal achievement effects. Niemiec, Sikorski, and Walberg (1989) also found CAI activities significantly more cost-effective than tutoring and suggested that computers be used more extensively in schools. And in their 1986 study of costs, effects, and utility of CAI, Hawley, Fletcher, and Piele noted that the cost differences between CAI and traditional instruction were insignificant and concluded that "the microcomputer-assisted instruction was the costeffective alternative of choice" for both grades addressed in the study.

Summary

The research base reviewed in preparation for this report indicates that:

- The use of CAI as a supplement to conventional instruction produces higher achievement than the use of conventional instruction alone.
- Research is inconclusive regarding the comparative effectiveness of conventional instruction alone and CAI alone.
- Computer-based education (CAI and other computer applications) produce higher achievement than conventional instruction alone.
- Student use of word processors to develop writing skills leads to higher-quality written work than other writing methods (paper and pencil, conventional typewriters).
- Students learn material faster with CAI than with conventional instruction alone.
- Students retain what they have learned better with CAI than with conventional instruction alone.
- The use of CAI leads to more positive attitudes toward computers, course content, quality of instruction, school in general, and self-as-learner than the use of conventional instruction alone.

- The use of CAI is associated with other beneficial outcomes, including greater internal locus of control, school attendance, motivation/time-on-task, and student-student cooperation and collaboration than the use of conventional instruction alone.
- CAI is more beneficial for younger students than older ones.
- CAI is more beneficial with lower-achieving students than with higher-achieving ones.
- Economically disadvantaged students benefit more from CAI than students from higher socioeconomic backgrounds.
- CAI is more effective for teaching lower-cognitive material than higher-cognitive material.
- Most handicapped students, including learning disabled, mentally retarded, hearing impaired, emotionally disturbed, and language disordered, achieve at higher levels with CAI than with conventional instruction alone.
- There are no significant differences in the effectiveness of CAI with male and female students.
- Students' fondness for CAI activities centers around the immediate, objective, and positive feedback provided by these activities.
- CAI activities appear to be at least as costeffective as— and sometimes more cost-effective than— other instructional methods, such as teacher-directed instruction and tutoring.

"Most programmes of computer-based instruction evaluated in the past," wrote Kulik and Kulik in 1987 "have produced positive effects on student learning and attitudes.

Further programmes for developing and implementing computer-based instruction should therefore be encouraged." Based on review of the research evidence published both before and after Kulik and Kulik's paper, the present report strongly supports this conclusion.

Computer Managed Learning (CML)

The Computer Managed Learning System is a suite of computer programmes for MS-DOS computers that has been developed by Dynamic Computer Solutions in Adelaide. It provides educators with state of the art tools to personalise, control and monitor each student's learning programme.

The CMLS controls and monitors the software installed on a computer or network and tracks the use of that software by each student. Educators can allocate software to students individually or en masse and monitor their progress. The software can be of any type: MS-DOS, Windows or CD-ROM. Educators, instructors etc. can write their own assessment/ assignment tasks using the CMLS's multimedia Assessment Module-naturally the computer marks it and provides a detailed analysis. Whatever software is being used, the CMLS monitors and reports on who is using the computer, when and for how long. Entire learning programmes, combining off the shelf curriculum software with assessment tasks created by the teacher can be created for each student.

The CMLS provides a tamper proof Windows environment and can be used on standalone or networked computers. The extensive online help and accompanying manual make it the most user friendly interface between technology and education available today.

At Dynamic Computer Solutions we have applied our considerable human and physical resources to developing the Computer Managed Learning System. A system that provides the ultimate in student centred learning environments.

The Computer Managed Learning System operating in conjunction with Microsoft Windows, transforms the computer into a powerful teaching tool. The various modules that make up the CMLS give teachers unprecedented power to manage each student's learning programme.

Until now, teachers have had very little control over the programmes students accessed through Windows because, once installed, a programme is available to everyone. Windows in its native state affords no security whatsoever. The CMLS changes all of that.

The software installation system within the CMLS is especially designed to enable all software—CD-ROM, MS-DOS and Windows-to be installed and run through windows. When installing software, teachers can nominate the suitable age or grade range of each title, so that each one can easily be allocated to the appropriate students.

The software allocation process allows teachers to establish and maintain each student's 'diet' of programmes. This means that students only have access to appropriate software. Through their unique Personal Menu, students can be given access to software selected to support and enhance a given curriculum area, while at the same time be given access to remedial and/or extension software especially chosen for them.

Not only is student access to software controlled. but the CMLS has in built control features that are student proof and teacher friendly. Students will not be able to alter Windows settings or access programmes that have not been allocated to them. When students login to the computer they are directed to their personal menu of programmes, or in the case of teachers, to the system's administration section.

Students see the usual Windows Programme Manager screen and, apart from the tamper proofing restrictions, Windows behaves normally. However, the system "secretly" records the programme that has been accessed and keeps track of the time spent on it, thus building the student's activity log.

Teachers can, at any time, login and obtain reports from the CMLS. The information contained in the reports, and the teacher's own professional judgement of the student's progress, will determine what new programmes are to be allocated to the student.

Indeed, teachers have a vital role to play in the initial and on going assessment of the programmes that each student should use. That initial choice will be based on a teacher's judgement of the needs of each student. Later, programmes can be removed and added to a student's allocated programmes based on data collected by the computer and the teacher's CMLS judgement of the student's progress.

Because the system maintains a continuous history of each student's learning activities, teachers from year to year can easily see what software each student has used in previous years. For the system to be an effective teaching tool, periodic editing and updating of system information is necessary-eg. new students added, those who have left the school deleted and any change in class or year group recorded. In addition, new programmes will need to be added to the system and some removed. But perhaps the most important maintenance task is the timely review and updating of each student's personal software menu.

You see, computer managed learning is not about throwing as many programmes at students as financially feasible and hoping that some good comes of it. It is based on the notion that the most effective learning path for most students is a structured, step by step, path. A 'free for all' on the computer makes learning a hit and miss affair. And it makes assessing the educational worth of each programme an impossible task.

The Impact of the Computer Managed Learning System on Each Sector of the Education Community

The Computer Managed Learning System will be acclaimed by all parties who have a stake in the education process....

For Students, computers are a natural tool because they:

- are non judgemental
- are non threatening
- are infinitely patient
- are friendly and discreet
- are 'hands on'-sight, sound and action
- provide instant feedback

For Teachers the CMLS:

- treats every student as an individual and helps teachers to follow suit

- allows students to be extended or remediated as required
- makes computer software accessible and relevant
- gives back huge amounts of time from testing and marking that is better spent on creative student learning
- provides previously unknown data on which to constantly refine and improve the teaching method

For School Principals and Management the CMLS:

- provides accurate measurement and analysis for informed decision making
- provides accountability and control
- traps, retains and shares valuable resources developed by teachers over time
- facilitates transfer of detailed student information from teacher to teacher from one year to the next
- facilitates quality control of the teaching process
- allows for new goal setting in measurable education outcomes

For Governments the CMLS:

- leverages the productivity of teachers
- collects data on computer usage
- fully utilises technology resources
- allows policy to be formed and funds allocated based on previously unobtainable data

The features of the system in summary:

- Available for network or standalone use.
- An easy to use programme installation procedure for all programme formats (Windows and DOS) and media (disk and CD-ROM).
- The ability to establish and maintain a unique menu of programmes for each student.
- A system for bypassing Windows for those programmes that only operate under DOS.

- Monitoring procedures that automatically record the programmes used by each student and the software access time in hours.
- A data base management facility for maintaining student records-which can include a photograph of the student.
- Numerous report formats that: summarise students' use of programmes; provide student lists by class and year group; list the software installed on the system.
- A report module for generating tailor made reports.
- A tamper proof Windows environment.
- Online Help features for teachers using the administrator's module plus an extensive manual for teachers.

Educational Broadcasting

Pioneers of wireless telegraphy (radio), such as Marconi, working 100 or so years ago, believed the new technology would soon be put to useful purposes. Shortly after it was set up in 1922, the British Broadcasting Company, later the British Broadcasting Corporation (BBC), began to see how it could use "wireless", as it was first called, to assist learning. John Reith, who, as a public service broadcaster, aimed to "educate, inform, and entertain", set up the first National Advisory Committee on Education in 1923 and appointed a Director of Education, a school inspector, who, in 1924, wrote an article in the BBC's programme listings magazine the *Radio Times,* proposing a Broadcasting University.

The earliest experimental broadcasts to schools emanated from Glasgow and London in 1924 and by the autumn of that year regular secondary school and adult education broadcasts were in place, with regular supporting publications coming soon after. A new weekly publication, *The Listener,* began publishing transcripts of educational talks from 1929 and developed into a magazine until 1991, when it ceased. As the services grew, education officers were appointed to liaise with the educational world and to advise on policy. Separate Advisory

Committees for School and Adult Education were set up and, for the latter, a Group Listening movement was encouraged. During the 1930s the whole system flourished, with most subjects on the curriculum treated. Mathematics was, interestingly, an exception.

Among initiatives at this time were new ways of learning, emphasizing a more imaginative, child-centred approach. Programmes in Gaelic and Welsh were introduced for children in Scotland and Wales. In the early 1930s it was not thought appropriate to make broadcasts for younger pupils. However, largely because of improved broadcasting practices, using drama and music in place of straight "talk", such broadcasts quickly became successful later in the decade. History and foreign language teaching series were firm favourites.

The Impact of Educational Broadcasting

The British system of educational broadcasting, transmitted nationally, was soon widely studied and used as a model in many countries, notably those in what, later, became the Commonwealth, and in more distant countries, such as Japan. It was realized that radio had great potential in both formal and informal education by adding to what teachers could provide, reaching isolated groups of learners, filling in for non-existent teachers, and acting as an agent of in-service training. Before long, "radio schools" were operating in countries with dispersed and remote populations, a notable example being the School of the Air in Australia, where two-way radio supplemented correspondence courses.

World War II severely disrupted life in Britain, but school broadcasting flourished and by 1945 some 2,000 more schools were using the service than in 1939, with 30 weekly series offered. Music, drama, and arts and crafts became popular subjects, along with civics and current affairs. Educational broadcasts became an anchor for teachers who, in the words of one headmistress, saw them as "lifebuoys in a queer, turbulent, scholastic sea". As the war ended, Forces Educational Broadcasts were devised to help demobilized service people with their return to civilian life. Television then became the centre of interest, with pilot experiments in school television in 1952 leading to a permanent service in 1957.

By the mid-1960s a comprehensive system of school broadcasts was being provided both by the BBC and Independent Television (ITV), which had started school television broadcasts just ahead of the BBC in 1957. Channel 4, which was launched in 1982, now handles school broadcasting for commercial television. The visual medium added a new dimension to learning and, significantly, mathematics became a successful subject for educational broadcasting, helping pupils and teachers to deal with the "new maths", then much in the news. Apart from continuing series in such subjects as modern language teaching, science, and history, adult education broadcasts began to address social issues such as parenting, old age, illiteracy, and unemployment—what became known as Social Action broadcasts.

In less-developed countries, educational broadcasts became a tool in social and political development, with campaigns treating health and farming issues. By the 1960s there was considerable evidence that educational broadcasting was a powerful branch of distance learning.

Much work had been done worldwide, when, in 1969, a major step was taken in the United Kingdom with the setting up of the Open University (OU). This combined the practice of correspondence learning, a well-proven distance learning technique, with educational broadcasts. It was effected by an alliance with the BBC, which created a department to make the radio and television programmes. These were first broadcast in 1971, accompanying the OU printed courses, prepared by course teams, including the BBC producers. The OU model is now being used worldwide and uses a very broad range of new educational technology.

In the late 1990s the consultative method of deciding educational output with councils, started in the 1920s, was changed. An important strand of programmes supported pupils taking new national examinations, and the Internet came into play. The "new" technology was now more interactive.

Technology in Educational Broadcasting

The Internet is the latest "new" technology to propel a development in educational broadcasting. Prominent examples in the past have been the transistor, which allowed many more people to use radio conveniently, especially in developing countries where teachers were scarce; stereo sound; black and white television, followed by colour television, which was an important addition to programmes dealing with subjects such as natural history and geography; improvements in recording techniques, cassetting, and disc recording (CD-ROMs); and the growth of transmission systems, such as cable and satellite, resulting in much-increased coverage. There have been many successful and unsuccessful attempts using satellites to transmit educational radio and television. India, in 1975, saw the Satellite Instructional Television Experiment, aimed at small, distant villages, supported by money and know-how from the United States. Canada and Australia, among many other countries, devised distance learning projects.

Most of these earlier, often ambitious, schemes, faced the problems experienced by their earthbound forerunners in the 1920s, namely inefficient transmitting and receiving apparatus, unreliable liaison between users and providers, inadequate back-up print material, inappropriate syllabuses, and ultimately the need for human contact. Most of these problems have been solved to some degree in developed countries, with even liaison and interactivity partially solved. Efficient postal systems, the telephone (fixed and mobile), and various recording and playback systems based on computer technology all have a part to play in educational broadcasting in the new millennium. The Internet and its websites are now familiar to many children in developed countries and among educational elites elsewhere, but it remains of little significance to very many more, who lack the most basic means for subsistence.

Telecasting

The educational programmes produced by the SIET have won wide acclaim and appreciation from the student-teacher-parent community of the Kerala State. At present the SIET telecasts educational programmes through Doordershan from 6.30 a.m to 7.00 a.m in DDI on a daily basis. SIET Kerala now also telecasting educational programmes through the EDUSAT Channel of the Dept. of Education, Govt. of Kerala from 7.00 am to 11.00 p.m everyday.

The Institute has adopted itself to play a catalytic role in fostering as well as supporting and supplementing the educational movement in the state particularly in the arena of secondary and higher secondary education. Its area of operation covers the preparation of video/audio programmes for the children of 5 to 17 years of age (Class I to Class 12) and the teachers in the regional language in the form of supportive materials for the conventional class room teaching.

Well equipped with a panel of technical personnel and programme producers, SIET is competent to produce world class dig ital learning materials to meet the needs of students. For the ETV productions topics are identified by the subject experts where the content outlines work as the guiding factor.

The major thrust of production enfolds curriculum (Science, Math, Language, Environment, Moral Education and Teachers' programmes), enrichment and educational entertainment. The brain storming efforts of the in-house and outside script writers, producers, media experts, Lecturers-in-production and Research and evaluation wing collaborate in breeding a good programme.

Occasionally the SIET also organises workshops where the subject experts, media experts, persons writing for TV & A.I.R., academicians/Educationists, Doctors, state and national awardee teachers and other experts ponder over developing ideas and script for production. Keeping the quality enhancing inputs in view, the scripts are tabled at a Script Review Committee Consisting of the Head of production, the producers, Lecturers-in-production, Scriptwriters and the Research and Evaluation officer where the script receives a finer shape for production.

After the script is ready, the producer, as the co-ordinator of the production, sits across the table with other constituent wings such as the cameraman, the Set Designers, the Graphic Artiste, Editors to chalk out the production strategy before the countdown starts. The planning meeting is important in view of the fact that all the concerned people in the programme are able to interact with the goal of contributing their best in the out-put. Then only the producer goes for recording of the programmes depending upon the design of the script whether to be accomplished outdoors or indoors.

After the Audio and Video recording is over, certain refinement is achieved at the editing table to give a concrete and final shape to the programme.

The producer submits the completed programme before the in-house preview Committee where a detailed discussion is taken up and necessary alteration suggested, if any.

Another programme preview meeting is held under the chairmanship of the Director of SIET once in every month.

The programmes, complete in all respects, are transmitted through Doordarshan Kendra at 6.00 A.M. on all days of the week excepting Saturday and Sunday.

All the constituent wings of production & Academics such as the Lecturers-in-Production, the Producers, Production Assistants, Script Writers, the Cameraman, the Scenic Designer, the Graphic Artists, Editors and the Floor Manager etc. are high up in their technical skill and experience.

The high professional excellence, technical quality and educational value of its programmes have earned the laurels of victory for its efforts in the different National Educational Video/film Festivals in different years.

Interactive Video

The term interactive video usually refers to a technique used to blend interaction and linear film or video.

Interactive Video on Broadband

Since 2005, interactive video has increased online as the result a number of factors including:

- the rise in numbers of users accessing the internet at broadband speeds
- the addition of video as a media type to Flash

Because users are often reluctant to pay for online content, it is perhaps unsurprising that many of the new online interactive videos (including all the examples given below) are either sponsored content or part of advertising campaigns. A number of these pieces of these have won major awards.

Some principal forms of online interactive video that have emerged are listed below.

"Customizable" Online Interactive Videos

Customizable videos allow the user to adjust some variables and then play a video customised to the user's particular preferences. However the user does not actually interact with the video while it is playing. Recent examples of this form of video include:

- Miss Helga — customizable video ad for Volkswagen Golf created by The Barbarian Group
- Ave a Word — customizable video ad for Mini created by Glue London-Silver Cannes Lion 2006. Ave a word is no longer online (formerly at www.aveaword.com)- but a customizable video ad for TV show Dexter at http://www.icetruck.tv/ offers similar functionality, created by http://www.ralphandco.com.
- Electric Feel — customizable music video for the so-titled song by the band MGMT.

"Conversational" Online Interactive Videos

Conversational videos allow the user to interact with a video in a turn-based manner, almost as though the user was having a simple conversation with the characters in the video. Recent examples include:

- Subservient Chicken — a "conversational" interactive video ad for Burger King created by The Barbarian Group Cannes Grand Prix 2005.

- A Conversation with Sir Ian-Interactive video interview with Sir Ian McKellen on Shakespeare. Created for the National Theatre by Martin Percy. BAFTA nominee 2007.

"Exploratory" Online Interactive Videos

Exploratory videos allow the user to move through a space or look at an object such as an artwork from multiple angles, almost as though the user was looking at the object in real life. The object or space is depicted using video loops, not still, creating a more "live" feel. Recent examples include:

- The BT Series-Interactive video exploration of the works of Tracey Emin, Anthony Gormley and Rachel Whiteread. Created for the Tate Gallery by Martin Percy. Webby Nominee 2006 and Honoree 2007 .
- Tate Tracks-Interactive video exploration of various works, allowing the user to listen to music while looking at art. Created for the Tate Gallery by Martin Percy. Part of integrated campaign winning Cannes Gold Lion 2007.

Aside from online use, interactive video may be found in a variety of applications, as listed below.

Modular Interactive Video

Modulated streaming video that allows the viewer to direct the course of the interaction at any point during playback while still remaining in the video experience. Rather than a solid block of linear video, Modular Interactive Video uses modular video files to reduce load time and keep the streaming video and menu sections integrated and continuously functional. Applications are endless. This technology is available free of charge for Job Seekers looking to create an Interactive Video Interview on AskMeHireMe.com and Cinume.com.

Interactive Video in Early Computer Games

The term interactive video or interactive movie sometimes refers to a nowadays uncommon technique used to create computer games or interactive narratives. Instead of 3D computer graphics an interactive image flow is created using premade video clips, often produced by overlaying computer-generated material with 12-inch videodisc images (where the setup is known as "level III" interactive video, to distinguish it from "level I" or videodisc-only, and "level II" requiring specially made videodisc players that support handheld-remote based interactivity without using an external computer setup). The clips can be animation like in the video game Dragon's Lair or live action video like in the video game Night Trap. Compared to other computer graphics techniques interactive video tends to emphasize the looks and movement of interactive characters instead of interactivity. For more on this please see interactive movies.

Interactive Video in Cinema

Interactive video has been used in interactive cinema presentations.

Interactive Video in Youtube

In 2008 YouTube added Video Annotations as an interactive layer of clickable speech-bubble, text-boxes and spotlights. Users may add interactive annotations to their videos and by that a new trend of interactive videos arose, including choose-your-own-adventure video series, online video games using YouTube videos, spot-the-difference-game videos, animal-dubbing and more. In 2009 YouTube added a community aspect to its Video Annotations feature by allowing video owners to invite their friends and community to add annotations to their movies.

Interactive Video Art

Contemporary interactive video artists like Miroslaw Rogala, Greyworld, Raymond Salvatore Harmon, Lee Wells, Camille Utterback, Scott Snibbe, Doug Williams (visual artist), Aaron Miller, Alexander Horn, Naiko Tosa, have extended the form of interactive video through the dialog of gesture and the participatory involvement of both active and passive viewers. Perpetual art machine is a video art portal and interactive video installation that integrates over 1000 international video artists into a single interactive large scale emersive video experience.

Interactive Video in VJing

Technically VJing is also about creating a stream of video interactively. However it rarely involves interaction between the end user and the video stream.

Hypervideo

Hypervideo is interactive video that is akin to hypertext and allows for non-linear navigation of the video. Asterpix offers a free online service for creating hypervideo.

Tele Lecture

Convergence

The growth of the Internet, computer telephony, electronic banking, interactive media services, mobile communications and related technologies, has paved the way for a new global network to emerge in the twenty-first century, subsuming the Internet and telephone networks. Where in the twentieth century we had separate devices and transmission technologies for each communications function, nearly all data is now transmitted digitally, and there is increasing convergence between the devices used to connect to digital networks.

Mobile Communications

The voice and data communications industry is working to forge new technologies and standards to support mobile E-Commerce. These efforts are focusing on two key areas:

accessing information and services via the Internet from a phone other handheld device;

providing the necessary bandwidth to handle content in the fastest and most reliable way.

Product Code Technology

Some supermarkets, such as UK retailer Safeway, have already introduced do-it-yourself scanning to take the pressure off tills. Shoppers can:

- pick up a hand-held scanner on entering the supermarket;
- use it to monitor how much they are spending as they go along;
- print out an invoice when they have finished.

Content Providers

The global network's content may increasingly be provided by media giants, providing entertainment, news and sports and there is likely to be a great deal of crossover with the retail sector, as consumers shopping for entertainment are persuaded to shop for other things.

Interactive TV

One of the big developments of the last few years has been the introduction of digital television, which in addition to providing a digital image has facilitated a range of interactive services, including:

- the provision of online programme information;
- interactive games on the television;
- the provision of pay-per-view programmes, such as big sporting events or recent films;
- the provision of online shopping services;
- an email service via your television.

All these services can be accessed using your remote control, although a special wireless 'qwerty' keyboard has also been developed to make use of the services easier.

Electronic Cash and Banking

Online banks are already appearing on the Internet, and established banks are having to adapt for the future.

It has been possible for a while to manage your banking from software on a PC, but these types of facility are becoming enhanced and integrated with the emergent mobile technologies.

Voice Recognition and Disabled Access

Voice control is likely to become a viable alternative for Internet access as well as the control of domestic appliances.

Computer Telephony

By merging computer and telephone technologies, Computer Telephony Integration (CTI) can change the way we do business. Call centres and automated call reception are just the tip of the iceberg–CTI technology can be merged with Internet and web systems to create a customer interface.

Voice over IP (VoIP)

Voice over IP (VoIP) is voice delivered using the Internet protocol. This means sending voice information in digital form in discrete packets rather than in the traditional circuit-committed protocols of the Public Switched Telephone Network (PSTN). VoIP and Internet telephony avoid ordinary telephone charges.

Videoconferencing

A videoconference (also known as a *videoteleconference*) is a set of interactive telecommunication technologies which allow two or more locations to interact via two-way video and audio transmissions simultaneously. It has also been called visual collaboration and is a type of groupware. It differs from videophone in that it is designed to serve a conference rather than individuals.

History

Videoconferencing uses telecommunications of audio and video to bring people at different sites together for a meeting. This can be as simple as a conversation between two people in private offices (point-to-point) or involve several sites (multi-point) with more than one person in large rooms at different sites.

Besides the audio and visual transmission of meeting activities, videoconferencing can be used to share documents, computer-displayed information, and whiteboards.

Simple analog videoconferences could be established as early as the invention of the television. Such videoconferencing systems consisted of two closed-circuit television systems connected via cable. Examples are the German network set up between 1938 and 1940, and the British GPO lines at the same period.

During the first manned space flights, NASA used two radiofrequency (UHF or VHF) links, one in each direction. TV channels routinely use this kind of videoconferencing when reporting from distant locations, for instance. Then mobile links to satellites using specially equipped trucks became rather common.

This technique was very expensive, though, and could not be used for more mundane applications, such as telemedicine, distance education, business meetings, and so on, particularly in long-distance applications. Attempts at using normal telephony networks to transmit slow-scan video, such as the first systems developed by AT&T, failed mostly due to the poor picture quality and the lack of efficient video compression techniques. The greater 1 MHz bandwidth and 6 Mbit/s bit rate of Picturephone in the 1970s also did not cause the service to prosper.

It was only in the 1980s that digital telephony transmission networks became possible, such as ISDN, assuring a minimum bit rate (usually 128 kilobits/s) for compressed video and audio transmission. The first dedicated systems started to appear in the market as ISDN networks were expanding throughout the world. Video teleconference systems throughout the 1990s rapidly evolved from highly expensive proprietary equipment, software and network requirements to standards based technology that is readily available to the general public at a reasonable cost. Finally, in the 1990s, IP (Internet Protocol) based videoconferencing became possible, and more efficient video compression technologies were developed, permitting desktop, or personal computer (PC)-based videoconferencing. In 1992 CU-SeeMe was developed at Cornell by Tim Dorcey et al., IVS was designed at INRIA, VTC arrived to the masses and free services, web plugins and software, such as NetMeeting, MSN Messenger, Yahoo Messenger, SightSpeed, Skype and others brought cheap, albeit low-quality, VTC.

Technology

The core technology used in a videoteleconference (VTC) system is digital compression of audio and video streams in real time. The hardware or software that performs compression is called a codec (coder/decoder). Compression rates of up to 1:500 can be achieved. The resulting digital stream of 1s and 0s is subdivided into labelled packets, which are then transmitted through a digital network of some kind (usually ISDN or IP). The use of audio modems in the transmission line allow for the use of POTS, or the Plain Old Telephone System, in some low-speed applications, such as videotelephony, because they convert the digital pulses to/from analog waves in the audio spectrum range.

The other components required for a VTC system include:

- *Video input* : video camera or webcam
- *Video output*: computer monitor, television or projector
- *Audio input*: microphones
- *Audio output*: usually loudspeakers associated with the display device or telephone
- Data transfer: analog or digital telephone network, LAN or Internet

There are basically two kinds of VTC systems:

1. Dedicated systems have all required components packaged into a single piece of equipment, usually a console with a high quality remote controlled video camera. These cameras can be controlled at a distance to pan left and right, tilt up and down, and zoom. They became known as PTZ cameras. The console contains all electrical interfaces, the control computer, and the software or hardware-based codec. Omnidirectional microphones are connected to the console, as well as a TV monitor with loudspeakers and/or a video projector.

There are several types of dedicated VTC devices:

1. Large group VTC are non-portable, large, more expensive devices used for large rooms and auditoriums.
2. Small group VTC are non-portable or portable, smaller, less expensive devices used for small meeting rooms.
3. Individual VTC are usually portable devices, meant for single users, have fixed cameras, microphones and loudspeakers integrated into the console.

2. Desktop systems are add-ons (hardware boards, usually) to normal PCs, transforming them into VTC devices. A range of different cameras and microphones can be used with the board, which contains the necessary codec and transmission interfaces. Most of the desktops systems work with the H.323 standard. Videoconferences carried out via dispersed PCs are also known as e-meetings.

Echo Cancellation

A fundamental feature of professional VTC systems is acoustic echo cancellation (AEC). Echo can be defined as the reflected source wave interference with new wave created by source. AEC is an algorithm which is able to detect when sounds or utterances reenter the audio input of the VTC codec, which came from the audio output of the same system, after some time delay. If unchecked, this can lead to several problems including 1) the remote party hearing their own voice coming back at them (usually significantly delayed) 2) strong reverberation, rendering the voice channel useless as it becomes hard to understand and 3) howling created by feedback. Echo cancellation is a processor-intensive task that usually works over a narrow range of sound delays.

Multipoint Videoconferencing

Simultaneous videoconferencing among three or more remote points is possible by means of a Multipoint Control Unit (MCU). This is a bridge that interconnects calls from several sources (in a similar way to the audio conference call). All parties call the MCU unit, or the MCU unit can also call the parties which are going to participate, in sequence.

There are MCU bridges for IP and ISDN-based videoconferencing. There are MCUs which are pure software, and others which are a combination of hardware and software. An MCU is characterised according to the number of simultaneous calls it can handle, its ability to conduct transposing of data rates and protocols, and features such as Continuous Presence, in which multiple parties can be seen onscreen at once.

MCUs can be stand-alone hardware devices, or they can be embedded into dedicated VTC units.

Some systems are capable of multipoint conferencing with no MCU, stand-alone, embedded or otherwise. These use a standards-based H.323 technique known as "decentralized multipoint", where each station in a multipoint call exchanges video and audio directly with the other stations with no central "manager" or other bottleneck. The advantages of this technique are that the video and audio will generally be of higher quality because they don't have to be relayed through a central point. Also, users can make ad-hoc multipoint calls without any concern for the availability or control of an MCU. This added convenience and quality comes at the expense of some increased network bandwidth, because every station must transmit to every other station directly.

Problems

Some observers argue that two outstanding issues are preventing videoconferencing from becoming a standard form of communication, despite the ubiquity of videoconferencing-capable systems. These issues are:

1. *Eye Contact:* It is known that eye contact plays a large role in conversational turn-taking, perceived attention and intent, and other aspects of group communication. While traditional telephone conversations give no eye contact cues, videoconferencing systems are arguably

worse in that they provide an incorrect impression that the remote interlocutor is avoiding eye contact. Telepresence systems have cameras located in the screens that reduce the amount of parallax observed by the users. This issue is also being addressed through research that generates a synthetic image with eye contact using stereo reconstruction.

2. *Appearance Consciousness:* A second problem with videoconferencing is that one is on camera, with the video stream possibly even being recorded. The burden of presenting an acceptable on-screen appearance is not present in audio-only communication. Early studies by Alphonse Chapanis found that the addition of video actually impaired communication, possibly because of the consciousness of being on camera.

The issue of eye-contact may be solved with advancing technology, and presumably the issue of appearance consciousness will fade as people become accustomed to videoconferencing.

Standards

The International Telecommunications Union (ITU) (formerly: Consultative Committee on International Telegraphy and Telephony (CCITT)) has three umbrellas of standards for VTC.

1. ITU H.320 is known as the standard for public switched telephone networks (PSTN) or VTC over integrated services digital networks (ISDN) basic rate interface (BRI) or primary rate interface (PRI). H.320 is also used on dedicated networks such as T1 and satellite-based networks;
2. ITU H.323 is known as a standard for transporting multimedia applications over LANs. This same standard also applies to older implementations of voice over IP VoIP. In recent years, the IETF's Session Initiation Protocol (SIP) has gained considerable momentum in practice for these two services.;

3. ITU H.324 is the standard for transmission over POTS, or audio telephony networks. 3G-324M is a 3GPP implementation for video call on 3G mobile phones.

In recent years, IP based videoconferencing has emerged as a common communications interface and standard provided by VTC manufacturers in their traditional ISDN-based systems. Business, government and military organizations still predominantly use H.320 and ISDN VTC. Though, due to the price point and proliferation of the Internet, and broadband in particular, there has been a strong spurt of growth and use of H.323, IP VTC. H.323 has the advantage that it is accessible to anyone with a high speed Internet connection, such as DSL.

In addition, an attractive factor for IP VTC is that it is easier to set-up for use with a live VTC call along with web conferencing for use in data collaboration. These combined technologies enable users to have a much richer multimedia environment for live meetings, collaboration and presentations.

E-tutoring

Do you need that added edge to help you excel in school and college? Are you facing increasing competition and need higher scores for college entrance? Do you wish you did not have to travel all that distance to that coaching class? Are you looking for an expert teacher to answer the specific doubts that you have in a subject? Or, are you looking for a teacher who will explain a concept in a way that you understand?

We bring high quality, personalised coaching directly to your home wherever you are, whenever you need it.

E-Tutoring provides LIVE, online coaching, homework help and focused exam preparation from the best tutors, irrespective of geographical location-all from the comfort and safety of your home. The result-higher marks, demonstrably better academic performance and less stress for both student and parent!

Each student is offered personalised learning and individual interaction with a tutor. The coaching is live using audio and a shared whiteboard. The process uses simple, easy to install technology, that we provide.

Every student is evaluated on his or her capability to learn and the tutoring is designed to take care of each student's individual capability. Good feedback and quality processes ensure that you achieve your goals. See how it works. It is convenient, proven and affordable!

How e-tutoring Works

The student and the teacher speak to each other on a one-to-one basis using a hands-free headset, much like talking on a telephone. The student and the teacher also write questions and answers on the same workspace using a digital pencil and a digital writing pad. This workspace is displayed on both both their computer screens simultaneously. Broadband connectivity and workstations are needed. 4C is currently looking for partnerships with the Supplemental Educational Service providers and schools to offer a cost-effective and high-quality offshore tutoring service from our corporate office in Bangalore, India.

Software in Commerce and Accountancy

Accounting software is application software that records and processes accounting transactions within functional modules such as accounts payable, accounts receivable, payroll, and trial balance. It functions as an accounting information system. It may be developed in-house by the company or organization using it, may be purchased from a third party, or may be a combination of a third-party application software package with local modifications. It varies greatly in its complexity and cost. The market has been undergoing considerable consolidation since the mid 1990s, with many suppliers ceasing to trade or being bought by larger groups.

Modules

Accounting software is typically composed of various modules, different sections dealing with particular areas of accounting. Among the most common are:

Core Modules:

- Accounts receivable—where the company enters money received
- Accounts payable—where the company enters its bills and pays money it owes
- General ledger—the company's "books"
- Billing—where the company produces invoices to clients/customers
- Stock/Inventory—where the company keeps control of its inventory
- Purchase Order—where the company orders inventory
- Sales Order—where the company records customer orders for the supply of inventory

Non Core Modules:

- Debt Collection—where the company tracks attempts to collect overdue bills (sometimes part of accounts receivable)
- Electronic payment processing
- Expense—where employee business-related expenses are entered
- Inquiries—where the company looks up information on screen without any edits or additions
- Payroll—where the company tracks salary, wages, and related taxes
- Reports—where the company prints out data
- Timesheet—where professionals (such as attorneys and consultants) record time worked so that it can be billed to clients
- Purchase Requisition—where requests for purchase orders are made, approved and tracked

(Different vendors will use different names for these modules)

Implementations

In many cases, implementation can be a bigger consideration than the actual software chosen when it comes down to the total cost of ownership for the business. Most midmarket and larger applications are sold exclusively through resellers, developers and consultants. Those organizations generally pass on a license fee to the software vendor and then charge the client for installation, customization and support services. Clients can normally count on paying roughly 50-200% of the price of the software in implementation and consulting fees. Other organizations sell to, consult with and support clients directly, eliminating the reseller.

Categories

Personal Accounting: Mainly for home users that use accounts payable type accounting transactions, managing budgets and simple account reconciliation at the inexpensive end of the market suppliers include:

Low End

At the low end of the business markets, inexpensive applications software allows most general business accounting functions to be performed. Suppliers frequently serve a single national market, while larger suppliers offer separate solutions in each national market.

Many of the low end products are characterized by being "single-entry" products, as opposed to double-entry systems seen in many businesses. Some products have considerable functionality but are not considered GAAP or FASB compliant. Some low-end systems do not have adequate security nor audit trails.

Mid Market

The mid-market covers a wide range of business software that may be capable of serving the needs of multiple national accountancy standards and allow accounting in multiple currencies. In addition to general accounting functions, the software may include integrated or add-on management information systems, and may be oriented towards one or more markets, for example with integrated or add-on project accounting modules. Software applications in this market typically include the following features:

- Industry-standard robust databases (eg PostgreSQL, MySQL, Microsoft SQL, Oracle, Pervasive)
- Industry-standard reporting tools (eg Cognos, Crystal)
- Tools for configuring or extending the application (eg an SDK, access to programme code, the ability to be controlled via Visual Basic for Applications (VBA))

High End

The most complex and expensive business accounting software is frequently part of an extensive suite of software often known as Enterprise resource planning or *ERP* software. These applications typically have a very long implementation period, often greater than six months. In many cases, these applications are simply a set of functions which require significant integration, configuration and customisation to even begin to resemble an accounting system. The advantage of a high-end solution is that these systems are designed to support individual company specific processes, as they are highly customisable and can be tailored to exact business requirements. This usually comes at a significant cost in terms of money and implementation time.

Vertical Market

Some business accounting software is designed for specific business types. It will include features that are specific to that industry. The choice of whether to purchase an industry-specific application or a general-purpose application is often very difficult. Concerns over a custom-built application or one designed for a specific industry include:

- Smaller development team
- Increased risk of vendor business failing
- Reduced availability of support

This can be weighed up against:

- Less requirement for customisation
- Reduced implementation costs
- Reduced end-user training time and costs

Some important types of vertical accounting software are:

- Banking
- Construction
- Medical
- Nonprofit
- Point of Sale (Retail)
- Daycare accounting (a.k.a. Child care management software)

Hybrid Solutions

As technology improves, software vendors have been able to offer increasingly advanced software at lower prices. This software is suitable for companies at multiple stages of growth. Many of the features of Mid Market and High End software (including advanced customization and extremely scalable databases) are required even by small businesses as they open multiple locations or grow in size. Additionally, with more and more companies expanding overseas or allowing workers to home office, many smaller clients have a need to connect multiple locations. Their options are to employ software-as-a-service or another application that offers them similar accessibility from multiple locations over the internet.

Use by Non-Accountants

With the increasing dominance of having financial accounts prepared with Accounting Software, as well as some suppliers' claims that anyone can prepare their own books, accounting software can be considered at risk of not providing appropriate information as non-accountants prepare accounting information. As recording and interpretation is left to software and expert systems, the necessity to have a Systems Accountant overseeing the accountancy system becomes ever more important. The set up of the processes and the end result must be vigorously checked and maintained on a regular basis in order to develop and maintain the integrity of the data and the processes that manage these data.

UNIT-VI

Managing Classroom

Classroom Management

Most college students embark on a learning experience with a new instructor with various anxieties and questions on their minds. They also wonder, Does the teacher care? Is the teacher fair? Does this instructor know the subject matter? Will I get something out of this course? You will, of course, want your students to arrive at affirmative answers to these concerns and questions. You wish to earn the respect of your students, and you want to provide a setting where each individual can gain as much as possible from the course. This will require the use of skillful classroom managementa broad concept which touchos in one way or another on every component of effective teaching. Your management goals should be:

- to adopt efficient methods of handling logistical details, some of which are mundane, but others of which have a more profound impact on the quality of the course;
- to inspire the students' confidence in your mastery of the subject matter, and their faith in your ability to conduct the course in a competent, fair and well-organized manner;
- to establish and maintain a positive and supportive atmosphere in the classroom, an environment of mutual respect, courtesy and consideration for others.

Even though these objectives are far-reaching, achieving them comes down to fundamentals:

The best management technique? Get the students interested, involved in, even excited about, the material you are presenting!

A well-prepared and well-executed class in mathe-matics (in English literature, in psychology, in your particular discipline) is the number one way to establish the positive control and authority necessary for an effective learning environment. Enthusiasm is contagious; it commands attention and inspires concentration. The behaviour of students will rarely be a problem when they are interested and focused on the subject matter.

Besides enthusiasm, organization is one of the keys to achieving the management goals listed earlier. Organization applies to clear and consistent policy statements, to the appearance and content of board-work, transparencies, hand-outs and other printed materials, to managing the various aspects of the physical environment, to the timeliness of the beginning and ending of class and of returning tests and assignments, to careful and accurate record-keeping, and even to something as trivial as the orderly distribution and return of materials.

Policy statements are vital. The article on syllabus construction (see page 9) explains the need to pre-determine and to carefully communicate your policies concerning attendance, assignments, make-up tests and grading schemes. Students need to know your expectations, and they want to have an idea of how they stand as the course progresses. In particular, your students should have received at least one major grade before the last "drop date," after which they will receive a WF rather than a W should they withdraw from the course.

Similarly, it is important to observe the published schedule for examinations, as well as the prohibition against tests and quizzes in the last few classes. (See Bulletin for details.) Sometimes students will tell you of extenuating circumstances and difficulties they are facing, and it is important to be sympathetic and supportive. You realize, of course, that there may be other students with equally compelling personal situations who do not say anything.

Be careful to deal with requests for special consideration in an even-handed way. It is important to offer "extra credit" or any similar opportunities in a uniform and impartial manner. In addition to establishing fairness and consistency, your policies should convey to the students your concern for their progress and the fact that you want them to succeed in your course. Office hours that are convenient for the students, optional review sessions before major tests, private conferences to discuss research papers or group projectsthese are some of the possible ways to underscore your concern for the students as individuals.

(*Note: You should refer students with serious emotional or personal problems to the appropriate counseling and support services on campus.)

Seek help for problems with the physical plant, or for students with special needs. Some of the important physical elements of the classroom (light, heat, air conditioning, glare on the blackboard, an adequate number of desks, etc.) may be within your control, but others may not. A staff member in your departmental office will be able to assist you if there is a problem in this area. If you are teaching away from your home building, it would be good to locate the departmental office closest to your classroom. Occasionally you may find the door locked (this is especially true of early morning classes) and it helps to know the location of the nearest master key. There may be special physical or procedural considerations if you have students in wheelchairs or students with vision or hearing impairments. The Educational Support Services Office can assist you in this case.

Printed materials reflect organization. Use a typewriter or word processor if time and available equipment permit; otherwise aim for legibility in hand-written work. A simple trick like attaching lined paper with a paper clip before writing on a ditto master, or using blank paper over lined paper when preparing an original for xeroxing, may produce neater copies. Neatness and legibility are also important when using the blackboard or overhead projector. The necessary size of the writing will depend on the dimensions of the room; it is a good idea to go to the back of the room at the end of a class to see if the writing is clear and large enough.

Board-work is usually best if it unfolds from left to right, although important principles may be "boxed in" and left throughout the period. Be careful not to talk to the board or to stand in front of what you have just written. (Note: you may have to carry chalk to class with you if you teach in a building away from your own department.) If it is available, an overhead projector allows you to face students, to take advantage of more vivid colours, and to go back to work written earlier. Transparencies can be prepared in advance, perhaps "burned" on a xerox from printed material for a professional touch. When using prepared transparencies, be sure to allow time for students to take notes.

Logistical methods depend on the size of the class. In a large class, it may help to count out materials in advance, according to the number of students in each row. Returning work to the students also varies with the numbers involved. In a small class this presents a wonderful opportunity to learn names, as you place each student's paper in his or her hand, but in a large class, this one-to-one method may be too time consuming. One possible solution is to ask students to put their last name near the top or on the back of their papers, which can later be returned by being alphabetized and placed face down on the front of the table, spread out so that names are showing. It is important to preserve each student's privacy in returning papers. Be sure to learn and to follow the policies of your department concerning the posting of grades and privacy restrictions.

Learning names, showing concern for individual progress, giving outside assistance to students either separately or in groupsthese are some of the practices already mentioned which will help to build rapport and a positive relationship with your students. During the actual class period, you should be conscious of your eye contact with each person in the room. It is tempting to focus on the most expressive faces, and right-handed speakers have been shown to favour the right side of the room; so be careful to spread your attention throughout the room, and to make eye contact with each student. Other nonverbal encouragement involves body language and physical proximity. Move around the room and use whatever gestures you feel natural to you as you communicate with your students. This will make the presentation even more lively and animated.

Mutual respect requires sensitive interaction. Never embarrass a student for a wrong answer, a foolish question, or an inappropriate comment or opinion. With practice, you can learn to rephrase the thought and redirect the discussion without damaging the self-esteem of the student. Usually the class will follow the instructor's lead in treating each other with courtesy and kindness. Expect this same consideration if you make a content or computational error while you are teaching, or if you are asked a question about the subject matter and you do not know the answer. Handle the situation in a low-key, confident manner. Correct the mistake when you discover it, or promise to answer the question at the next class meeting. Your credibility will not be diminished; instead you will seem more human to your students.

Use positive reinforcement. Recognize exceptional effort and outstanding performances in front of the whole class. Compliment students, with sincerity, whenever you can. Reward student contributions to class discussion by your facial expression and by referring to particular offerings later in the hour. Remember that you can commend students for good work with a remark in class, with a written comment on an assignment or test paper, or in a private verbal exchange. Individual differences should be considered here. Some students are somewhat embarrassed by too much public recognition; a quiet word before or after class may be more comfortable for them. The student who shows dramatic improvement or much greater effort should be especially bolstered and encouraged. A student who has an unusually bad performance on one particular test or assignment may need some reassurance. Whatever the circumstance, the most effective feedback is positive in tone and content; criticisms and put-downs are to be avoided. However, some behaviours should not be reinforced. In spite of your best efforts to establish rapport and a positive atmosphere in the classroom, occasionally you will have to contend with students who disrupt the class by talking continuously, or by arriving late or leaving early, or by other negative behaviours. The time-honored advice on authority and control is to start out strict and loosen up later when things are going well. This is particularly important for inexperienced teachers, especially those who may be close in age or even younger than some of their students. "Starting out strict" does not involve lengthy reprimands or protracted lectures on behaviour. Here again, clear communication of expectations, through effective use of voice, eyes, facial expression, and body language will establish firmness and control. An image of authority and professionalism will be enhanced by appropriate dress and appearance, and perhaps by having students call you "Ms. Smith" or Mr. Jones" rather than by your first name.

What is the best way to handle persistent socializing? Try direct eye contact with the offenders, perhaps underscored by a period of silence. To counteract a general buzz, use a dramatic change in the pitch and pace of your voice. Try using a much lower, much slower speaking style. (The worst approach is to allow your voice to become higher and louder, in a vain attempt to talk over the din.) If all else fails, flipping the lights off and on in the room will certainly regain everyone's attention. When a small group of students persist with disruptive or negative behaviour, you should separate their seats and/or arrange to speak with them privately. Do not resort to sarcasm or to public humiliation. If you are polite but firm, you can correct the problem and still maintain the positive atmosphere you have worked to establish. Through clear and consistent policies, an organized approach to logistical details, and an insistence on courtesy and mutual respect in the classroom, you will be taking advantage of effective management techniques. With good rapport and a positive atmosphere established, you will be able to concentrate more fully on the preparation and delivery of excellent lessons in the subject matter, which will stir interest and motivate active involvement. Students will leave your course knowing that you have treated them fairly, and that you do care about them. Because of your effective management of the classroom, your students will benefit from a good environment in which to learn and to grow in their mastery of the discipline. You will have set the stage for academic achievement. You will have offered a valuable learning experience to your students.

Factors Influencing Classroom Management

Elements of commerce is basically a subject of the nature of survey course and in it we can divide the course content into specific units of instructions. In it we do not have any sequential arrangement for various units and various units are arranged according to logical sequence of study plan. By teaching elements of commerce we aim at the development of following competencies

(i) To provide to students a comprehensive picture of business in its economic setting.

(ii) An understanding of the relationship of business services and functions as they affect the individual directly as a consumer as well as a producer.

By presenting the units in a logical sequence it is hoped that it will be more advantageous for the students to comprehend the concept. It should be kept in mind that each unit is built upon the skills and knowledges developed in the preceding units.

The tentative list of units of teaching for attaining the above stated objectives is given below.

Units

1. Evolution and growth of commerce.
2. Meaning of business, commerce and trade.
3. Organisation of Business House-Types of business.
4. Organisation of Home Trade and Foreign Trade.
5. Organisation of Business Office.
6. Commercial correspondence.

7. Postal information.
8. Banks, Insurance, Transport etc.

System Approach—Input Process—Output and Feedback—Aspects in Commerce Teaching

The subject 'Elements of Commerce' is also knows as 'Business Methods' or as 'General Business'. Its objectives are as follows:

1. Knowledge Objective

(a) Ability to recall facts, concepts, items and principles in Elements of Commerce.

(b) Ability to recognise facts, concepts, performs etc., in Elements of commerce.

(c) Ability to locate commercial informations in books, reports, periodicals, newspapers, charts, diagrams and advertisements etc.

2. Understanding Objective

(a) Ability to distinguish between relevant and irrelevant, essential and incidental etc.

(b) Ability to discriminate between different facts and different concepts in commercial operations.

(c) Ability to locate, classify, compare and contrast commercial information.

(d) Ability to cite illustrations.

(e) Ability to detect and rectify errors.

(f) Ability to interpret data presented in various forms,

(g) Ability to recognise underlying assumptions and to identify relationships.

(h) Ability to give reasons for occurrence of phenomenon.

3. Application Objective

(a) Ability to analyse new problems to identify the issues involved in it.

(b) Ability of selecting the facts relevant to new situations and to eliminate irrelevant matter.

(c) Ability to verify a new hypotheses.

(d) Ability to draw inference.

(e) Ability to predict.

(f) Ability to suggest improvements in the process.

4. Skill Objective

(a) Ability to write effective business letters and documents.

(b) Ability to prepare models, sketches etc., of business appliances.

(c) Ability to handle instruments and office appliances properly.

(d) Ability of collecting, preserving and displaying relevant in formations.

5. Interest Objective

Student gets interested:

(a) to read newspapers, magazines, books etc., related to Elements of Commerce.

(b) to collect specimens, pictures, charts, data, cuttings etc.

(c) to discuss social, economic and commercial problems, with his fellows, teachers and parents.

(d) to visit places of social, economic and commercial interest.

(e) to exhibit his artistic talents of commercial subjects.

6. Attitude Objectives : The student

(a) Develops an ability to critically examines new developments in the field of business, trade and commerce.

(b) Develops an attitude of realistic thinking towards new

(c) Develops a spirit of healthy competition and cooperation.

(d) Exhibits sympathy and good behaviour in his dealings.

(e) Develops habits of hard work.

(f) Develops enterprising spirit.

(g) Considers inter-dependence of nations as essential for economic growth.

7. *Appreciation Objective The student*

(a) Appreciates the interrelationship between the growth of civilisation and commerce.

(b) Appreciates the fact that it is through commercial process that human wants are satisfied.

(c) Appreciates minimisation of disparity and inequality of physical resources.

(d) Appreciates the contribution made by the business agencies and commercial houses to well being and prosperity of society.

(e) Appreciates that personality factors are important for the success of business.

Methods of Teaching

There 'are large number of methods for teaching of `Elements of Commerce'. Harma and Stehr has laid down more than a score of methods for teaching 'General Business'. e.g. in 'Elements of Commerce' we find such methods as 'Whole Method'; 'Part Method'; 'Traditional Method'; 'Functional Method' etc. Any method involves a great deal of 'why' and leaves much of 'How' to the individual teacher. Method is a procedure by which the teacher meets the learner at his level starting with his interests and with his problems, and then establishes conditions that enable him to proceed to reach set goals in as effective manner as possible.

For teaching "Elements of Commerce' most useful suggested procedures are:

1. Lecture Method,
2. Lecture-blackboard Method,
3. Question-Answer Method,
4. Problem-solving Method,

5. Demonstration Method, and
6. Discussion Method.

All these methods have been discussed in detail in separate chapter on ' Methods of Teaching'.

Approaches of Teaching

1. Cyclic Approach

For achieving teaching objectives of teaching 'Elements of commerce'. Cyclic approach is considered to the most effective. The cycle may be broadly divided into following three divisions:

(i) How the business serves,

(ii) How different systems promote business activities, and

(iii) How the business is influenced by the environment.

The students gets an overview of business in the part:

(i) of cycle, learn about business services and how to use them in part

(ii) and gets a more complete understanding of business system in part (iii).

(i) How the Business Serves

In this part of the cycle the students becomes aware of the following:

(a) His personal business transactions,

(b) How the business serves consumers,

(c) How the business is organised to produce and distribute goods and services,

(d) How the business is organised and managed, and

(e) What kind of workers are required in our economic society.

(ii) How the Different Systems Promote Business Activities

It is the part of the cycle in which students are told about various types of business organisation and different types of business services. It is the part in which an effort is made to explain, to students, functional aspects of business and economic enterprises, student acquires efficiency in the management of his personal finances and with this knowledge becomes more intelligent in determining prices, values, need and use of goods and services offered by different kinds of businesses.

(iii) How Business is Influenced by the Environment

It is the final phase of the cycle and in it students feels more concerned about advanced business principles and issues rights and duties of labour, management and government.

Keeping the above three cycle an experienced teacher can plan his units of instructions and develop them accordingly. It will be quite helpful to the students in learning of different facts and concepts in 'Elements of Commerce'.

2. Role Playing

It is another technique used for teaching. It is also known as psychodrama' when it refers to deeper personal emotional problems, encountered by the individual in his own life. This is the most appropriate technique for high school students.

In it the students are assigned the actual role like the roles in a drama. They play the roles with interests. It is an unprepared, unrehearsed dramatisation. This technique helps in developing a democratic attitude among students. The values of the technique lies in the spontaneity of presentation. In this technique the individual makes full use of his creative experiences. For the role-playing there are three perquisites. These are as under:

1. The class must have a cooperative group feeling and common interest on the issue in mind.
2. The participants should have the issue in mind.
3. The experience should be regarded as a means of learning and not-entertaining,

Following are the steps involved in role-playing:

1. Selecting the situation,

2. Choosing the participants,
3. Setting the stage,
4. Preparing the audience,
5. Acting out the situation, and
6. Follow up.

3. Team-Teaching

For teaching 'Elements of Commerce' is a preferred. This is so because this subject is inter-mingling of various concepts of business world and thus the students and commerce teachers must realise the importance of team work. It is better to allow the students to work in small groups before teaching them the concept of team teaching. For the successful execution of team-teaching plan, the teacher has to select the topic and outline the outcomes. He has to organize committees and provide for supervision, help and coordination of the work. He should contain the students to show a more responsible behaviour in planning and executing the activities. Each team should have limited members and the membership should not be large. In this approach some problems may arise because of the following reasons

(i) Shyness of the students,
(ii) Lack of supervision,
(iii) Poor planning,
(iv) Poor execution,
(v) Lack of motivating force for all the members, and
(vi) Variance in teachers efforts.

Truely speaking team teaching is the modern refinement of committee technique. It involves specialisation and departmentalisation in Education. In it we assume that no single teacher can do justice to all the topics and team of teachers work with a team spirit, each taking up various aspects of same problem. For success of this technique team members should be selected to complement each other. All teachers must have equal authority and equal recognition.

Advantages of Team-teaching

Following are the advantages of team-teaching:

1. In it a specialist provides the instructions.
2. It helps in better utilisation of staff members.
3. It helps to eliminate boredom of one teacher approach and motivates students to learning through variety of approaches from different persons.
4. It helps to solve the individual problems of the students.
5. It provides occasions of learning to teachers from each other.

Disadvantages of Team-teaching

1. In the absence of proper adjustment of *pschedules* this type of teaching is not possible.
2. It is an expensive approach.
3. Sometimes it leads to personality conflicts amongst teachers.
4. Special trained teachers are generally not available in some institution.

Classroom Interaction Analysis—Classroom Climate Types of Teachers based on Leadership Styles—Teacher Dominated Pattern

Every society expects its educational institutions to help in developing competent citizens who would at the same time maintain the existing values and adopt fresh ones. Every school subject must, either through the matter taught or through the ways of learning it, contribute to the growth of knowledge and competence in learners.

Teacher occupies an important place in the process of education and a great responsibility therefore devolves upon the teacher. According to Binning, 'Teaching is a progressive occupation and the teacher must ever be a student".

From the point of view of society as well the teacher occupies an important place, Dr. Radha Krishnan has rightly remarked,

'The teacher's place in society is of vital importance. He acts as the pivot for the transmission of intellectual traditions and technical skill from generation to generation and helps to keep the lamp of civilisation burning".

In order to prove worthy of the trust reposed in him the teacher must have certain qualities and characteristics. The qualities and characteristics are required for teachers of every subject. This is true about teacher of commerce as well.

Qualities and Requirements of a Commerce Teacher

The teacher of commerce is expected to possess certain qualities and characteristics. Such qualities are described in brief in the following pages:

In a nut shell it can be said, 'The teacher of commerce must be properly qualified person and should possess the training qualifications to teach."

For any improvement in commerce education a well qualified and trained commerce teacher is a must. The most important of the several qualities expected of a commerce teacher is the he should be *devoted to the profession of teacher.* It has been observed that per-sons generally after taking training in commerce teaching profession switch-over to some other profession. The subject of commerce has now received wide recognition and acceptability, second only to science subjects. Therefore, it has become essential that profession of commerce teacher is taken up very seriously.

Since the first and foremost duty of a commerce teacher is to teach so it is desirable that he fulfils the requirements of the profession and possesses the necessary qualifications.

Qualifications of a Commerce Teacher

A teacher of Commerce should have

(i) A master's degree in commerce.

(ii) A bachelor's degree in education.

(iii) Specialisation in Commerce education.

(iv) A good academic background in Economics.

(v) Proficiency in skill subjects.

(vi) A thorough understanding and knowledge of theories of skills.

Besides these, he should have special aptitude and training in the audio-visual aids and vocational guidance. He should have enough of professional experience and training to undertake the teaching of type-writing and short-hand efficiently. The success and prospect of vocationalisation at secondary stage largely depends upon this aspect of specialisation on the part of the commerce teacher.

Specially on instructor or a teacher. Who is required to teach short-hand and type-writing must have specialisation in these subjects and a good background in teaching methods of commerce subjects. Knowledge of teaching short-hand and type-writing in English or any other regional language should be essential for a commerce teacher. Teachers for teaching short-hand and type-writing should be professional rather than M.Com. with specialisation in short-hand and type-writing. It is better to appoint a person, to teach short-hand and type-writing, who has practiced these subjects as stenographers at more than 100 words per minute for more than five years. These persons will fare well and try to develop the vocational skills of students.

Qualities of a Commerce Teacher

Various qualities which are desirable in a commerce teacher are as follows:

Personal Qualities

(i) He should have a good personality.

(ii) He should be graciously dressed.

(iii) He should be man with qualities of integrity, fairness and moral fitness.

(iv) He should have a pleasant speaking voice.

(v) He should possess a good physical and mental health.

(vi) He should be socially acceptable to his colleagues.

(vii) He should have interest and aptitude in teaching profession. In this respect Mudaliar Commission observed, 'Teachers must develop a new orientation towards their work. They should look upon their work as a great social and intellectual adventure".

(viii) His relationship with his students be polite, submissive and friendly.

(ix) He must have an urge of learning new trends in this subject of Specialisation.

(x) He should be able contrive and use a variety of teaching-learning procedures.

(xi) He should be trained in use of various instructional techniques such as committee of work, question-answer, demonstration, project, discussion etc.

(xii) He should be competent to develop, construct and use a wide variety of teaching aids.

(xiii) He should be able to use variety of methods to evaluate pupils progress and his own growth as teacher.

(xiv) He should be able to function efficiently in the guidance programme of the school.

(xv) He should be able to function well in organisation and supervision of cocurricular activities.

(xvi) He should have a good understanding of the needs of stu-dents in relation to knowledge.

(xvii) He should have a good understanding of current world conditions and problems.

(xviii) He should have a good proficiency of observation and records of behaviours, interest and development of students.

(xix) A good habit of study and research in commerce education.

Interests of Commerce Teacher

A commerce teacher to be successful should have a variety of interest. These may be summarised as under

Community Interests

(i) He must be an active member of parent-teacher association.

(ii) He should be actively interested in community activities.

(iii) He should be interested in student's clubs and other school activities.

Professional Interest

(i) He should have a knowledge of equipments of business and industry.

(ii) He must remain in touch with the latest researches in his filed of interest.

(iii) He should have a personal library of books and magazines of Commerce, Economics and Education.

(iv) He should try to acquire professional growth through higher education in Commerce, Economics and Education.

(v) He should make it a point to participate in summer schools, work-shops, refresher courses and other in-service education programmes organised for commerce teachers.

(vi) He should contribute articles to magazines of Commerce, Education, and Economics.

Training of a Commerce Teacher

In the present educational set up the commerce teacher has to be resourceful and fully equipped with all necessary informations which can help them in training students properly. To equip himself with desirable qualities a commerce teacher is expected to pass through the following phases of training programme.

(I) University education in Commerce subjects.

(II) Office experience or practical business.

(III) Training course Inn Teaching-Commerce subjects.

(IV) In-service training.

(I) University Education in Commerce Subjects

M.Com. degree is a must but it would be desirable if the teacher specialises in any one or two of the commerce subjects. For becoming a teacher in short-hand and type-writing. Certain degree of efficiency must be acquired in these subjects from professional institutes or other institutes teaching and training in the art of teaching the skill. Before appointment of commerce teachers, his specialisation and degree of efficiency, he has acquired, should be taken into consideration. Thus we can say that a person being appointed as commerce teacher should be M.Com., should have office experience or practical business experience or the stenography experience of taking dictation at a high speed,

(II) Office Experience or Practical Business Experience

For becoming a successful teacher it is desirable for the would be teacher, to have some experiences of handling *office* procedures and situations in business. This type of experiences provide him with the confidence that is so essential to become a successful teacher. Actual experience in handling accounts book, labour saving appliances, office practice and correspondence, banking-work, import and export documents, activities concerning sale and purchase of goods etc. will help the commerce teacher to equip himself with the necessary skills and technical know-how of the various commerce programmes. These experiences will provide the commerce teachers with the necessary reliable materials required by the commerce teacher. Only theoretical knowledge is not enough for a commerce teacher to farewell in his profession and in the absence of *office* experience or business experience or vocational skills he is likely to cut sorry figure in his class.

Thus a proper training be organised, for commerce graduate/ post graduate in universities followed by a minimum of six months practical training or actual experience in service in a business firm or an office before the award of degree to them.

(III) Teacher Training Course

After completing his formal education in university the

prospective commerce teacher should be given a course of teachers training. During this course he should be imparted training in various teaching techniques. Educational psychology, History of education etc.

Teachers training in the field of Commerce started in India only in *1963-64* when such a course was offered by four regional colleges of Education. Priór to this the following provisions were made for training of commerce teachers

(i) Training in methods of teaching elements of commerce and bookkeeping in C.I.E., New Delhi, and also in secondary training college Bombay.

(ii) Somė Seminars and courses were organised by Ministry of Education Govt. of India during the period *1958-1960.*

(iii) In some states, short-hand courses were held for training teachers who were already in service.

(IV) In-Service Training

Since the persons, who became commerce teachers prior to *1965,* did not receive any specialised training in commerce methodology they were not familiar with the modem methods of teaching of commerce subjects so it was essential to arrange in-service training courses for such persons. Teachers already in service should acquire some technical know-how of the latest methods of teaching, new educational trends and researches made in the field of commerce. He should try to develop and use some audio-visual aids, film slides etc. and should also try to maintain a profile of papers and documents used in business transactions.

Commerce teachers should try to attend seminars, training courses and work-shops organised by Regional Colleges of Education and other training colleges that have now specialised in commerce pedagogy. They should also try to keep themselves in touch with latest publication on educational philosophy and methodology of teaching and try to keep themselves abreast of latest innovations brought about in the field of education. Commerce teachers should make it a habit to study latest journals, magazines, periodicals etc. concerning commerce subjects and allied subjects. All these will help a commerce teacher to become a successful commerce teacher.

Professional Growth of Commerce Teacher

In addition to teaching, which is the primary duty of a commerce teacher, he has to carry out many other duties in the school. Some of these are as follows:

(i) To maintain discipline in the class.

(ii) To keep in touch with the business community.

(iii) To act as a guide to students and help them in the choice of their subjects.

(iv) To evaluate the students.

(v) To maintain a proper record of the progress of each stu-dent.

(vi) To prepare the lesson-plan.

(vii) To provide guidance and counselling services.

(viii) To prepare written reports.

(ix) To prepare requisition for supplies.

(x) To organise cocurricular activities.

(xi) To take care of the equipment.

For carrying out these duties efficiently it is desirable that working teachers improve upon their knowledge, skill etc. and keep it upto date. It is in this perspective that teachers try their best to enhance their professional abilities. There are many a ways for professional growth, by which they can enrich and enhance their experiences. Some of these are described here

(I) Mastery on the Subject

Without a mastery on his subject a teacher is not likely to command a good respect among students.

(II) Teachers Training

It is quite desirable that only trained teachers be appointed in schools. A course in teachers training makes him a perfect teacher. In a school the teacher has to deal with adolescents and he is expected to apply the psychology of learning. It is desirable that he be well versed in the learning process. Moreover a trained teacher will be able to look after the sociological and philosophical concepts that he is required to deal while dealing with students.

(III) Professional Attitude

A teacher should be sincere to his duties and profession and should possess a professional attitude towards his job. In India we find that most of the teachers including commerce teachers adopt a negative attitude and on most of occasions, they state:

> *"Whatever we had to become, we have become. Now we are not going to become district magistrates. We should work to the extent that entitles us to get the pay."*

Such an attitude is quite derogatory and is not in consonance with the professional ethics. Such an attitude is likely to degenerate the standard of teaching.

The products of such teachers will be de-barred from right type of education. It is thus quite logical for teachers to have a sense of realisation as long as they work as teachers.

(IV) Keeping Abrest of Changes

A teachers occupies an important position in the educational set up. He is a nation builder and to carry out his job in right earnest the teacher has to have an overview of the present and peep into the future. He has to make modifications in the patterns of education. For all these it is essential for a teacher to keep himself abrest of the changes.

(V) Dynamic in Thought and Action

The best teacher is one who tries to equip himself with the latest, know-how and information required in his area of specialisation. A teacher should therefore keep himself engaged in learning new things continuously. In this way he can serve better and do more justice to his profession.

(VI) Store of Knowledge

The teacher should try to become the library of vast stores of knowledge. He should collect various types of books. For promising teaching this is quite important.

(VII) Attending Seminar and Conferences

A good teacher is always on the look out of an opportunity to participate in a seminar or a conference. By participating in such seminars and conferences the teacher broadens his outlook and expands his knowledge.

(VIII) Contribution in Paper and Journals

A good teachers contributes his mite by communicating his ideas in black and white. This is possible if he publishes his papers in journals of repute. In this way he will be helping other to benefit from his ideas.

(IX) Organisation of Exhibitions and Fairs

It is only in exhibitions and fairs that a teacher contributes his best ideas. In this way students community gets the maximum benefit. By participating in these exhibitions and fairs the students get practical experience of most of the things they have understood. Organisation of such exhibitions and fairs helps in enhancing the knowledge and skill of the teacher as also of the students. It is thus desirable to organise such an activity once a year.

(X) Setting up of Association

Teachers generally set up such associations to make their bar-gaining capacity stronger. But the teacher can discuss and solve their difficult problems during meetings of such associations. Such an association can, therefore, easily become a forum for discussions and publications of professional articles. Through this association teachers are likely to enrich their experiences.

(XI) Practice Oriented

No improvement in education is possible until it becomes practice oriented. Both for teachers and students it is essential to maintain a profile of business, trade and industry and school. The syllabus be modified to cater to the business needs and emphasis be laid on such courses in commerce for which ready market exists in different sec-tors of economy.

Research Hobbies of Commerce Teachers

In the sphere of commerce education only a limited research work has been done. There is enough scope and so every innovative idea of teacher should be tried out. However, before any idea may be put to trial the teacher is expected to prepare a design of the idea. Let us illustrate with an example.

If a teacher is interested to standardise an achievement test in elements of commerce, he should adopt the following procedure.

(i) Weightage to Objectives

The teacher should write down various objectives and assign marks to each objective. The marks be assigned to an objective keeping in mind the importance of the objective.

For a test of 75 marks, the marks be allotted as under:

(a) Acquisition of knowledge	40
(b) Development of understanding	30
(c) Application of skills	5
Total	75

(ii) Weightage on Content Areas

For allotment of marks, the syllabus be analysed and the scope of each topic be delimited and then the marks be allotted on the basis of the scope of the area

(iii) Weightage to Forms of Questions

The weightage for various type of question be given, suggested allotment is as under

(a) Objective type questions *20*

(b) Very short answer questions 5

(c) Shrrt answer questions 20

(d) Essay type questions 30

Total 75

(iv) Scheme of Options

The questions should be put in increasing order of difficulty.

(v) Preparation of Blueprint

The Blueprint should include the different types of questions in regard to:

(a) Objective to be tested,

(b) Area to be covered, and

(c) Form of questions to be set.

(vi) Administering the Test on a Sample Population

Various test items finalised may be printed and the test be administered to a sample population.

(vii) Statistical Analysis

The score of the sample test be statistically analysed and on the basis of this analysis some poor items may be eliminated and best items retained. In this way most of the items retained will be those whose score is between 31-70% in sample test.

Another sample test will then be conducted on the basis on these items and the test will be analysed.

Adopting this procedure the teacher will finally be able to standardise the test.

There is an acute necessity in this field and so the teachers should make a hobby to carry out researches in the field of commerce education.

All the above mentioned points are essential for the professional growth of a commerce teacher.

Classroom Climate

Descriptions, definitions, synonyms, organizer terms, types of Classroom climate is defined as the type of environment that is created for students by the school, teachers, and peers. Teachers are continually looking to create a "positive" classroom climate in which student learning is maximized. According to Julie Crotty, author of Seizing the Days: Engaging All Learners website, having an environment where students feel safe, nurtured, and intellectually stimulated is a must for students to learn to their potential. This type of positive classroom climate allows for students to meet their basic needs of physical and mental health described by Glasser, William. While there is no specific definition of what creates a negative classroom climate, it is considered to be one in which students feel uncomfortable, whether physcially, emotionally, or academically, for any reason.

Application in Classrooms and Similar Settings

According to the website Seizing the Days: Engaging All Learners, Glasser believes that "misbehavior of most students results from the failure of teachers and schools to fulfill their needs. He believes that students want to experience success, they want to have feelings of self-worth, and they want to learn? (Crotty, 2002). Before we can expect a child to learn, the physical needs such as food, clothing, shelter, and safety must be met. While some of these needs are beyond a teacher's circle of influence, one can work with guidance counselors, social workers, and community service agencies in identifying those in need beyond the teacher's help. In addition to these physical needs, humans have mental needs that must be met in order for them to be happy, emotionally healthy, successful people. These needs must be met in a way that does not harm anyone else. There are four basic mental needs: love, or the need for belonging, power to be in control of our own lives, fun, and freedom. Freedom in terms of the classroom is giving students the chance to make choices about assignments and other lesson planning as well as to help make decisions about the classroom (Crotty, 2002).

Thus, by working to fulfill these needs, the teacher is applying the idea of a positive classroom climate because it is helping the students met their full learning potential. To leave any need unmet would be making the classroom experience a negative one for students. When interacting with students it is important to recognize individual differences, learn names, arrange the seating where all students are angled to receive instruction, establish expectations immediately, make yourself (as the teacher) available to your student and encourage students positively to achieve.

It has been seen that meeting the needs of students creates a positive climate for learning, but, according to Linda Starr of Education World (2004), effective classroom management is necessary as well. Howard Miller, Associate Professor of Education at Lincoln University, has established 12 steps for the beginning of the year to help teachers promote effective classroom management. These are as follows (taken from Creating a Climate for Learning: Effective Classroom Management Techniques):

1. Develop a set of written expectations you can live with and enforce.
2. Be consistent. Be consistent. Be consistent.
3. Be patient with yourself and with your students.
4. Make parents your allies. Call early and often. Use the word "concerned." When communicating a concern, be specific and descriptive.
5. Don't talk too much. Use the first 15 minutes of class for lectures or presentations, then get the kids working.
6. Break the class period into two or three different activities. Be sure each activity segues smoothly into the next.
7. Begin at the very beginning of each class period and end at the very end.
8. Don't roll call. Take the roll with your seating chart while students are working.
9. Keep all students actively involved. For example, while a student does a presentation, involve the other students in evaluating it.

10. Discipline individual students quietly and privately. Never engage in a disciplinary conversation across the room.
11. Keep your sense of perspective and your sense of humor.
12. Know when to ask for help.

Using all of these tips helps the teacher set clear guidelines for the student so that there is no confusion or uncertainty from the students. As the former U.S. Department of Education teacher-in-residence, Mary Beth Blegan, said, "Setting the classroom environment is key. For a new teacher that means pretending that you know what you're doing" (Starr, 2004). Unecessary and constant confusion from unclear expectations can cause students to be uncomfortable in the classroom which leads to a depleted climate. Besides the classroom management techniques, inner-city high school teacher Robert Bencker gives several tips of daily interactions that help create a positive learning environment. He recommends starting the day by greeting each student personally, which then sets the tone for the day as well as establishes rapport. He also reccomends dealing with all the minor problems before they can escalate into big ones (Starr, 2004).

It is also suggested that to continue to maintain control without confrontation, use other techniques such as: establishing eye contact, moving around the room to be nearer to restless students, have a silent signal and give a quiet reminder, know ways to re-direct a student's attention, begin a new activity when the other one is out of control, offer students a choice, be prepared to use humor to diffuse situations, provide positive reinforcement, wait quietly until everyone is on task, make use of directed questions, and understanf that when all else fails, try something else! (Starr, 2004).

Another way to apply the ideals of a positive classroom climate, according to the Indiana University Center for Adolescent Studies, is to create a peaceful classroom. The center promotes seven guidelines:

1) have a genuine interest in your students;

2) communicate classroom rules clearly;
3) be objective, not judgmental;
4) show that you are human;
5) minimize the power differential in everyday communication;
6) address problem behaviour directly and immediately; and
7) adopt a collaborative approach (Hawley, 1997).

A suggested way to combine all of these ideas and start a positive classroom climate from day one is to use Icebreakers. These are a good way to get students emotionally started for the school year with a positive attitude. The students need to buy what you as a teacher say about the classroom climate being important and very valuable for both their personal school experience as well as their learning experience. Name games are very good Icebreakers as students want to know each other, they want to know you as a teacher, and, of course, you want to know your students as quickly as possible too. It is also easier to remember the names because with each name you can associate now a personal story, a hobby or favorite movie etc.. Finally it sets the basis for future group activities. Students should productively interact with each other and with the teacher and for this interactive classroom climate, it is important to know and trust each other. This should be the message given to your students from your icebreaker used in the first day of class.

Due to differing teaching styles and personalities of teachers, the way the positive classroom climate is implemented will change. Some teachers may see the open forum between teachers and students approach as disrespectful to the teacher, and so they would prefer the peaceful classroom approach. Also, the students will vary in what will make them feel comfortable within the classroom and so their needs will require being met in different ways. As long as all needs of all students are met the classroom climate will be positive, but the way in which all these needs will be met will need to be changed to address the wide variety of student and teacher personalities.

Tips for Managing the Classroom Environment:

1. Start class on time, sending a message that being there is important. If a student arrives late several days in a row, say something before it becomes a habit. If it does become a habit, take further action.
2. End class on time. If you begin letting students out early, they will begin routinely packing up their backpacks before class is over; if you go over time on a regular basis your students will become resentful.
3. Announce your office hours and keep them faithfully. Being accessible can prevent many problems. If students know you are there for them they may be more willing to come to class and participate because they know help is available.
4. Set policies at the beginning of the course. In particular, make sure attendance and grading policies are clear, preferably in writing. Don't stray from these policies or students may see you as a pushover.
5. Be conscious of signs of racial or sexual harassment, whether by you, towards you, or towards other members of the class. Make it clear by your words and actions that put-downs or derogatory comments about any groups for whatever reason are simply not acceptable.
6. Refer students with psychological, emotional, academic, or financial trouble to the appropriate counselors. You can be sympathetic and supportive, but becoming a student's counselor can cause problems.
7. When acting as a teaching assistant, involve yourself only to the extent that you are expected to be involved. If the professor you are assisting is in charge of determining grades and you receive complaints about grades, have the students deal with the professor. Do not foster a "me against you" attitude, and do not side with the students against the professor.

These tips are adapted from those provided by the Center for Teaching Effectiveness at Pennsylvania State University.

Laissez Faire Pattern and Democratically Planned Pattern Significance

Targeting the Field of Analysis

Informal, shadow, underground, black, parallel and hidden are only some of the terms used to refer to economic activities conducted without full respect for the law and whose outputs may be either legal or illegal. Given this stressed heterogeneity which often leads to misunderstandings and overlaps, it may be of use to start by briefly pointing out what lies behind these whimsical names.

According to vast literature, the unofficial economy basically encompasses four branches distinct from one another: household, informal, irregular and illegal (Thomas 1992). In the first, all outputs are produced and consumed within the domestic walls so that this economy relies on self-production in which no monetary transaction is undertaken. Two examples of this are a peasant working the land to nourish his family and a woman sewing to clothe her children.

The informal economy differs from that of the household economy in having consumption occur outdoors rather than indoors. The assets offered into the market may be either finished or intermediate: the former case can be exemplified by a homemade-bread street-seller, the second by a home-seamstress making hand decorations as an intermediate phase of a dress manufacturing.

The irregular economy externalizes both manufacturing and consumption. The most common definition outlines this sector as the one where final goods and services are legal whereas ways of producing them are not. This is the first type of the unofficial economy that garners examples coming from developed countries also. Tax evasion, lack of official work contracts, and emission of noxious fumes close to human settlements are just some of them.

While in the previous branch the final output was legal, in the illegal economy this is outlawed. According to the specific country under consideration and the relative laws in force, examples may include drug traffic, prostitution, smuggling, and gambling.

Given the breadth of the topic, one needs to approach it by narrowing his/her field of analysis. Accordingly, I will be dealing with only the irregular economy. Still, even the "only" irregular economy can be tackled from several standpoints. There are scholars who have studied the historical origins of the phenomenon (De Soto 2000, Capecchi 1989), highlighted the role played by strong, albeit informal, institutions (Assaad 1993), explained the structure of irregularity (Contini 1982), detected the causes underlying its growth (Del Boca and Forte 1989), worked the specific burdens of these out (Schneider 2000, Cebula 1997), and investigated the conditions experienced by people involved (Cortese 1996; Fortuna and Prates 1989). These multifold views are essentially due to the wide range of social scientists interested in the subject. Economists, sociologists, social psychologists, and anthropologists may all study different aspects of this same topic.

Here, I shall seek to examine a relation that has often been oversimplified in this wide literature. That is the role that the state can play, wittingly or not, in helping the irregular economy grow.

Most scholars have overlooked this aspect, claiming a universal attitude of state laissez-faire toward the "flip-side" of economy.

From this perspective, informal and irregular economic activities would be seen favorably by both third and first world governments: for the former, they would act as a sort of "urban growth safety valve" (Thomas 1992) enabling people of favelas and bidonvilles to survive without voicing their own miserable condition; for the latter, they would allow the real unemployment rate to decrease, making the working class meeker (because of lesser rights and the presence of an income, however small) and the entrepreneurial class freer in its action. The final result would be an economy released of many legal constraints running more smoothly. In both cases the state is considered a neutral observer that does not interfere with the irregular economy. Although this assumption is sometimes correct, I argue the story may be different since the state also controls the means that can affect the expansion of this phenomenon. To advocate this statement, I will resort to two Italian local histories (Reggio Emilia and Siracusa) that demonstrate how both laissez-faire and a strong state intervention can bring about the emergence of irregularities in labour settings. Most importantly, I will be showing how the final outcome in terms of local development in the two cases is completely different.

Reggio's Industrial Downturn and the Emergence of a District Economy

Reggio Emilia and Siracusa do not share a great deal from economic, historic, and cultural standpoints. At first glance, the only seemingly characteristic in common is their size (roughly 140,000 inhabitants in each town and 400,000 in each province). Public opinion and academics often look up to Reggio as a paragon for local governance in Italy and most socioeconomic indicators supply grounds for this argument by displaying Reggio's province on the top. For instance, it boasts the best public kindergarten and has one of the national highest per-capita incomes.

On the contrary, if we were to find Siracusa in these classifications, it would be better for us to start from the bottom. Located in south-east Sicily, Siracusa is Italy's most southern province and one of the most economically depressed. Among the bleakest indicators, it has the lowest amount of bank-deposits and one of the highest youth unemployment rates.

Nonetheless, making a parallelism between the last half-century histories of these two provinces may turn out to be of interest, as it enables us to see how two similar industrial downturns have sparked opposite processes of economic development in spite of both being based on the expansion of the irregular economy.

The first town struck by economic hardships because of a factory's downsizing was Reggio: in the wake of the Italian defeat in World War II the state-owned Reggiane had to close the munitions department and to cut back on staffing by 12,000 units (Ovi 2001). Not only technical factors but also political considerations underlay the withdrawal of the state from Reggio's economy. The Emilian town vaunted a longstanding tradition of peasant cooperation based on socialist and anarchist ideals that had promptly revealed themselves in the first general polls and that were in manifest conflict with the conservative bent of the first republican right-wing governments.

However, the most important aspect for us involves the characteristics of the national welfare state in the late 1940s. At the time, the sole income protection for industrial laborers who went through a temporary reduction of working hours (i.e. labour hoarding) or a temporary layoff was Cassa Integrazione Guadagni (i.e. CIG). This was a wage guarantee fund which helped workers made redundant for events out of the employer's control by granting them two/thirds of the hourly wage for every working hour lost, within a maximum term of three months (Tronti 1993). No allowance was provided otherwise for workers definitely dismissed.

It ensues that Reggiane's employees were not sheltered by this income protection. Consequently, for those who did not decide to emigrate abroad, there was often "only one way out, which was to start their own entrepreneurial activity" (Capecchi 1989) and eventually hire some of their old companions. An industrial organization thereafter known by the term of "district" was on the brink of emerging.

Following Viesti (2000), we may hypothesize this sequence of events in Reggio. The presence of fairly mature markets and relatively developed infrastructures helped the rise of small and medium enterprises (SMEs) whose origin dated back to the "entrepreneurial spirit" rooted in ancient traditions of independent work in both agriculture and handicraft (Trigilia 1986). At the same time, the absence of large factories and the shortage of public employment reduced workers' expectations so that labour cost could be more easily restrained, especially in comparison with that of other northern regions like those of the "industrial triangle" (i.e. Milan, Turin, and Genoa). Additionally, a high rate of informality and irregularity contributed to the competitiveness of the region by making input costs lower and production of outputs faster.

In particular, situations of both complicity and exploitation were equally common. Home-workers integrating the family breadwinner's income and moonlighters adding concealed earnings to the official ones were examples of complicity, while lowskill workers obliged by their employers to register as artisans so as to shun social contributions illustrated exploitation (Brusco 1982). Hence, flexibility and informality in, to use a contemporary term, "human resource management" definitely played a major role since they made it possible high proceeds usually reinvested in technologically advanced machinery. In so doing, Reggio's SMEs progressively moved from price-based to process-based competitiveness.

The high degree of irregularity was also facilitated by the laissez-faire-prone attitude of the state, which was certainly underes-timating the real size of the phenomenon, but also acknowledging the fact that this part of the country was making the name of Italy renowned all over the world (thanks to the label of "made in Italy") and guaranteeing large revenues despite partial fiscal evasion (Cortellese 1988). For example, two reggiane world famous firms Max Mara (fashion garments) and Fantuzzi (machine tools) started from scratch in the 1950s. The former was founded by an artisan tailor whose son is nowadays one of the richest businessmen in Italy, while the latter by a young man who, due to his poor family's conditions, had to leave school early (Ovi 2001). These firms are today two of the Italian foremost exporters and, as we will see, one of them also holds powerful financial ties.

Companies like the aforementioned were important to the whole surrounding area for several reasons, three of which are worth mentioning. First, they helped the region develop further by relocating intermediate phases of production to smaller enterprises. Second, they nurtured processes of spillover and spin-off as they upsized.Third, they bolstered the local "entrepreneurial spirit" by acting as role models for other novel businessmen. Last but not least, local institutions sharing a common sub-culture (Trigilia 1986) sympathized with this small-scale industry because they were aware that, on account of political reasons, national governments would barely support, at least directly, their local economies.

Hence, they cooperated with each other, establishing horizontal and egalitarian relationships which helped them refrain from a conflict-oriented approach in problem-solving so as to successfully pursue the interest of the overall community (Locke 1995). The achievement of this goal was also eased by a political demand which, especially at the beginning, was influenced by societal rather than individual interests (Trigilia 1992).

The final outcome of this puzzling process was a system of production rested on the key-concepts of "horizontal integration" and "flexible specialization" (Brusco 1982, Capecchi 1989, et al.). Here, only few firms gain direct access to the final market, while most of them specialize in manufacturing a single component which is subsequently sold to the firms placed in the following stage of production. A simultaneous condition of cooperation and competition is, thus, unavoidable. The former involves the firms located in different steps of the "manufacturing ladder," while the latter with the enterprises on the same stage of production. Altogether the reggiano case shows us that high level of irregularity and informality may be provoked by the state's absence in the wake of industrial distress and that this situation can even spawn dynamics of economic growth. Yet before we draw general conclusions from this example we need to verify what has happened in Siracusa in a similar situation throughout the 1970s and 1980s. To better accomplish this parallelism we shall start from the post-war period as done with Reggio to subsequently pass to the decisive span of the industrial downturns.

UNIT-VII

Instructional Materials

Text-book

Text-book and an important and most widely used teaching aid. According to Dr. D.S. Kothari, "The question of textbooks is the most important and urgent one for our country. Energetic on State and National basis is required to progress the preparation of high quality school textbooks".

Importance of Textbook

"Few tools have been so misused as textbooks in teaching." It will be no exaggeration to say that textbooks have become ends in education. The teacher follows them blindly. They are read out loudly, para by para in class by each of the pupils in turn; brief explanations and comments are given by teachers, and all the matter covered is to be memorised by the pupils in the class as well as at home.

Teacher may use any of the methods of teaching he feels a necessity of textbooks. The work of the teacher does not end in the classroom he has to see that the pupil can readily apply the knowledge gained by him in the classroom.

For this it is desirable to provide the student with a record of class-work and also some questions for practice. This record can be had, by the pupil, by taking notes in the class, but these lengthy dictation and notes may prove to be most-time consuming. A good textbook saves the times of the teacher as well as of the taught.

A textbook is probably the cheapest and most reliable source of information. It also serves as a reference book for the teacher.

A textbook is a concise source of material for reviews. It helps the students to acquire the required information with speed. While revising his lessons a pupils can work independently making use of textbooks at his disposal.

A textbook helps this students in thoroughly understanding the subject matter. It also helps the students to make up his deficiency because of his failure to attend certain classes due to unavoidable reasons.

A teacher can make use of the textbook to give homework and assignments to the pupils.

The textbook specifies the standards expected to be attained by a particular class. It also gives suggestion about the use of various teaching aids and activities to be undertaken. A textbook also helps the teachers in teaching and correlating the subject with other things.

It lays down the order of procedure.

In lower classes textbooks with coloured illustrations provide an incentive to learning and they provide attraction for the young learner.

That is why a textbook for every child has become an essential equipment.

How to Use a Textbook?

A textbook is valuable only if it is used properly. The teacher should not consider that his work the textbook into the heads is confined to transferring the contents of the pupils. The textbook should not be used as the only source of instructional material. It should be used as an aid in teaching not a substitute for teaching. It is a means and not an end in itself. Its place in teaching can only then be real if the teacher supplements it by his oral exposition, by reference reading and by all his illustrating and objective techniques. It should be followed carefully and intelligently aid not slavishly. For an average teacher the textbook is all his stock-in-trade. The greater the capacity, knowledge, professional training and experience of the teacher, the less he needs to depend on his textbooks, However, no teacher can afford to work entirely without a textbook. It is not a master to be feared, it is rather a servant to be ordered.

The contribution of the textbook can be increased by creating situations where the pupils have a real purpose for turning to the text-book. Assignment Method, Dalton Plan and Project work provide a larger scope for creating such situations.

Essentials of Good Textbook

According to Hall Quest "A good textbook" is

(i) a source of knowledge,

(ii) a guide,

(iii) a tool,

(iv) a means of interpreting truth, and

(v) an inspiration to the pupil.

At present there is a great need of good textbooks in all the regional languages. But books are generally of low standard, excepting very few, due to apathetic attitude of authors, tendency to prefer quantity to quality, partiality in evaluating the textbooks and so on.

Criterion of Good Text-Book

1. *Author:* The author should have a considerable experience of teaching the subject. The minimum academic and professional qualifications may also be prescribed for the author.
2. *The Language and Structure:* The textbook should be written in lucid, simple, precise and scientific language which is within the approach of an average stu-dents. Diagrams will add to the value of the book.
3. *The Subject-Matter:* A good textbook in home-science should deal with the subject matter in a systematic and orderly manner in psychological sequence. The standard should be gradually increased. The matter should create

interest in the pupils and the variety of topic should correspond to the variety of interests which the pupils are expected to have.

The presentation of matter should be more psychological than logical.

4. *Exercises:* A good textbook not only teaches, it also tests. For consolidation of learning, there should be new thought-provoking exercises followed by good summary. There should be problems graded in difficulty at the end of each chapter. In addition to this in a good text-book there should be a good index.

   The exercises should not be merely of recaptulatory nature rather they should be such as to help to develop further concepts, desirable attitudes, technical skill and creative power. The exercises should offer further experience in developing the pupils power of thinking and reasoning.

5. *Illustration:* The pictures in a good textbook should be well drawn, realistic and coloured wherever necessary so that they make the learning very much convenient and quick. The pictures as far as possible should be proportionate in size, otherwise the information about them contained in the book is very likely to be misinterpreted.

   Some times, too many details are stuffed into a small space with the result that no detail is clear to the young mind. The effort to save space results in loss of utility on the whole. Illustrations should be attractive and useful because they play a vital roll in raising the standard of a textbook. Therefore it is correct to say, " One picture is worth a thousand words". For very young pupil they should be coloured and not in black and white.

6. *Technical Considerations:* For the physical appearance and set up of a good textbook due consideration be given to the following points.

   (i) It should be printed on a good white paper.

(ii) The type used should be in accordance with the reading ability of the pupils, headings and sub-headings should be in still bolder types. The type-faces should be appropriate.

(iii) The building should be proper and strong to withstand rough use. It should not make the book-difficult to open. The cover page should be well designed and attractive.

(iv) There should be no mistake in printing.

(v) The size of the textbook should be handy for the children for whom it is meant.

(vi) The price should be reasonable which the majority of learners can easily afford to pay.

In addition to the above the following qualities are expected in a good textbook.

(i) It should be up-to-date in its subject-matter.

(ii) The symbols and terms used must be those which are popular. All new terms should be clearly and accurately de-fined.

(iii) There should be suggestion to improve study habits.

(iv) It should offer detailed suggestions for correlation, project work, assignment work and field work.

(v) There should not be any irrelevant matter.

(vi) It should facilitate the use of inductive, analytical heuristic and laboratory methods.

(vii) It should satisfy the demands of the examinations.

(viii) It should conform to the recommendations of various committees.

Criteria of a Good Textbook as Prescribed by the UNESCO Planning Mission

(i) It should first of all meet the requirements of the syllabus.

(ii) The facts, concepts etc. should be modern and within the comprehension of the pupils.

(iii) It should help in linking up the subject with the fife practice. The pupils should be equipped with the "know how" of utilising the knowledge in everyday life.

(iv) The contents should contain only the established facts aiming at shaping integrated modern world out look. The con-should be simple, brief, exact, definite and accessible.

Textbook for Commerce Subjects

In contrast to arts subjects, commerce subjects are of practical utility. For these subjects we need very good textbooks to serve to the needs of the teachers and the students. In commerce subjects we find a death of highly specialised and authoritative textbooks. Because of these facts it becomes quite difficult to make a proper selection of a textbook in commerce subjects.

The following points may be kept in view while selecting a text-book in commerce subjects.

(i) *Attractiveness of Book :* It should be attractive.

(ii) *Name of the Book :* Its name should not be too technical and frightening. It should be such which is appealing, arouses interest of the students and indicates the nature of the subject matter.

(iii) *Author :* He should be an authority on the subject and must also be conversant with the methods of teaching of commerce subjects.

(iv) *Date of Publication or Revision :* The book should be a recent publication and the year of publication must be mentioned on the textbook. In some subjects (e.g. Income Tax) old textbooks may be out of date.

(v) *Language :* It should be simple, flowing, easy, grammatically correct.

(vi) *Nature of content :* The textbook should include all the topics of the subject.

(vii) *Teaching Procedures Followed :* It should include variety of teaching procedures of business subjects.

(viii) *Kind of Questions and Number of Questions :* It should have question based on information, rules, principles, definitions and other data. The questions should be thought provoking and should deal with what, why and how? Some questions on application of rules etc. must be included. Such questions are of more importance in subjects such as Bookkeeping, Arithmetic, Shorthand etc.

(ix) *Illustrations :* in a good textbook there should be sufficient illustrations such as pictures of peoples, things and places etc. The illustrations should be of reasonable size and should be related to textbook material. It is desirable that illustrations appear on the same side of the page, where principles have been discussed. They should have outlay captions and must be up-to-date.

Periodical and Journals

A periodical publication, or just periodical, is a published work that appears in a new edition on a regular schedule. The most familiar examples are the newspaper, often published daily, or weekly; or the magazine, typically published weekly, monthly or as a quarterly. Other examples would be a newsletter, a literary journal or learned journal, or a yearbook.

These examples all are related to the idea of an indefinitely continuing cycle of production and publication: newspapers plan to continue publishing, not to stop after a predetermined number of editions. A novel, in contrast, might be published in monthly parts, a method revived after the success of *The Pickwick Papers* by Charles Dickens. This approach is called part-publication, particularly when each part is from a whole work, or a serial, for example in comic books or *manga*. It flourished in the middle of the nineteenth century, for example with Abraham John Valpy's *Delphin Classics*, and was not restricted to fiction.

The International Standard Serial Number (ISSN) is to periodical publications what the ISBN is to books: a standardized reference number.

Newspapers

A newspaper is a publication containing news, information, and advertising. General-interest newspapers often feature articles on political events, crime, business, art/entertainment, society and sports. Most traditional papers also feature an editorial page containing columns that express the personal opinions of writers. Supplementary sections may contain advertising, comics, and coupons.

Newspapers are most often published on a daily or weekly basis, and they usually focus on one particular geographic area where most of their readers live. Despite recent setbacks in circulation and profits, newspapers are still the most iconic outlet for news and other types of written journalism.

Features a newspaper may include are:

- Editorial opinions and op-eds
- Comic strips and other entertainment, such as crosswords, sudoku and horoscopes
- Weather news and forecasts
- Advice, gossip, food and other columns
- Critical reviews of movies, plays, restaurants, etc.
- Classified ads

History

Before Movable Type: In Ancient Rome, *Acta Diurna*, or government announcement bulletins, were made public by Julius Caesar. They were carved on stone or metal and posted in public places.

In China, early government-produced news sheets, called tipao, circulated among court officials during the late Han dynasty (second and third centuries AD). Between 713 and 734, the *Kaiyuan Za Bao* ("Bulletin of the Court") of the Chinese Tang Dynasty published government news; it was handwritten on silk and read by government officials. In 1582 there was the first reference to privately published newssheets in Beijing, during the late Ming Dynasty;

In 1556, the government of Venice first published the monthly *Notizie scritte*, which cost one gazetta. These avvisi were handwritten newsletters used to convey political, military, and economic news quickly and efficiently throughout Europe, and more specifically Italy, during the early modern era (1500-1700CE) — sharing some characteristics of newspapers though usually not considered as fully being ones.

Modern Era

Newspapers printed with movable type date to the beginning of the 17th century.

Asia

By 1638 the *Peking Gazette* had switched from woodblock print to movable type.

Europe

Johann Carolus' *Relation aller Fürnemmen und gedenckwürdigen Historien*, published in 1605 in Strassburg, is often recognized as the first newspaper. Strassburg was a free imperial city at that time in Germany; the first newspaper of today's Germany was the *Avisa*, published in 1609 in Augsburg.

The Dutch *Courante uyt Italien, Duytslandt, &c.* of 1618 was the first to appear in folio-rather than quarto-size. Amsterdam, a center of world trade, quickly became home to newspapers in many languages, often before they were published in their own country.

The first English-language newspaper, *Corrant out of Italy, Germany, etc.*, was published in Amsterdam in 1620. A year and a half later, *Corante, or weekely newes from Italy, Germany, Hungary, Poland, Bohemia, France and the Low Countreys.* was published in England by an "N.B." (generally thought to be either Nathaniel Butter or Nicholas Bourne) and Thomas Archer.

The first newspaper in France was published in 1631, *La Gazette* (originally published as *Gazette de France*).

Post-och Inrikes Tidningar (founded as *Ordinari Post Tijdender*) was first published in Sweden in 1645, and is the oldest newspaper still in existence, though it now publishes solely online.

Opregte Haarlemsche Courant from Haarlem, first published in 1656, is the oldest paper still printed. It was forced to merge with the newspaper *Haarlems Dagblad* in 1942 when Germany occupied the Netherlands. Since then the Haarlems Dagblad appears with the subtitle *Oprechte Haerlemse Courant 1656* and considers itself to be the oldest newspaper still publishing.

The first successful English daily, *The Daily Courant*, was published from 1702 to 1735.

North America

In Boston in 1690, Benjamin Harris published *Publick Occurrences Both Forreign and Domestick*. This is considered the first newspaper in the American colonies even though only one edition was published before the paper was suppressed by the government.

In 1704, the governor allowed *The Boston News-Letter* to be published and it became the first continuously published newspaper in the colonies. Soon after, weekly papers began publishing in New York and Philadelphia.

These early newspapers followed the British format and were usually four pages long. They mostly carried news from Britain and content depended on the editor's interests. In 1783, the *Pennsylvania Evening Post* became the first American daily.

In 1751, John Bushell published the *Halifax Gazette*, the first Canadian newspaper.

Industrial Revolution

By the early 19th century, many cities in Europe, as well as North and South America, published newspaper-type publications though not all of them developed in the same way; content was vastly shaped by regional and cultural preferences.

Advances in printing technology related to the Industrial Revolution enabled newspapers to become an even more widely circulated means of communication. In 1814, *The Times* (London) acquired a printing press capable of making 1,100 impressions per minute.

Soon, it was adapted to print on both sides of a page at once. This innovation made newspapers cheaper and thus available to a larger part of the population. In 1830, the first penny press newspaper came to the market: Lynde M. Walter's Boston *Transcript*. Penny press papers cost about one sixth the price of other newspapers and appealed to a wider audience.

UNIT-VIII

Community Resources

Micro-teaching is a new kind of approach and strategy in teaching In it a small group of 4-5 students are taught and the unit to be taught is very small, say of 5-6 minutes duration. It is a laboratory technique of teacher training in which the complexities of normal classroom teaching are simplified.

The term micro-teaching was first coined by A. W. Dwight Allen of the Stanford University in 1963.

Various Educationists have defined the micro-teaching in different ways. Some of these are as follows:

"Micro-teaching is a system of controlled practice that makes it possible to concentrate on specific teaching behaviour and to practice teaching under controlled conditions." —D. W. Allen and A.W. Eve

"Micro-teaching is scaled down teaching encounter in a class size and class true." —Dr. Allevn D. W.

"A teacher education technique which allows to apply clearly defined teaching skills to carefully prepared lessons in a planned series of five to ten minutes encounter with small group of real students often with an opportunity to observe the same video-tape." —Dr. Bush R N.

"Micro-teaching is most often applied to use of closed circuit television to give immediate feed back of trainee teacher's performance in a simplified environment. Micro-teaching is best viewed as a form of simulated teaching, usually incorporating reduced complexity and

some feedback placed along a simulation spectrum ranging from the purely abstract textbook of teaching practice through to actual classroom teaching." —Mc Alesse and Unwin

"The term micro-teaching is most often applied to the use of close circuit television to give immediate feed back of a trainee teacher's performance in a simplified environment." —Mc Allesse and Unwin

"Micro-teaching is a `scaled down teaching encounter' in which a teacher teaches small unit to a group of 5 pupils for a small period of 5-20 minutes. Such a situation offers a helpful setting for an experienced or inexperienced teacher to acquire new teaching skill and to refine old ones." —L. C. Singh

"Micro-teaching is a training technique which requires student teachers to teach a single concept using specified teaching skill to a small number of pupils in a short duration of tune." —B.K. Passi and M.S. Lalita

"Micro-teaching is a training setting for the student teacher where complexities of the normal classroom teaching are reduced by:

(i) One component skill at a tune,

(ii) Limiting the content to a single concept,

(iii) Reducing the size to 5-10 pupils, and

(iv) Reducing the duration of lesson to 5-10 minutes. —N. K. Jangira and Ajit Singh

"Micro-teaching is teaching training procedure which reduces the teaching situation to a simpler and more controlled encounter achieved by limiting the practice teaching to a specific skill and reducing teaching time and class size." —Clift and Others

Propositions of Micro-teaching

In micro-teaching the lesson is scaled down in length of class time as also in terms of teaching tasks which include the practicing and mastering of a specific teaching skill such as lecturing, questioning, discussion etc., or teaching strategies such as flexibility, discussion making etc. Micro-teaching helps in both how to teach and what to teach. Allen and Ryan has given the following main propositions of micro-teaching,

1. Micro-teaching is real teaching, although a teaching situation is constructed in which the student-teacher and pupil's work together in a practice situation. Bonafide teaching does take place.
2. Micro-teaching lessens the complexities of normal classroom teaching class size, scope of content and time are all reduced.
3. Micro-teaching focusses on training for the accomplishment of specific tasks. These tasks may be the practice of instructional skills, the practice of techniques of teaching, the mastery of certain curricular material or the demonstration of teaching methods.
4. Micro-teaching allows for the increased control of practice. In a micro-teaching setting, the time number of pupils, methods of feedback and supervision etc. may be manipulated.
5. Micro-teaching greatly expands the normal knowledge of results of feedback dimensions in teaching. Immediately after teaching a brief micro-lesson, the trainee is engaged in a critique of his performance. All this feedback can be immediately translated into practice when the trainee reteaches shortly after the critique conference.

The related areas can be pointed out where there are clear advantage-(i) training in teaching skill, (ii) research in teachertraining.

Important Features of Micro-teaching

Important features of micro-teaching are as follows:

1. *Micro-Element:* It is based on the supposition an$_d$ before one attempts to understand, learn and perform effectively the complicated task of teaching, one should first master the components of that task.

2. *Technical Skills of Teaching and Teaching Strategies:* A repertoire of teaching skills like lecturing, questioning or leading a 'discussion and mastery of teaching strategies is another important feature of micro-teaching,
3. *The Feed-Back Element* : It is another important element of micro-teaching. At present, "feed back" in the students teachers is ordinarily based m supervisor's recall and selective note-taking. The evaluation of student teacher's performance is based on overall impressions. In it subjective factors affect the evaluation and in the absence of objective criteria the student teacher may overtly or covertly oppose supervisor's evaluations and suggestions.

   Following are some of the important sources of feedback in the micro-teaching laboratory

   (a) Oral feedback of the laboratory supervisor.
   (b) Questionnaires filled in by the pupils learning in the microlesson.
   (c) Audio-tape recordings.
   (d) Video-tape recordings.
4. Safe Practice Grounds.
5. *The Teaching Models* : There are many styles of good teaching and trainees will develop their own individual styles using these models as guide.
6. *The Research Laboratory* : According to Allen and Ryan, the following areas of research appear to make the most effective use of micro-teaching setting

   (a) in-house studies designed to optimise the procedures and sequences in micro-teaching situations.
   (b) research in modelling and supervising techniques.
   (c) task-analysis of the teaching act and the investigation of the relationships between teaching behaviour and student performances.
   (d) Aptitude treatment interaction studies to try to provide optimal training procedures for teachers with different abilities, interests and backgrounds.

Merits and Limitations of Micro-teaching

Merits of Micro-teaching:

1. It is a useful innovation in teacher education.
2. It develops greater awareness of individual differences.
3. It helps the teacher traince of many problems such as indiscipline and anxiety.
4. It helps the teacher to prepare in better way.
5. It helps to reduce strain on practicing school.
6. It is quite suitable for refresher courses.
7. It is quite helpful in faster motivation of the students.
8. It is concerned more with self-improvement and self-evaluation.
9. It helps in creating more interest and enthusiasm towards teaching.
10. It helps to develop greater understanding of teaching.
11. It generates self-confidence.
12. It helps to develop a healthier attitude towards criticism.
13. It makes teaching more enjoyable.
14. It creates greater awareness of verbal and non-verbal communication.
15. It helps in proper planning of lessons.
16. It is quite useful in teaching the same unit again.

Limitations of Micro-teaching:

1. It fails of provide necessary training to teacher to teach in a normal classroom.
2. Limited number of students fail to arouse interest in teaching.
3. It is only of a limited application.
4. They require more time for planning
5. Some-times it becomes difficult for the teacher to divide a bigger unit into smaller units.
6. Many times it creates administrative difficulties.

7. It hampers the classroom climate.
8. It is-an artificial situation.
9. It requires the supervisors to be more critical.
10. It requires insightful supervisors.

Micro-teaching in India

Micro-teaching is an innovation in teaching education. By adopting it is a systematic and meaningful way, it is possible to bring about a revolution in teacher education in India. This technique is quite useful both at pre-level as well as at in-service teacher education programmes. By adopting this technique a wide range of experiences could be provided with economy in time and resources. It can be altered to suit many circumstances.

This techniques was adopted in 1967 at Government central Pedagogical Institute at Allahabad. G. B. Shah tried it in 1970 at the Faculty of Education and Psychology Baroda. Later on it was adopted at many places such as at Technical Teachers Training Institute, Madras; Technical Teachers Training Institute, Chandigarh; Technical Teachers Training Institute, Calcutta etc.

To integrate micro-teaching into the 'student teaching' programme following procedure is used

(i) *Lectures* on theory connected with 'student teaching are given.

(ii) *Demonstration Lessons* are given to student-teachers.

(iii) *Diagnostic Lessons* are evaluated to find the areas in which the teacher traince is deficient and then remedial measures are undertaken.

(iv) *Micro-lesson for practice* are arranged for training teachers is 'student teaching'.

Stimulated Teaching

Simulation may be defined as a role playing in which the process of teaching is enacted artificially and an effort is made to practice some important skill of communication through this. Under this, the student teacher and the students simulate a particular role and try to develop an identity with the actual classroom environment. Thus stimulated teaching stands for imitation of role playing in which such a skill is used that the students are compelled to be curious. Simulation is the basis of sensitivity training, socio-drama, role playing and psychodrama. It is, therefore, a dramatic technique of teaching

It is based on the assumption that certain underlying skill to teaching can be modified, described and practiced like any other skill. It is further presumed that through role perception the psychological appreciation of the classroom problems will grow and develop in the student teacher a basis for handling the problems in the class.

Use of Simulation

In the words to stone, "Simulation techniques for all their artificiality can often be preferable to putting students in the classroom to learn on their own or to lecturing to them about the classroom.

In other spheres pilots trained in the `artificial' circumstances of the link trainer, driving schools have their traffic simulators and medical students their cadavers. And this is eminently sensible. By the same token, classroom simulation removes the risk from the first steps of a neophyte and enables him to come to terms with the demands of a complex skill learning without the stress of the real situation. At the same time it. is to be preferred to merely `telling' the students, for much the same reasons as it is better to allow the beginning pilot to practice operating the dummy controls rather than telling him to do it when he find himself in air".

Steps in Simulation

Following steps have been recommended by Flounders:

1. Letters A, B, C, D, etc., are assigned to each person in the group and role assignments are rotated by letters so that each individual has a chance to be an actor or observer.

2. The skills to be practiced are discussed and topics of conversation that fits the skill are suggested.
3. Consideration as to who will initiate the conversation, who will intervene, who will stop the interaction and when it will be stopped are decided.
4. First practice session is conducted and the actor is provided with feed back on his performance. If found essential, the procedure of the second session is altered so as to improve the training procedure.
5. If any need arises, one should be ready to change the procedure and the topic and move on to the next skill in order to present a meaningful challenge to each actor to keep his interest as high as possible.

Characteristics of Stimulated Teaching

1. The teacher-traince gets a chance of role-playing even before entering the profession.
2. They get training in dramatization.
3. They develop role-playing skill.
4. They are taught to play the role of new teachers.

Limitations of Simulations

Some of the limitations of simulations are as under

1. The beginner participant may find it difficult to ask different type of questions.
2. During an exercise the observer may record incorrectly.
3. It is a misconception that adults can play the role of pupils. Simulators

'Simulator' refers to a single set of apparatus capable of representing to its operator a very large portion of the situation required in the use of a weapon system. Air-craft simulators are the best examples. The pilot, during the trial period, observes instruments and operates controls which simulate those of the real aeroplane with a high degree of precision.

Generally simulators are designed for procedures for adjusting electronic representation of motor skills, identification of targets or emergence signals, conceptual tasks involving reasoning and team functions. The simulator is deliberately designed to omit certain parts of the real operational situation.

Community Resources—Meaning—Types—Their Uses in the Teaching and Learning of Commerce and Accountancy

It was Aristotle who first defined the word "community" as a group established by men having shared values. That initial definition has been refined and expanded through the years. We have come, for example, to recognize that people can belong to a number of different "communities" simultaneously—communities of place; cultural communities; communities of memory, in which people who may be strangers share "a morally significant history"; and psychological communities "of face-to-face personal interaction governed by sentiments of trust, co-operation, and altruism."

The world, we are repeatedly reminded, has contracted into a "global village." One effect of this contraction is the bringing together of hitherto isolated peoples, allowing for the development of new patterns of civilization—but also creating new tensions. Thus, challenges now confront communities at local, national, and global levels. For example, new information technologies have created "networks" and "cybercommunities" in the world of the Internet that link individuals and organizations around the globe without regard for national boundaries; small communities around the planet are affected by urban migration or by degradation of the natural and built environment; the existence of national communities—nation states—is under threat from assaults by ethnic or tribal enclaves. Ironically, while the emergence of a global community wielding effective power is seen by many as a necessity in order to combat the ill effects of unfettered market economics, the whole idea that a real global community can ever come into existence is met with deep misgivings or complete skepticism by others. How, then, can we understand "community" at the end of the twentieth century—and what will its future be in the next millennium?

Analysis

Most of the beyond the school constructive learning activities that we mapped involve school related learning, such as homework, research and tutorials. However, learning a language or a musical instrument were also commonly reported. Other types of types of activities were not reported as being related to learning. These activities might have included participating in leisure activities that involve reading, writing, problem solving, or decision making; recreational activities like watching TV, playing games, doing hobbies, or group sports; and health maintenance activities (Clark, 1992). We interpret the fact these other activities were not mentioned as an indication that they are not highly valued as school related learning activities, rather than as an indication that they are not taking place.

Whilst there are many benefits to be gained from easier access of the parents and the community to schools as sites of learning, there are also many benefits to be gained from a broader of recognition and acknowledgement of sites of learning beyond the school fence. Many of the goals for schooling that have been identified in *The Adelaide Declaration on National Goals for Schooling in the Twenty-First Century* (MCEETYA, 1999) can be supported through constructive learning activities based in the community. These goals include:

- the capacity for, and skills in, analysis and problem solving and the ability to communicate ideas and information, to plan and organise activities and to collaborate with others;
- self-confidence, optimism, high self-esteem, and a commitment to personal excellence;
- the capacity to exercise judgement and responsibility in matters of morality, ethics and social justice;
- the capacity to think about how things got to be the way they are, and to be active and informed citizens;
- employment related skills, the use of technology and the ability to contribute to ecologically sustainable development.

In our view, there is great potential for these goals to be supported within the community if more resources are allocated for this purpose. Maintenance of current levels of government funding through DET will ensure that a narrow, but necessary, focus on engaging student at risk continues. Increased funding could be put towards raising the levels of awareness of community organisations of the important educative role they can play-independent of schools. This is premised on the need to break down the pervasive views that learning *only* takes place at school and that teachers are *the* experts when it comes to curriculum matters.

A core consideration in publicising and promoting sites of learning beyond the school fence is the continuing need to challenge deficit views of families and communities, especially those views held by school-based personnel. This has been a long-term focus of targeted programmes such as the Priority Schools Funding Programme, and the Disadvantaged Schools Programme before it, but deficit views persist and play a significant role in limiting the nature of school community links initiated and supported by schools and, more particularly, by school principals. Challenges to these views should be set against clear and explicit agreements about the purposes and values of education. Whilst it is necessary for schools to exercise some autonomy in this regard and to respond to their perceived local conditions, Australia's long history in the provision of redistributive funding to achieve more equitable outcomes from schooling, aligned with policy support, reinforces the importance of common and agreed goals for all public schools. Our research suggests that systemic leverage, perhaps in the form of targets for community involvement in decision making, are required in order to move schools towards more democratic processes that are accessible to their communities.

There was a strong sense that the key link in the middle school years was between the teacher and the student; that this is a time when students needed the most support; and that it is also when teachers felt they could still make a difference. Our interviews with students at risk in Years 5 and 8 confirm the critical role that relationships with teachers play in the levels of satisfaction they express with their participation and success at school. It appears as though students in the middle years view teachers as members of their community and, therefore, important facilitators and supporters of their daily traverse across the school fence. The two main issues most commonly mentioned as barriers to effective school community links were lack of time and limited resources. Although participants acknowledged the importance of school community links other concerns took priority. For parents, this was due to juggling work and other family commitments. School personnel expressed a reluctance to be involved, in the absence of specific release time to carry out school community activities, given all the key functions and tasks they were required to perform within their schools. For District staff, their time pressures were due to the large number of schools they had to work with and hence the limited amount of time they were able to spend with each individual school. While community workers faced increasing pressures on their time and few if any of their projects were funded to work with young people in the middle school years or to focus on learning issues with young people, limiting their ability to effectively engage with schools.

The lack of funding and resources for programmes was also seen as an important barrier. While policies encouraged school community interaction, little extra funding was being provided to support and enable projects and new initiatives to develop. Among parents, school and district staff, and community workers there was a view that additional funding was needed to support ongoing activities, but they claimed that funding had been cut back over recent years.

According to parents the main barriers to effective-school community links were:

- poor communication with teachers about student learning issues;
- lack of information from schools about educational programmes;
- language barriers; and
- lack of interest by school staff.

There were a number of factors identified by school and district office staff as barriers to more effective school community links. They included:

- the lack of time and resources;
- the difficulties of making connections with parents;
- the cultural and social diversity among the local community;
- the culture of the school;
- lack of school community 'champions' in a school;
- lack of appropriate skills in the community on student learning issues; and
- school community links are not a core activity and are of marginal value to student learning.

Among the community organisations the community workers felt the main barriers to more effective school community links were:

- schools were not interested in community based projects and initiatives or contact with local community organisations when these projects did not focus on young people and their needs;
- school teachers indicated that involvement with community creates extra work; and
- there was often no real reason for a school to establish or maintain a link with a community organisation.

Field Trip

A field trip is a journey by a group of people to a place away from their normal environment.

The purpose of the trip is usually *observation* for education, non-experimental research or to provide students with experiences outside their everyday activities. The aim of this research is to observe the subject in its natural state and possibly collect samples. In western culture people first come across this method during school years when classes are taken on excursions to visit a geological or geographical feature of the landscape, for example. Much of the early research into the natural sciences was of this form. Charles Darwin is an important example of someone who has contributed to science through the use of field trips.

To mitigate these risks and expenses, most school systems now have formalized field trip procedures that considers the entire trip from estimation, approval and scheduling through planning the actual trip and post-trip activities.

Work Experience

Work experience is the experience that a person has working, or working in a specific field or occupation.

Volunteer Work and Internships

The phrase is sometimes used to mean a type of volunteer work that is commonly intended for young people — often students — to get a feel for professional working environments. This usage is common in the United Kingdom, while the American equivalent is intern.

Though the placements are usually unpaid, travel and food expenses are sometimes covered, and at the end of the appointment, a character reference is usually provided. Trainees usually have the opportunity to network and make contacts among the working personnel, and put themselves forward for forthcoming opportunities for paid work.

Many employers in the more sought after professions (eg TV, politics, journalism) demand that every new entrant undergo a period of unpaid "work experience" before being able to get paid work. In most cases this is effectively "experience through work" and is contrary to the Minimum Wage regulations if unpaid. Such is the demand for this kind of work that very few complain about this and so the practice continues illegally.

Educational Work Experience at Secondary Level in Australia and the United Kingdom

Work experience is offered on the national curriculum for students in Years 10 and 11 in the United Kingdom (4th year in Scotland) and Australia); every student has a statutory right to take work experience if he or she wishes. Work experience in this context is when students in an adult working environment more or less act as an employee, but with the emphasis on learning about the world of work. Placements are limited by safety and security restrictions, insurance cover and availability, and do not necessarily reflect eventual career choice but instead allow a broad experience of the world of work.

If a student fails to find a placement then he or she may sometimes be forced to attend school everyday, aiding the caretaker for example, or helping out elsewhere in the school, such as with language and PE departments, or with ICT technicians.

Students are not prohibited from working at a company outside the conurbation of the city or abroad. Routine safety checks on the companies are now more thorough and students who arrange placements at failed companies are forced to find a new placement; companies which fail to comply with statutory requirements for insurance and child protection may be prohibited from officially taking students (this depends upon the LEA).

Most students do not get paid for their time doing work experience, as this is considered part of their education. The duration varies according to the course the student is on and various other personal circumstances; the vast majority of students will go out on work experience for one or two weeks in a year, while some students will work in a particular workplace perhaps one or two days a week for extended periods of time throughout the year, either for vocation reasons and commitment to alternative curricula or because they have social and/or behavioural problems.

University-level Work Experience

At the university level, work experience is often offered between the second and final years of an undergraduate degree course, especially in the science, engineering and computing fields. Courses of this nature are often called *sandwich courses*, with the work experience year itself known as the *sandwich year*. During this time, the students on work placement have the opportunity to use the skills and knowledge gained in their first two years, and see how they are applied to real world problems. This then can offer then useful insights for their final year and prepares them for the job market once their course has finished. Some companies also have the means to sponsor students in their final year at university with the promise of a job at the end of the course. This can act as an incentive for the student to perform well during the placement as helps with two otherwise unwelcome stresses: the lack of money in the final year, and finding a job for when the University course completes.

Guest Speakers

Including a guest speaker at your event makes for a memorable occasion. To help you get an idea of who might be right for your event we have put our speakers into categories for you. If a guest speaker overlaps from one category to another we've included them in both for you. So, if you have no idea or a strong idea of who you are looking for they will be easy to find.

Attitudes toward free markets and interest in pro-market organizations: evidence from students in free enterprise.

It is not surprising that students who study free markets tend to have a positive attitude about free markets. For example, Breeden and Lephardt (2002) find that the higher the level of economics course the surveyed student is enrolled in, the more pro-market the student is. What they do not show, however, is if these students are in higher level economics courses because of their beliefs or if they have these beliefs because they are in higher level economics courses. In this note, we explore this question by examining whether students exhibiting an extracurricular interest in free markets without having necessarily studied economics or business tend to be pro-market. Surprisingly, we find that students who express an interest in joining Students In Free Enterprise (SIFE SIFE Students in Free Enterprise

SIFE Second ISLSCP Field Experiment

Actually significantly less pro-market than their peers. Beyond this finding, our characterization A rather long and fancy word for analyzing a system or process and measuring its "characteristics." For example, a Web characterization would yield the number of current sites on the Web, types of sites, annual growth, etc.

SIFE is a non-profit organization A non-profit organization (abbreviated "NPO", also "non-profit" or "not-for-profit") is a legally constituted organization whose primary objective is to support or to actively engage in activities of public or private interest without any commercial or monetary profit purposes. with teams on college and university campuses around the world. Its mission is to "provide college and university students the best opportunity to make a difference and to develop leadership, teamwork and communication skills through learning, practicing and teaching the principles of FREE ENTERPRISE" (SIFE USA, 12). As the name implies, SIFE is decidedly business oriented o·ri·ent *n.*

1. Orient The countries of Asia, especially of eastern Asia.
2. a. The luster characteristic of a pearl of high quality.
   b. A pearl having exceptional luster.
3. but strives to attract students from all majors and backgrounds. SIFE team members plan, manage, and implement projects with the goal of teaching others principles that will increase their quality of life. The SIFE team on our campus started its first full year in the fall of 2004 with an intensive recruiting campaign. Student leaders visited approximately 30 classes in the College of Business Administration. We surveyed (1) students from these classes to learn more about the type of student who is likely to be interested in SIFE.

Our work can be linked to two distinct bodies of literature. The first deals with attitudes and beliefs regarding free markets. According to according to *prep.*

1. As stated or indicated by; on the authority of: according to historians.
2. In keeping with: according to instructions.
3. Breeden and Lephardt (2002), male students and students with higher grades in economics courses are more pro-market. Parker, Spears, and Jones (2002) use factor analysis to show that a student's degree of economic conservatism is influenced by locus of control locus of control *n.*

A theoretical construct designed to assess a person's perceived control over his or her own behaviour. The classification *internal locus* indicates that the person feels in control of events; *external locus* and by gender and personality. Gender and personality are also shown to influence individual economic decision-making in Parker and Spears (2002). Barilla barilla see halogeton glomeratus., Parker, and Paul (2005) use the Rotter conceptualization con·cep·tu·al·ize

v. con·cep·tu·al·ized, con·cep·tu·al·iz·ing, con·cep·tu·al·iz·es *v.tr.*

To form a concept or concepts of, and especially to interpret in a conceptual way: of locus of control to determine student personality types and find that different personality types impact students' perceptions of free markets. Students who believe they have control over their environment are more likely to be pro-market than are students who believe they have no control over their success. A second body of literature deals with the benefits of students becoming engaged on campus outside of the classroom. See Astin (1975 and 1984), MacKay and Kuh (1994), DeSousa and Kuh (1996), Watson and Kuh (1996), and Furr and Elling (2002) for research on this topic.

Data and Results

Our survey included basic demographic questions, questions about whether or not the student heard the SIFE recruitment presentation, their response to the presentation if they heard it, and questions from a survey created by Breeden and Lephardt (2002) on student attitudes toward free markets. These were used to determine the characteristics of students interested in SIFE. Ten classes were sampled, all of which heard the presentation from the same student. Responses were received from 359 students. Thirty percent of the respondents In the context of marketing research, a representative sample drawn from a larger population of people from whom information is collected and used to develop or confirm marketing strategy.

reported majors in the College of Business Administration compared to only 20% of students university-wide, but eight of the ten classes sampled were freshmen level, meaning that even these students had a limited exposure to business in an academic setting. The other colleges represented in the responses were those of Liberal Arts liberal arts, term originally used to designate the arts or studies suited to freemen. It was applied in the Middle Ages to seven branches of learning, the trivium of grammar, logic, and rhetoric, and the quadrivium of arithmetic, geometry, astronomy, and music. and Social Sciences (15%), Health and Human Sciences (15%), Science and Technology (10%), Education (9%), and Information Technology (3%). The survey was completed at a regional comprehensive public university in the southeast with about 16,000 students. Approximately 90% of the students were full-time, 52% were female, 72% were white, and 23% were African-American. (2)

Females were more likely than males to sign up for more information (females made up 48% of those who responded and 54.1% of those who signed up). African-Americans also signed up in higher proportions than other races (15% of respondents and 18.8% of those who signed up), a result that is consistent with that pf other researchers (e.g., see Watson and Kuh, 1996). We conducted means tests means test *n*.

An investigation into the financial well-being of a person to determine the person's eligibility for financial assistance.

Means test:

Noun *to compare the free market attitudes of those who responded to the recruitment talk with those who did not. Table gives results for means with significant differences. Variance ratio tests determined whether we used T tests with unequal variances or with equal variances. All differences are significant at the 5% level unless otherwise noted.*

Those who signed up for more information upon hearing the presentation were significantly more likely to attend the first meeting. For those who did not attend the first meeting, students who signed up for more information were significantly more likely to report scheduling conflicts or forgetting about the meeting, and were also more likely to report either having attended another meeting or plans to attend another meeting. Those who neither signed up for more information nor attended the first meeting were more likely to report having not attended because they were not interested, or because they didn't know about the meeting. These results are important because they imply that students did not feel pressured to sign up for information regardless of interest.

Our most interesting finding is that students who signed up for more information about SIFE were actually more likely to hold a negative view of the free market system than students who did not sign up. They were more likely to report believing that the free market system encourages greed Greed

Shakespearean symbol of avarice. [Br. Lit. and materialism materialism, in philosophy, a widely held system of thought that explains the nature of the world as entirely dependent on matter, the fundamental and final reality beyond which nothing need be sought., and that it leads to the abuse of natural resources. We examined the differences between male and female students to see if these results were being driven by the fact that the majority of students who signed up were female. In most cases, females had less favorable fa·vor·a·ble

1. Advantageous; helpful: favorable winds.
2. Encouraging; propitious: a favorable diagnosis.
3. views of free markets than males, although neither group reported particularly strong beliefs. The only cases where males had less favorable beliefs than females were for the statements that "free markets

encourage unethical unethical said of conduct not conforming with professional ethics. business behaviour" and "lead to excessive risk of business failure." Breeden and Lephardt (2002) and Parker, Spears, and Jones (2002) find that females are less pro-market than males. Our results (3) confirm these earlier findings, but it is important to note that the significant differences between those who signed up for information on SIFE and those who did not are not the same as those between males and females. We take this as an indication that our results are NOT being driven by the makeup makeup.

In the performing arts, material used by actors for cosmetic purposes and to help create the characters they play. Not needed in Greek and Roman theatre because of the use of masks, makeup was used in the religious plays of medieval Europe, in which the angels' faces of the group.

Finally, we sent an email survey to all 71 members of the SIFE team. Fifteen students responded for a response rate of 21%. We asked students for basic demographics The attributes of people in a particular geographic area. Used for marketing purposes, population, ethnic origins, religion, spoken language, income and age range are examples of demographic data. To rank how active they had been in SIFE during the year, and how they heard about SIFE originally. The survey also included the Breeden and Lephardt (2002) survey on attitudes about free markets. Seventy-three percent reported having attended more than five meetings during the year, while 66.7% reported actively participating in one or more SIFE projects.

The significant differences between the group of people who sought more information about SIFE and the smaller group that actually actively participates in SIFE. Neither group strongly believed that the free market leads to insufficient provision of important public services Public services is a term usually used to mean services provided by government to its citizens, either directly (through the public sector) or by financing private provision of services., although those who are members of the team were less likely to believe this than those who only sought information. (4) In this respect, members of Students In Free Enterprise had a more favorable view of free markets. Members of SIFE were significantly more likely to believe that free markets lead to inflation. While this result is surprising, it is in line with our other findings that students interested in SIFE have less favorable views of free markets.

Conclusion

Our findings seem to support the idea that students' positive attitudes towards free markets are the result of education rather than an inherent interest in business or market activity. We were surprised to learn that, of the students in our survey, students interested in SIFE and members of SIFE held less favorable views of free markets than those who were not interested in the organization. Since the goal of this organization is to teach the merits of free enterprise, this is not as expected and warrants further study. It may be that the curriculum being taught in business courses focuses on the benefits of a free market system while the popular press focuses on its negative effects. Students with a primarily extracurricular interest in markets would thus have more exposure to the negatives.

Over the next few years, it will be interesting to see if a greater understanding of free markets through hands-on experience in SIFE will lead to more favorable views about free markets for these students. Alternatively, their understanding and awareness of the free enterprise system may lead them to cautious support as they learn of both the merits and the ethical and social dilemmas A Social dilemma is a paradox arising from social decision situations in which contributions are needed to attain a common goal and where the rational choice of the individual is to "free-ride". that a market economy creates.

UNIT-IX

Commerce Department

Commerce Department

Like any other subject there should be separate room/ rooms for the commerce. The setting and arrangements of these rooms should be such that it creates an atmosphere for the study and teaching of commerce. The students entering the room would find themselves interested in learning of mathematics.As a matter of fact, the department of commerce of a school should have a block of three rooms at least

(i) One room to be used as a general classroom for teaching subjects of commerce i.e. Book keeping. Elements of commerce, commercial geography etc. This room should be big enough to accommodate as many students as possible in a class.

(ii) One room for teaching of shorthand and type-writing, trasscription and business machines. If possible, it should be provided with a flexible partition into two parts-one for short-hand and other for type-writing.

(iii) One room for business machines wherein Adding and Calculating machines, Tape recording machine, Duplicating machines, Record players, Dictaphones, Stock registers etc. be kept.

Business like atmosphere has to be created in the department of commerce. Audio-visual aids should be kept in the department in sufficient number to provide various experiences needed in the commerce programme.

Commerce Laboratory

It is a room of 12'x 20' i.e. area of 240 sq. foot. On three sides of this room the systems of racks are introduced to save space for storage of the necessary material for the class:

Filing Cabinet	1
Chairs for Students	10
Almirahs	2

At a time only upto ten students be accommodated under the guidance of the teacher or the instructor or the mechanic. Practical work of duplicating, filing and office practices should be done in this room. This should be provided with the following equipment facilities:

Type Writer	-25 (including 25% as reserve)
Duplicating Machine	-1
Adding and Calculating Machines	-5
Tape recorder	-1
Copy Holders	-21
Interval Time Bulletine Boards	-3
Overhead Projector	-1
Opaque Projector	-1
Films strip	-1
Paper binder Machine	-1
Paper Cutter	-1

[Note-It should be specially seen by the commerce teacher that nothing is lent out (even temporarily) to any one from the above].

Type-writing Room

It is a room of 24' x 20' i.e. an area of 480 sq. foot. Two room is to be used for the following purposes:

(i) Type-writing instruction for the commerce students.

(ii) Transcription instructions for commerce students.

(iii) Types-writing instructions for non-commerce students who have offered it for their personal or professional use.

The arrangement of the room should be such that the demonstration be made visible to all students. It is always better to have a demonstration stand-Which may be flexible as well as adjustable. It should be provided with a good black board which may be used to give instruction and illustration to the students properly. The seating plan of the class be such that the teacher may have an access to the individual students. This facility must be made avail-able to the students. While supervising the work of the students teacher should identify the defects and demonstrate before them how to adopt correct procedures of doing the practical work.

Office Machines Room

It is a room of 12' x 20' i.e. 240 sq. foot area. It should be located adjacent to the typing room, preferably interconnected by a door. In some of the schools the same teacher has to supervise the work of students both in type-writing as also of students working on the office machines. It also facilitates the movement of the students who may like to move from the office machine room to the type-writing room to use the duplicating machine.

For displaying material a bulletin board be provided in the room. This should be located near the door of the room and should be extensively used.

This room may be used for instructions on duplicating, adding and calculating machines. A part of this room may be used for stor-age of supplies and accessories needed for the equipments used in this room.

For taking their instruction on various office machines the commerce students be divided into groups of 10 each. The machines kept in the room may be used for imparting instruction in Elements of commerce and also in office practices. The extensive use of Adding and calculating machine be done for imparting instruction in Bookkeeping. When the stencils have been cut do type-writer the duplicating machine be used freely.

The supervision of this room be done by all the members of the commerce department i.e. teachers instructors. Type-writing instructors etc. For convenience it is better if this room is located between typing room and Bookkeeping room. All the three rooms may be inter-connected.

Records and Registers to be Maintained

It is a room of 28' x 20' i.e. 560 sq. foot area. Thus it is a quite spacious room. This room may be used for imparting instructions in the following commerce subjects:

(i) Book Keeping,

(ii) Elements of Commerce,

(iii) Commercial Arithmetic,

(iv) Commercial Geography,

(v) Economics, and

(vi) Short-hand.

Note: For teaching of short-hand the room should be equipped with special type of blackboard arrangement (Ruled).

For class demonstrations the following facilities be provided in the room.

(i) Demonstration stand-For demonstrating the machine being used and for explaining its various basic concepts.

(ii) Black-board-Large one and adjustable. For Bookkeeping problems such a blackboard is convenient.

(iii) Charts and diagrams.

(iv) Exhibits and Bulletin-boards.

(v) Files strip projector, overhead projector, opaque projector etc. Arrangements should also be made to make the room dark when it is to be used as a dark-room.

Equipment Essential and Desirable

The following is the list of minimum equipment facilities that should be provided in commerce rooms:

(i) Blackboard (20' x V),

Note : Blackboard provided in bookkeeping room should have Journal and ledger rulings. For short-hand room the blackboard should have horizontal lines at a distance of 6".

(ii) Bulletin boards,

(iii) References, tables

(iv) Magazine racks,

(v) Book-cases or shalves,

(vi) Pencil sharpner,

(vii) Stapler,

(viii) Paper Punch,

(ix) Paper cutter,

(x) Individual table and chair for each student,

(xi) Teacher's desk and chairs,

(xii) A standing desk for the teacher,

(xiii) Map stand and pointer (for Commercial geography),

(xiv) Show cases for storage of articles like rice, wheat, silk etc., Mineral products, Models of agricultural processes, Industrial products etc.,

(xv) Demonstration stand,

(xvi) Type-writers, and

(xvii) Various audio-visual aids such as Epidiascope, Film projector, Slide projector, Tape recorder, Dictating Machine, Record Player etc.

UNIT-X

Professional Development

Commerce Teacher—Professional Growth of Teacher—Pre-service and in Service Programme Qualities Required for a Good Teacher

The success or failure of a Commerce and Accountancy course rests mainly with the Commerce and Accountancy teacher. He may be provided with all the possible facilities in terms of laboratory, apparatus and equipment. Given an ideal syllabus and sufficient time for teaching of Commerce and Accountancy but he is not likely to achieve success unless he is enthusiastic about his work, knows the subject and really knows how to teach Commerce and Accountancy. On the other hand a keen and well informed teacher who loves his subject and believes in its value will succeed inspite of difficulties and handicaps.

In this regard the Kothari Commission report (1966) says, "Of all the different factors which influence the quality of education and its contribution to national development, the quality, competence and character of teacher are undoubtedly the most significant."

Dr. S. Radha Krishan emphasises the role of teacher in the following words, 'The teacher's place in society is of vital importance. He acts as the pivot for transmission of intellectual traditions and technical skills from generation to generation, and helps to keep the lamp of civilisation burning. He not only guides the individual, but also, so to say, the destiny of nation. Teachers have therefore to realise their special responsibility to the society. On the other hand it is in content on the society to pay due regard to the teaching profession and to ensure that the teacher is kept above want and given the status which will command respect from his student".

Importance of Teacher

"A teacher is more like a gardener who tends each plant, examines water and seen that plant may take its own nourishment. The teacher should be a guide, helper and a friend. The teacher must study the child, must know the effect of environment on the child, and should know the laws of learning for which a study of psychology is necessary."

The teacher is an integral part of the process of education. He imparts education and teaches his students the subject matter prescribed for them. He has to perform a difficult job. If the teacher because an embodiment of sight conduct in thought, word and deed, the students by their association will learn virtue and develop manly qualities.

Since the teacher is the pivot of any educational system for younger pupils so on her rests the failure or success of the systems.

The teacher is the dynamic force of the school. "There is no greater need for the cause of education today than the need for strong manly men and womanly women as teachers for the young."

The teacher is the yardstick that measures the achievements and aspirations of a nation. The work and potentialities of a country get evaluated in through the work of a teacher. 'The people of a country are the enlarged replica of their teacher." They are the real nation-builder.

Functions of a Teacher

Some of the important functions to be discharged by a teacher are as under:

(1) He is expected to bring about the successful teaching and build up understanding and motivation among the students.

(2) He is expected to study and organise the learning plans of the students and distribute the load for each student in a proper and scientific manner.

(3) The teacher is also expected to give due regard to individual differences.

(4) The teacher is also expected to create in the students the interest for the subject through proper appreciation of the achievement of the students. Through personal contact and knowledge, he can create love for the subject.

Qualities of a Commerce and Accountancy Teacher

As in the case to other teachers, many things are expected of the teacher of Commerce and Accountancy. Teaching is not an easy job. A teacher has to bear in mind many factors-the children with their individual objectives of the subject, the selection of suitable subject-matter, method of teaching etc. His obligations are not only confined to the classroom but also extend in many other directions.

No teacher can do a thorough good job of teaching Commerce and Accountancy unless he is willing to make a careful analysis of his job and be guided by that analysis in making his preparations and in conducting the work of his class.

Following qualities are expected in a good Commerce and Accountancy teacher:

(i) Thorough Knowledge of the Subject

If a teacher has a thorough knowledge of his subject it gives him confidence in his teaching. If a teacher is not clear about certain facts or rules. She will be afraid lest she should be caught somewhere. Suppose a pupils asks a question and the teacher is not able to give a satisfactory answer. She will fail to exercise her influence on the students. They will no longer listen to her attentively. She may have some problems of indiscipline as well.

(ii) Knowledge of Methods

Only having good knowledge of Commerce and Accountancy is not sufficient. The teacher should be able to communicate his knowledge to the pupils. For that, teacher must be well conversant with the various methods of teaching the subject. She should have professional training. She must know the latest methods and techniques of teaching. As far as possible, the teacher should be trained, particularly in case of secondary school teachers.

There are two equally important aspects of any true profession, viz., significant knowledge and effective technique. One can not be efficiently professional if there is any serious weakness in either of the two.

In the beginning of his carrier the teacher will need to spend most of his time in improving his knowledge of teaching field and her technique of teaching.

(iii) Interest in the Subject

The Commerce and Accountancy teacher must have a love for his subject. Such a love and interest in subject would help him to create a similar love and interest for Commerce and Accountancy in her students.

(iv) Love for the Students

A teacher must love his students. Unless the teacher likes them, they will not like him. Like or dislike is reciprocal process. If the students do not like the teacher, the students will riot like his subject. So the first essential before a teacher is to establish rapport with the students. She should understand them, their abilities, interests, achievement etc.

(v) Impressive Personality

The teacher should process an impressive personality. She should have a thorough command on the subject and should be able to present it in such a manner that students grasp what she says or does in the classroom.

The teacher should keep himself properly dressed and should possess presentable physical features. There should be an aptitude of sobriety and seriousness in the teacher. This helps in discipline. The teacher should have healthy qualities. Her behaviour should serve as an ideal to the students.

(vi) Knowledge of Educational Psychology

The teacher must have knowledge of child psychology. It is then possible for her to know the psychophysical requirements of her students and organise her teaching accordingly.

(vii) Capacity to Inspire Confidence in his Students

The teacher of Commerce and Accountancy should have the capacity to inspire confidence in her students. This can be done only by example and devotion to duty and certain other qualities. If the teacher can inspire confidence in her students, she can very safely carry them along with herself.

(viii) Proper Habits and Attitudes

A good Commerce and Accountancy teacher is expected to possess good habits like patience, confidence, hard work, initiative etc. She is expected to have rational and Heuristic attitude. She is expected to possess a strong will power and a power of concentration. She is also expected to possess neat and systematic habit of work. She is expected to possess qualities of cooperation and sympathy.

(ix) Awareness of Aims

The teacher must be clear about the aims and objectives of teaching of Commerce and Accountancy at various stages. Such a knowledge helps him in carrying out his job thoroughly.

(x) Originality

The quality of originality is a must for every teacher and so is the case with a Commerce and Accountancy teacher. This helps the teacher to devise ways and means for imparting knowledge effectively and properly. Her approach should be original and he should not depend on any particular book-text or help book.

(xi) Knowledge of Application of Commerce and Accountancy

The teacher should have a good knowledge of the application of Commerce and Accountancy to other subjects, vocations, real life etc. Such a knowledge is quite helpful in making the teaching meaningful and interesting.

(xii) Organising Ability

A good teacher is expected to be a good organiser. She is required to organise her teaching work and other co-curricular activities such as activities of Commerce and Accountancy club, library etc. She has also to organise tests etc.

(xiii) Capacity of Analysis and Comprehensive Description

While teaching a subject a teacher is required to give even minute details to explain things to his students. For giving such details teacher should possess the capacity of analysis. A Commerce and Accountancy teacher should also possess skills such as computational skill, drawing and sketching skill, problem solving skill etc.

(xiv) Up-to-date Knowledge of the Subject

A teacher must keep his knowledge up to date. She should study various journals and other useful books on the subject. She should attend refresher courses, work shops, seminars etc. on the subject. She may do professional research work. She may join various Commerce and Accountancy Organisation, visit good schools and hold discussions with requited teachers of the subject.

(xv) Capacity to Prove Things More by Action than by Words

"Practice is better than precept". This is true for a Commerce and Accountancy teacher like any other teacher. The teacher has to prove things by example and not by words. If she can do that, he is sure to influence her students and so she will be able to make them interested in her subject.

(xvi) Studiousness

The teacher is expected to be studious. Studiousness is essential to keep ones knowledge up-to-date.

(xvii) Presence of Mind

Presence of mind is the basic requirement of any teacher. Unless she possess this quality she will not be able to solve the difficulties that beset her path in the teaching of her subject in the classroom.

(xviii) Aesthetic and Artistic Outlook

Such an outlook helps the teacher in presenting things in proper perspective in an attractive manner.

Ethics of Teacher—Social and Environmental Responsibilities of the Commerce Teacher

A Commerce and Accountancy teacher is expected to possess certain academic qualification as also certain professional qualifications.

As regards the academic qualifications it is usually a pass in matriculation/senior secondary examination for becoming a Commerce and Accountancy teacher in a primary school. A pass in B.Sc. examination for being a Commerce and Accountancy teacher in a middle or high school and pass in M. Sc. examination in the subject for becoming a teacher to teach the subject in a senior secondary school (grade 11 and 12).

In addition to the minimum academic qualification any one who wish to be appointed a teacher in Commerce and Accountancy has to undergo a teachers training course. For this purpose a person for appointment as a teacher in primary school has to undergo 1 or 2 years Junior Basic Training (J.B.T.) course and for appointment in high and higher secondary school the graduate or postgraduate teacher has to under a B.T. or B.Ed. course. This professional training is all the more important these days when new techniques of teaching, evaluation etc. are being introduced.

Trained Commerce and Accountancy teachers also require the stimulus of a refresher course to keep himself informed about the latest methods of teaching and to refresh his knowledge of Commerce and Accountancy. Such a refresher course also provides him with an opportunity to see some of the latest books and apparatus concerning Commerce and Accountancy teaching and to obtain instructions in arts and scientific hobbies. During such refresher course he also gets practical training in the organisation of Commerce and Accountancy clubs, fairs, etc.

For keeping himself in touch with latest in Commerce and Accountancy the teacher may visit some nearby schools where Commerce and Accountancy is taught by new methods. He can also take up the membership of a good library or good science association. He can think of other such institutions and industrial houses nearby from where he can get the latest knowledge of Commerce and Accountancy. All this is quite essential because a good teacher must always keep himself informed of the latest development in the field. This aspect of a teacher has been brought out in the following words by Dr. Rabinder Nath Tagore, "A teacher can never teach unless he is still learning himself. A lamp can not light another lamp unless it continues to burn its own flame".

Continuing professional development refers to an attempt to increase the competency of present Commerce and Accountancy teacher through seminars, workshops, conference, study groups, courses, lectures etc. For this purpose any formed or informed programme can be undertaken but such a programme should contribute to the professional growth of the teacher who are already in service. Some of the activities that could be undertaken are as follows:

(i) Providing opportunities to observe and participate in outstanding educational programmes.

(ii) Conducting parent-teacher meetings. During such meeting many an educational problems such as "Post-school adjustability of the pupils" can be discussed and sorted out.

(iii) Organising seminars and workshops so as to demonstrate modern teaching devices. It is desirable to demonstrate to in service teachers such modern teaching devices as 'term teaching', 'micro-teaching', 'open space' etc.

Term Teaching is a process where by teachers can cooperate in planning, teaching evaluating and observing the learning environment. Such a term approach provides for 'a teacher-teacher visibility, interaction, sharing and thus provides the potential for collaborative supervision".

Micro-Teaching may be considered as, "belong down a teaching situation in terms of time, methodology and content." It provides an opportunity for teachers and supervisors to try out teaching ideas without risk of an actual situation.

Open Space is a way that helps in promoting "Cooperative teaching and learning, availability of specialised resources, differentiated staffing, independent study and use of multi media." It frees the teacher to see each other work to collaborate, to evaluate each other and to describe each other.

(iv) To help the teachers in acquiring special skills such as curriculum development, instructional improvement, demonstration, research and dissemination etc.

(v) To facilitate teachers to go to some other schools and to see for themselves other teachers and instructors at work.

(vi) Organisation of faculty meetings. Such meeting are quite helpful in improving the quality of staff and an opportunity for cooperative thinking. Such meetings also help to know the total school.

(vii Promotion of creative teaching. "Creativeness is a conscious state of experimentation" This experimentation has three phases viz., planning, testing and revising. A clear sense of direction be provided by the supervisor for promoting creativeness in teachers.

(viii) To provide opportunities to teachers for the conduct of action research in their respective classrooms.

(ix) To arrange extension courses to provide opportunities to in-service teachers for active participation in them.

Commerce and Accountancy Teacher's Diary

Just like other teachers a Commerce and Accountancy teacher should also keep a diary. In this diary the record of the syllabus drawn up by the Commerce and Accountancy teacher be maintained. It should clearly indicate the particulars of quarterly and weekly distribution of work. A copy of timetable be also kept in diary. The timetable should clearly show the distribution of available time for: (i) class room and laboratory work, (ii) Project and other allied activities (iii) Outdoor activities (excursions, visits etc.).

A record of daily work be entered in the diary regularly and it should be dated. In keeping this daily record teacher should clearly mention the details of lecture-cum-demonstration work, individual experimental work, slides etc. to be shown and any such other details. He should also enter in his diary: (i) those parts of the proposed work that have been accomplished, (ii) those parts of the proposed work that could not be accomplished, (iii) any other extra work that has been attempted.

The diary should also show details of written works, questions set. Entries of any comments on assignments and practical work must also find a place in teacher's diary.

If possible teacher should also mention the mistakes that were committed by a majority of students. Such as entry will be helpful to the teacher and he can explain these mistakes to the class. The results of the class tests and house examinations must also be recorded in the teacher's diary. A Commerce and Accountancy teacher can also keep a record of various chemicals, apparatus etc. ordered, for his reference, in his diary. Such a record will be quite useful for him when he is placing the orders at the beginning of the year.

Student's Note-Books

It is expected of each students to have three notebooks, one of these should be practical notebook, the remaining two are ordinary notebooks, one of these two be used for taking notes and copying blackboard summaries and the other for assignments. It would be much convenient if all the students have some type of practical notebooks and the two notebooks to be used for talking notes and for assignment purposes are of different colours. Teacher should emphasise that all notebooks must be kept clean and maintained properly. It would be useful if right hand page is used for writing and left-hand page is left blank for corrections, diagrams and calculations. This blank page can also be used for further notes from textbooks, library books etc.

Record of individual practical work should be kept in practical notebook. The observation should always be directly recorded in fair practical notebook.

For practical class some teachers use printed notebooks but such notebooks be avoided in higher classes.

Pupils Home Task

The teacher should give home work to the students and check their notebooks regularly and should also maintain a record of it. In Commerce and Accountancy home work consists of preparatory work of *assignment* set or of learning the work covered in demonstration lesson or to write answers to one or two questions on the topic of demonstration. Occasionally keeping in view the availability of time teacher may ask her students to read from some popular Commerce and Accountancy books, magazines etc. and even ask them to write something on what they have read.

The correction of note books and the marking of errors in them takes a lot of teachers free time but it is useless to assign work to student it the teacher does not find time to mark and correct their work. All efforts be made to reduce this burden to the minimum. For this teacher may use some selected codes of symbols to make corrections and ask the students to make corrections themselves.

While making correction all efforts be made by the teacher to point out mistakes in style and language. He should encourage the students to use a simple and, straight forward language.

Inspection of Commerce and Accountancy Department

The teacher should always be prepared for the inspection of her department. Such as inspection is quite essential for the evaluation of whole educative process and thus improve the teaching of Commerce and Accountancy.

The inspection must be carried out at least once a year. It should be carried out by a team which must include at least one expert in Commerce and Accountancy. While carrying out inspection the team should pay special attention to the following points.

(i) *Teacher.* The inspection team should see that the Commerce and Accountancy teacher possess the required academic and professional qualifications. The team should also pay attention to his teaching method. The individuality of teacher's method should be respected and the team if it so feels may suggest an alternative method but it should not be insisted upon. The inspection team should see that the science teacher practice proper correlation and coordination of science with other science subjects and also with other school subjects and environment.

(ii) *Scheme of Work.* Inspection term should see that the teacher prepares a quarterly and weekly scheme and such a scheme as shown in his diary is followed by him.

(iii) *Teacher's Diary'.* The inspection team should see if the science teacher is maintaining his diary properly. Whether or not is he keeping a daily record of work done both in theory and practical, home work assigned etc. Has he noted down his timetable in diary? Is he having a good timetable? Is he having enough time for practicals? Is he teaching some other subjects? etc.

(iv) *Text Books and Library Books.* Are the students using approved and standard text books? What type of books are available in library? Are the students using library books?

(v) *Laboratory and Equipment.* The inspection term should see that adequate space and apparatus etc. are available in school. In the laboratory there is provision for the proper storage of the apparatus, equipment, chemicals etc. Inspection team must make a report about the upkeep and tidyness of the laboratory. While making remarks about laboratory the following points be clearly mentioned:

(a) Were the pictures, charts, models etc. properly displayed in the laboratory?

(b) Did the arrangement exist in the laboratory for supply of water, disposal of waste water, first-aid box etc.?

(vi) *Stock Registers.* Maintenance of stock registers is one of the duties of Commerce and Accountancy teacher and inspection team is expected to see that various stock registers are being maintained properly, accurately and regularly. It would not be improper if the inspection team carries out the physical verification of some items and find out for themselves if the actual stock agrees with the balance shown in the stock register. The checking of stock register includes the checking of requirement register and the preparation of indents etc.

(vii) *Class Work and Home Work of Students.* It can easily be seen from the note-books maintained by the students. The inspection team should satisfy itself that the amount of written work done by the students is sufficient. Practical' notebooks and assignments have been checked properly and regularly by the teacher and the mistake have been pointed out to the students.

(viii) *Commerce and Accountancy Library and Commerce and Accountancy Museum.* The importance of library and museum of teaching of Commerce and Accountancy is given elsewhere in the book. The inspection team while carrying out the inspection of Commerce and Accountancy department in a school should find if a library and museum of the department are of some good standard? Is the school library being used properly by the students? Are there arrangements for regular issue and return of books from Commerce and Accountancy library? What method is used by Commerce and Accountancy teacher to satisfy himself that his students regularly devote some time to the study of library books?

(ix) *Extra-curricular Activities.* The existence of Commerce and Accountancy club is a school provides an opportunity for carrying out extra-curricular activities. Inspection team should report, whether a Commerce and Accountancy club exist? What are the activities of Commerce and Accountancy club? How many tours excursions etc. have been arranged? How many of such excusions, tours were arranged to visit places of scientific interest? Has the school arranged any science fair during the year? How may films/slides shows were arranged during the year? What steps were taken to encourage students to prepare home-made apparatus? Have the students contributed any good charts/ models during the year? Have any debate/ declamation/paper reading contest/quiz contest etc. arranged?

The inspection team should also ask for the record of all such activities carried out by the school during the year.

In addition to carrying out the inspection, the inspection team is expected to give some constructive suggestion to the Commerce and Accountancy master for all the activities for making improvement in Commerce and Accountancy teaching in schools. Such suggestion should not be forced on Commerce and Accountancy teacher and only those of these suggestions be implemented by the Commerce and Accountancy teacher which are likely to bring about a qualitative, change in- Commerce and Accountancy teaching.

Research in Commerce Education—Computer in Commerce and Accountancy Teaching and Research

Skill is defined as, "The ability to use one's knowledge effectively and readily in execution or performance; technical expertness; a power or habit of doing any thing".

According to Prof. M. S. Khan, " Leaning a skill includes the necessity of acquiring knowledge and understanding, but there is also the necessity usually, of much effort and time developed to purposeful and controlled practice. Behind all this practice usually lies the necessity of filling many previously learnt complex knowledge and understanding into what appears to be a simple skill that once high skill is obtained in some thing, the act can be performed automatically without any `interference' from the highest brain centre".

Learning skills in practical commerce subjects is quite essential, particularly in type-writing and short-hand, bookkeeping, operating business machines, taking dictation etc.

Mastery of Basic Skill

The mastery of basic skill is considered to have been achieved when the skill can be performed sub-consciously. Sub-conscious a skill can be performed even if some thing else is in mind.

For example, in typing when a particular level of skill is achieved the typing can be done without booking at the keys of the type machine. The fingers move correctly without any effort.

Mastery is essential before a skill can function. Following steps are considered essential to attain mastery in a skill.

1. The pre-test step.
2. The teaching step.
3. The test the result step.
4. Adopt the procedure step.
5. The Reteach step.
6. The Restest step.

In teaching these steps be repeated till the attainment of mastery.

Teaching for Mastery

In skill subjects the students should thoroughly master whatever is presented before them so that it remains with the students even after the lapse of some time.

In case a student learn only to the horizon of minimal learning (indicated by horizontal line), he is likely to forget soon. If his learning is above this level of minimum learning, he is likely to forget but will definitely retain some thing in his mind. If he repeats constantly he learns maximum and in such a case he retains maximum.

Pre-test is essential to know the background of students. In skill subjects demonstration is considered as the best form of teaching. To teach skill subjects, the teacher will do better if he keeps following concepts in mind, "Before problems requiring the application of a skill can be solved, the learner must acquire a certain facility in the skill."

Following two things are important for acquiring the skills.

(i) Mastery formula

(ii) Order of emphasis.

Order of Emphasis

Teacher should emphasis on those skill which he feels have not been acquired by the students correctly. Some teachers concentrate on *accuracy, speed* and *technique* in that order, however, in true sense of the term this order of emphasis should be reversed i.e. the correct order would be *technique, speed, accuracy* or briefly 'TAS'.

Next thing is the *motion pattern of experts.* For this the students may observe the motion pattern of teacher. Striking key on the typewriting machine, the learner should observe how only one sound is being produced at a strike.

Similarly, short hand the learner observes how the expert (teacher) holds his pen., moves his hand and writes and turns the pages. These correct patterns must be correctly imitated by the learners. On the basis of scientific studies it has been found that the main features of expert performance are as follows:

(a) Establishment and maintenance of a steady even flow of motion.

(b) Imbibe easy and economical movements.

(c) Practice relaxed performance unhampered by nervous tension and hurry.

(d) Concentrate upon the task at hand.

(e) Use the senses intelligently. The expert sees, hears and feels correct techniques simultaneously.

There is a particular technique of teaching expert pattern. Some essential and proper techniques which must be mastered ed by any one who wants to master skill are given below

1. Recognise factors that comprise the pattern.
2. Demonstrate factors comprising the pattern.
3. Appeal to as many senses as possible.
4. Group drills are useful only to establish the desired patterns. Individual drill is more beneficial after the learner understands what he is working to attain.
5. Students should work at the speed just below that at which confusion begins to appear and just above that which is characterised by laboured and detailed movements.
6. Repetition without conscious direction is of little value.
7. Each period, in fact, each portion of period must have definite objectives.
8. Drill period should be a shorter and not a longer one.
9. More attention should be paid towards emotional stability. 10. Goals should be attainable.
11. Skills should be automatized and not intellectualised.
12. Positive approach and not the negative approach should be adopted by the teacher.
13. Drills must be varied before the law of diminishing returns starts to operate.
14. Lack of proper technique causes errors and adoption of correct techniques causes skill learning
15. Too much formal testing is a hindrance to the effective building of skill.

Teaching Machine Parts

Psychologically it is desirable to teach about the parts of

machine, while teaching type-writing, only when they are to be used in learning by the students. Teacher should avoid to introduce all the parts at a time. The use of cylinder knob be made only when the student wants to insert paper into machine. The use of paper margin released be taught only. When it is to be used.

For becoming a good typist the development of *correct technique* should be emphasised, without caring for the speed, in the beginning The typist should not allow any waste of moments.

While practicing on new keys the most essential thing is the *correct stroking patterns.* The correct stroking pattern be **demonstrated** to the students by the teacher. Correct stroking pattern can be achieved through building rapid stroking patterns. For a good typist *concentration on the copies* is of almost importance.

For this *correct reading habits be* developed. It is also desirable that students acquires the capability of manipulating the parts of machine with dexterity For this special drill is needed More practice be made on the following Backspacer key, the margin release keys, the tabulator set and clear keys, the space bar etc. The stroking of these keys is different from that of stroking of alphabet keys.

Any student who is desirous of becoming a good typist must automatise the following. For effective learning the following are very important

1. An urge, from within the learner, to learn a skill.
2. Good surroundings which are conducive to learning.
3. Matter to be learnt be of direct concern to the learner.
4. Security, less tension and success helps in learning a skill.
5. Interest in the skill.
6. Repeat that which gives satisfaction and avoid that which annoys the learner.
7. To learn a part in life it is better to play that part.

8. Learning condition should be real and life-like.
9. Learning should be continuous and repeated.
10. The more extensive the activity of the learner, the greater will be his learning
11. Abundant and realistic practice contributes to learning
12. First hand experience makes for lasting and move complete learning.

Standard Psychological Rules for Building Skills

Professors Mort and Vincent have compiled 30 psychological rules for building skills.

The thirty rules are as under:

1. No one learns without feeling some urge to learn.
2. A person learn more quickly and lastingly what has meaning for him.
3. What a person learn is influenced directly by his surroundings.
4. All learning occur through attempt to satisfy needs.
5. Individuals differ in all sorts of ways.
6. When an organism is ready to act, it is very painful for it not to act, and when an organism is not ready to act, is painful for it to act.
7. Security and success are the soil and climate for growth.
8. Interest is an indicator of growth.
9. Emotional tension decrease efficiency in learning.
10. Physical defects decrease efficiency in learning.
11. Interest is a source of power in motivating learning.
12. The best way to learn a part in life to play that part.
13. What gives satisfaction tends to be repeated, what is annoying tends to be avoided.
14. You cannot train the mind like a muscle.
15. Learning is more efficient and longer lasting when the conditions for it are real and life like.

16. Piece-meal learning is not efficient.
17. Participation enhances learning
18. Abundant, realistic practice contributes to learning.
19. A person learns by his own activity.
20. You start to grow from where you are not from some artificial starting point.
21. Growth is a steady continuous process and different individuals grow at different rates.
22. Unused talent lead to personal maladjustment.
23. General behaviour is controlled by emotions as well as intellect.
24. First hand experience makes for lasting and more complete learning
25. It is impossible to 'learn one thing at a time.
26. The average pupils is largely a myth.
27. Learning is reinforced when two or more senses are used at the same time.
28. It has been said that a person learns more in first three years of his life than all the years afterwards.
29. If you want certain results teach it directly.
30. Child develops in terms of all the influence which effect them.

Teaching of Type-writing Skill

Of the various approaches for teaching of type-writing skills the most commonly used in schools and colleges for teaching are:

1. The Home-Row Approach.
2. The Skip-around or word-pattern Approach.
3. The vertical Finger Approach.
4. The whole Key-board Approach.

1. Home-Row Approach

Adopting this approach for teaching the students is taught first the locations of the fingers. A good practice is given in the form of drills of the home-row keys. This is considered as the easiest way to introduce the key-board. In this row only one vowel "A" is provided so adoption of this approach provides nonsense typing and so wordtyping or phrase typing should not be expected.

2. *The Skip-around or Word Pattern Approach*

Adopting this approach for teaching those keys are presented first to the students, which are required to prepare meaningful typed material. To start with more emphasis on reaches controlled, by the stronger fingers of both the hands. By adopting this approach, no nonsense material is typed. To master key locations short and simple Words are typed putting more emphasis on double letters which is considered as easiest letter combination for beginners. When taught by this technique student's get a feeling of confidence and they strike the keys with more confidence.

3. *Vertical Approach*

In this approach of teaching type-writing all keys struck by one finger are presented at one time. For example j, h, b, u and y with for finger of right hand and f, g, c, v, r and t with for finger of left-hand. The material produced by this approach is quite nonsense as in case of Home-row approach.

4. *Whole-Keyboard Approach*

In this approach of teaching type-writing the entire alphabetic key-board is presented during the first day of typing. To help students to learn the locations of all the keys additional drills are provided on subsequent days.

Pre-requisites for a Beginner in Typing

Some of the pre-requisites for beginners in type-writing are as under:

1. *Position*

(a) Body should be erect directly in front of the machine.

(b) Body should neither be too close nor too far away from the type-writer.

(c) Feet should be on the floor-one little forward and the other a little backward.

(d) Spine should be straight.

(e) Head should not bent.

(f) Elbow should be close to the body and not too far from it.

(g) Wrist should not be too high and bended.

(h) Fingers should be curved just like the paws of the lion.

(i) All fingers should be on the home-row and eyes on the copies.

2. Handling Paper

(a) Paper should be put correctly on the type-writer. It should be practiced a number of times.

(b) The proper manipulation of the machine should be encouraged.

(c) Handling more than one paper together with carbon be practiced.

3. For Avoiding Reach Errors

(a) make use of right fingers with rights hands.

(b) never use wrong fingers with wrong hands.

(c) do not use wrong fingers with right hands.

4. For Avoiding Stroking and Touching Errors

(a) Students be encouraged to type in a right manner.

(b) Crowding of letters be avoided.

(c) Avoid typing in a way wherein there is a piling of various keys at a time.

(d) Avoid practice of Ghost-letters.

(e) Touching of keys should neither be too heavy nor too light.

(f) Always encourage even touching of keys.

5. Caring for Space Errors

(a) Encourage the students to type, by providing proper spaces, from the very beginning.

(b) Make it a habit to provide enough space between two words, two lines two paragraphs etc.

(c) The space provided should be according to need and avoid to provide too many spaces for the purposes mentioned in (b).

6. Manipulation of Special Parts of the Machine

Take necessary care for manipulation of special parts of the machine. Generally the beginners fail to keep their fingers on the home row, while operating the shift keys,. Sometimes they use shift lock instead of shift keys thereby causing errors in typing.

To use space bar use right hand thumb. Beginners must develop this habbit. A number of errors in typing are caused because of improper pressing of shift-keys and it is thus desirable to pay proper attention while using various parts of the machine.

Objectives Teaching of Type-writing Skill

The objectives of teaching type-writing skill can be summarised as follows:

1. To Develop the Ability to Operate Type-writer Efficiently

(a) Students should display good practice in key-strokes and in machine manipulation.

(b) Student should understand the mechanism of machines.

(c) The pupils should arrange his material so as to have an orderly flow of work through his type-writer.

(d) The Pupil should look after the machine carefully.

2. To Have Correct Knowledge of English and to Apply it

(a) Should have a knowledge of rules for spacing etc.

(b) Should know how to punctuate, use capitals and numbers in the material.

(c) Should know the procedure of setting of forms of letters.

(d) Should know the rules for word divisions in terms of letters.

(e) Should know the method of setting up a manuscript copy.

3. *Developing Ability to use the Machine*

(a) Should know the drafting of copies of writing, again editing and copying later.

(b) Should know how to think as-he types.

(c) Should know to prepare a usable copy by making neat erasures.

4. *Developing Habbits of Corrections*

(a) Should develop high standards for neat work.

(b) Should develop and improve his skill as proof reader.

(c) Should practice spelling, punctuation etc.

5. *Ability to Arrange Written Matter Efficiently*

(a) Should be able to make simple outlines.

(b) Should type from a rough draft.

(c) Should arrange a simple tabulation quickly and correctly.

(d) Should know how to display material to attract attention to it.

(e) Should centre the material vertically and horizontally on a paper of any size.

6. *To Acquire General Habits for Good-Work*

(a) Should acquire a cooperative attitude to work well with others.

(b) Should develop ability to work without emotional tensions.

(c) Should develop time saving techniques.

(d) Should know how to finish the job well once it has been started.

Standard Guide-Lines For Teaching Type-Writing

(i) Teacher should provide enough knowledge of type-machine, its important parts and its use.

(ii) Teacher should teach the techniques of operating the machine.

(iii) Teacher must tell how to recognise and mark the errors.

(iv) Teacher should also tell the method of carrying out minor repairs and adjustment of machine parts.

(v) Student should acquire a typing speed of 50-60 words per minute.

(vi) Teacher should teach him all forms of letters.

(vii) Students should learn to make out carbon copies according to requirements.

(viii) A complete record of machine such as its make, price, date of purchase and dates of repairs etc., must be maintained.

Teaching Alphabets of the Key-board of Type-Machine

Various methods of teaching of type writing skill such as Homerow method, First Finger Method etc., have already been discussed.

The general principles in teaching the key board are as given below.

1. To begin with the student should practice two, three or four letters.
2. In the beginning only those strokes be used which promote good and easy stroking
3. Pairing of keys, which do not promote easy stroking should be avoided.
4. Stroking of keys should be in continuity and not in isolation.
5. Try to follow a fixed pattern out of the new keys.
6. Teacher should give a correct demonstration about new keys which should be correctly imitated by students.

Guidelines and Principles for Teaching Numbers & Symbols

Dr. Khan has given following guidelines for teaching numbers and symbols

1. Touch method applies to the numbers and symbols also.
2. Alphabets precede the numbers and symbols in learning typewriting
3. Present numbers are continuous so that locational security is promoted
4. Sight, sound and touch senses are to be used in teaching numbers and symbols.
5. Gradually abandon the home-row system.
6. The numbers and words are to be practised together after establishing initial skill to enhance number proficiency.
7. Adequate and purposeful practice should be provided in typing numbers and symbols. (Commerce Education *1982* Ed.)

Teaching of Numbers and Symbols

The four important methods of teaching of numbers and symbols are as under:

1. The Traditional Approach.
2. WE-23 concept.
3. Pipe organ Method.
4. Top-row Method.
   1. *Traditional Method*: In this method both the hands are kept on the home-row and the respective fingers type out the numbers and symbols. If necessary the keys may be seen by the learner.
   2. *The Method of 'WE-23'*: In this method the learner is asked to type "WE " five times and then "23" five times. It helps in developing speed.

3. *Pipe Organ Method:* In this method left hand operates the keys and the right hand remains on the home-row.
4. *Tope-row Method:* In this method both the hands come up on the top-row and it is operated accordingly.

Method of Teaching Type-writing

The methods generally used are as follows:

(i) Demonstration Method.

(ii) Apprentice Method.

(iii) Problem solving Method.

(iv) Experimental Method.

(Details of Method are given in chapter).

Development of Mechanical Skill in Type-writing

For development of mechanical skills in type-writing following are essential:

(i) Correct movement of fingers.

(ii) Correct demonstration by the teacher.

(iii) Imitation and correct practice by the students must follow the teachers demonstration.

(iv) To type any given material with confidence.

Speed and Accuracy

Speed and accuracy are two important things that we look for in type writing skill. It is the duty of the teacher to see that the students gains speed with accuracy. Any deficiency in these may be considered as a failure on the part of the teacher.

It has been opined that, "When a person a properly skilled in operating type-writer, he does not look at the key of the machine. The strokes are automatic and there is not necessity of conscious application of mind, one is required to take certain definite steps in acquiring a skill. The teacher should be habitual demonstrator in teaching typelearning, short-hand and bookkeeping. In typing the sitting position of typist, position of the machine, the distance from the machines should be ideal and should be demonstrated by the teacher.

The learner should proceed from easy to difficult. First he can start from printed matter and later on start from hand-written copy. The teacher should teach the working methods of the type-writer and demonstrate every activity. He should issue necessary instructions at each step of practice, till the learner becomes master in the desired skill. Certainly `Practice makes the man perfect'. The learner should first master to do the skill accurately and then start increasing his speed".

Tonne, Propham and Freeman have suggested the main features of an expert performance as under

1. Establishment and maintenance of a steady even flow of motion.
2. Easy and economical movements.
3. Performance unhampered by nervous tension and hurry.
4. Concentration upon the task at hand.
5. Intelligent use of senses. 1 he expert sees, hears and feels each correct technique used.

Teaching of Short-hand

The skills of type-writing and short-hand should go together, however, the skill of typing can proceed alone. Short-hand is useless without the skill of typing.

Short-hand is a system of writing in symbols which can be written in few lines and dots and getting guidance from it a neat draft can be typed. The Pitman system of short-hand is the most popular system in the world.

Objectives of Teaching Short-hand

Important objectives of teaching of short-hand are as under

1. To prepare the pupil to undertake the job of a stenographer.
2. To improve skill in spelling, punctuation and paragraphing.

3. To help the students in binding a business vocabulary and to become word conscious.
4. To help pupil to develop good attitudes such as accuracy, neatness, perseverance and cooperativeness.
5. Automatizing high frequency words, phrases, short or brief forms and their derivatives for a limited vocabulary.
6. To make student understand the place of shorthand in commercial world.
7. To enable the students to form well contrasted outlines.
8. To develop fluency in writing and in reading short-hand.
9. To develop the ability to recognise sounds and to record in short-hand the sounds heard.
10. To develop the ability to take dictation with sufficient speed and with sufficient accuracy.

Methods of Teaching Short-hand

Some of the methods commonly used for teaching of short-hand are as under:

1. Basic Method.
2. Functional Method.
3. Demonstration Method.
4. Laboratory Practice Method.

1. *The Basic Method :* The three important features of this method are
   (a) It emphasises on verbalized generalizations. Teacher can make use of either deductive or inductive method.
   (b) Writing is introduced earlier and some authors even insist on reading approach in the beginning.
   (c) Penmanship drills are also provided for classroom practice.

2. *Functional Method:* Main characteristics of this method are as under
   - (a) Reading approach is important and basic to this method. In this the student is required to read well-constructed fluent outlines of about 15-20 lessons and then he starts writing.
   - (b) It emphasises automatisation of correct short-hand responses without learning the rules relating to them.
3. *Demonstration Method :* Refer to chapter
4. *Laboratory Method:* For this a laboratory provided with outlines, keeps, charts, diagrams and pictures of most of the difficult and complex concepts. It provides an atmosphere conducive to the learning of short-hand and helps in learning the skills quickly.

The most sough for system for teaching of short-hand is Pitman's system of short-hand.

For teaching by this method teachers has to use Pitman's Shorthand instructor which is actually a textbook This contains a complete theory of short-hand. Dictation is given from the text and supplementary publications of the same inventor-author,

Short-hand Teaching Technique

Dr. Khan has given ten techniques (or guidelines) for the teaching of short-hand which are as follows

1. The teacher should plan the learning situation so that the pupil have opportunity of doing their best.
2. He should know that the students have imagination which can be used by them under proper encouragement.
3. It is possible for the students to learn more than one thing at a time if an opportunity is provided to them.
4. The teacher should start with and build upon what is already known to the student.
5. Write down lesson-plan every day setting down

specifically what he wants to do in a particular period and the exact order in which the procedure will be followed.

6. Teacher should keep an experimental attitude in his instructions.
7. Teacher should make frequent use of individual dictation.
8. Teacher should remain in close touch with the students to know the daily growth of the child and to encourage his development in short-hand technique.
9. Teacher should set a good example by freely using shorthand.
10. Teacher should conduct work and make all assignments in terms of time in the class.

Developing Correct Study Habits in Short-hand

1. Keep your left hand fingers on writing material of short-hand and write with right hand fingers on the short-hand notebook.
2. Make extensive use of blackboard
3. Make it a habit to read connected materials daily.
4. Practice how to write correctly and how to lift the finger correctly and how to hold the pen correctly.
5. Correct pemenship be taught well to the students.
6. Give assignments for words, outlines, correct spelling, pronunciation etc. to the students. Ask them to practice reading, copying and transcribing at home.
7. Give dictations at varying speeds and that also with varying pauses.
8. Encourage the students to imitate the expert.
9. The class time should be properly divided providing for various activities such as Blackboard drills. Reading back from the dictation, Blackboard preview, Brief form recall drills Repetitive dictation, Reading back the material, Recall drills, Roll Call and class adjustments.

Course of Short-hand

The "Pitman's Short-hand Instructor" Covers the whole course that needs about six-months or year to complete. It is advisable to divide this course into several terms of short duration. All efforts be made to complete the unit in fixed time.

Some experts are of the opinion that the course in short-hand be completed in two years instead of one year. It would provide enough practice to the student and will help him in attaining full efficiency in the skill.

Dictation in Short-hand

An Educationist has opined, "the outlines of short-hand are required to be learnt. But the actual skill is developed in proper dictation practice.

While giving dictation the learner should also be taught the principle of taking dictation. The learner is to be guided to develop the power of learning accurately, with speed and make proper outlines of the matter. The group of learners should understand the exercises before the dictation is given. First dictation can be slow, later it can be taken with speed which is acquired with practice."

Teaching Transcription

To enable the students to produce mailable transcript is the most important aim of teaching short-hand. As transcription is a new skill, it should be introduced when students have some knowledge of shorthand and type-writing both. It has been realised by many experts that the following abilities in no way ensure superior transcription ability.

(a) Ability to write readable short-hand.

(b) ability to copy rapidly at the type-writer.

(c) ability to use English fairly well.

(d) ability to spell most words correctly.

Moreover, it is not necessary for a fast typist to be a fast transcriber. Similarly, the best speller may not be the best transcriber.

To become a good transcriber the development of following skills is essential:

(a) Development of the expert pattern.

(b) Adoption of proper techniques rather than emphasis on 'Perfect copy'.

(c) Isolation of troublesome items for special drill or group drills.

(d) Right kind of repetitive practice.

(e) Supervised transcription instilling good habits.

In the opinion of some other experts the learner will be able to transcribe if he has automatized the following skills:

(a) Spelling correctly.

(b) Ability to write from short-hand dictation materials.

(c) Ability of hear and retain maximum number of words in mind while taking dictation.

(d) Ability to recognise the symbols he has mentioned in his notebook.

(e) Ability to fill in the gap which has been left out while taking the dictation.

(f) Ability to arrange the materials systematically so that he does not feel any difficulty while transcribing.

Factors Conducive for the Rate of Transcription

(a) Nature of dictation; depending upon vocabulary-spelling, pronunciation etc.

(b) Knowledge of the learner with the meaning of the material.

(c) Varying degree of speed of which dictation was given.

(d) Degrees of legibility of the dictation notes taken.

(e) Period for which dictation is taken.

(f) Number of carbon copies to be taken out.

(g) Quality of the standard transcription required.

The transcription process includes the following:

(a) Keeping transcription materials.

(b) Keeping the type-writer in readiness.

(c) Writing the letter heads etc., such as-date, place, address, salutation etc.

(d) Reading the short-hand notes and typing.

(e) Making corrections.

(f) Proof reading of the transcribed materials.

(g) Addressing envelopes.

(h) Arranging finished work.

(i) Making refrences.

(j) Making use of correct punctuation marks.

(k) Capitalising the message.

(l) Making words into syllables at the end of the line.

(m) Designing proper correspondence marks.

(n) Capitalizing the message.

(o) Breaking words into syllables at the end of the line.

(p) Designing proper correspondence forms.

(q) Selection of proper title for the addressee.

(r) Paragraphing the message.

(s) Editing the message.

(t) Complimentary closing.

Bibliography

Ahmad, K.: *Economic Development in an Islamic Framework*, Leicester, The Islamic Foundation, 1979.

Alvesson, M. and H. Willmott: *Commerce Studies*, Sage, New Delhi, 1992.

Beaver, W. H.: *Financial Reporting: An Accounting Revolution*, Englewood Cliffs, Prentice Hall, 1981.

Belkaoui, A.R.: *Accounting Theory*, London, Academic Press Ltd, 1992.

Blanshard, B.: *The Uses of A Commerce Education*, La Salle, Open Court, 1973.

Bragg, S. M.: *Accounting Best Practices*, John Wiley & Sons, 2001.

Bruner, J.: *Toward a Theory of Accountancy*, Cambridge, Harvard University Press, 1966.

Choi, F. D.S. and Mueller, G. G.: *International Accounting*, New York, Prentice-Hall International Inc, 1992.

Cooper, D. J. and T.M. Hopper: *Critical Accounts*, London, The Macmillan Press Ltd, 1990.

Dancy, J.: *Introduction to Contemporary Epistemology*, Oxford,Blackwell Publishers Ltd., 1996

DeGeorge, R. T.: *Business Ethics,* London, Macmillan Publishing Co., 1990.

Donald N.: *The Rhetoric of Commerce Education,* Madison, University of Wisconsin Press, 1985.

Friedman, M.: *Capitalism and Freedom*, Chicago:University of Chicago Press, 1982.

Galbraith, J.K.: *A History of Economics: the past as the Present*, London: Penguin Books, 1987.

Keen, S.: *Debunking Economics: The Naked Emperor of the Social Sciences*, Pluto Press, Sydney, 2001.

Lehman, C.R.: *Accounting's Changing Roles in Social Conflict*, New York, Markus Weiner Publishing, 1992.

Loomes, G. : *"Experimental Commerce Education,"* New York, St. Martin's Press, 1989.

Merchant, K. A.: *Rewarding Results*, Boston, Harvard Business School Press, 1989.

Morris, J.: *Software Industry Accounting*, John Wiley & Sons, 2000.

Plott, C. R. : *"Policy and the Use of Laboratory Experimental Methodology in Commerce,"* Boston, Kluwer, 1999.

Roslender, R.: *Sociological Perspectives on Modern Accountancy*, London, Routledge, 1992.

Ross, D. : *Commerce Theory and Cognitive Science*, Cambridge, Mass., MIT Press, 2006.

Roth, A. E. : *"Introduction to Experimental Commerce,"* Princeton, Princeton University Press, 1995.

Scott, D.R.: *The Cultural Significance of Accounts,* New York, Henry Holt, 1931.

Sichel, D.: *The Computer Revolution: An Economic Perspective*, Washington, Brookings Institution, 1997.

Smith, V. L. : *Papers in Experimental Commerce*, Cambridge, Cambridge University Press, 1991.

Watts, R.L. and Zimmerman, J.L.: *Positive Accounting Theory*, Englewoods Cliffs, NJ:Prentice Hall, 1986.

Wyrick, Thomas L.: *The Writer's Guide to College Economics*, St. Paul, West, 1995.

Index

□□□□